PIES
sweet and savory

PIES
sweet and savory

CAROLINE BRETHERTON

with Jane Bamforth

LONDON, NEW YORK, MELBOURNE, MUNICH, AND DELHI

Photography William Reavell
Recipe Editor Kathy Steer

DK UK
Editor Alison Shaw
Project Art Editor Kathryn Wilding
Design Assistant Jade Wheaton
Managing Editor Dawn Henderson
Managing Art Editor Christine Keilty
Senior Jackets Creative Nicola Powling
Jacket Design Assistant Rosie Levine
Pre-Production Producer Andrew Hilliard
Senior Producer Jen Lockwood
Creative Technical Support Sonia Charbonnier
Publisher Peggy Vance

DK PUBLISHING
North American Consultant Kate Ramos
US Editor Margaret Parrish
US Senior Editor Rebecca Warren

DK INDIA
Senior Editor Chitra Subramanyam
Editor Ligi John
Assistant Editor Neha Samuel
Senior Art Editor Anchal Kaushal
Art Editors Vandna Sonkariya,
Isha Nagar, Pankaj Bhatia
Managing Editor Glenda Fernandes
Managing Art Editor Navidita Thapa
DTP Manager Sunil Sharma
DTP Operator Satish Chandra Gaur

13 14 15 16 10 9 8 7 6 5 4 3 2
002–187843–Feb/13

First published in the United States in 2013 by
DK Publishing
345 Hudson Street, New York, New York 10014

Published in Great Britain by Dorling Kindersley Limited.

A catalog record for this book is available from the Library of Congress.

ISBN: 978-1-4654-0203-5

DK books are available at special discounts when purchased in bulk for sales
promotions, premiums, fund-raising, or educational use. For details, contact:
DK Publishing Special Markets, 345 Hudson Street, New York, New York
10014 or SpecialSales@DK.com.

Color reproduction by Opus Multi Media Services, India

Printed and bound by South China Printing Co. Ltd, China

PUBLISHER'S NOTE
The recipes contained in this book have been created for the ingredients and
techniques indicated. The Publisher is not responsible for your specific health or
allergy needs that may require supervision. Nor is the Publisher responsible for any
adverse reactions you may have to the recipes contained in the book, whether you
follow them as written or modify them to suit your personal dietary needs or tastes.

Discover more at **www.dk.com**

CONTENTS

FOREWORD

It's time that pies and tarts had their moment in the sun. For too long these versatile dishes have been neglected, thought by many to be old-fashioned and heavy. There are, however, as many different types of pie and tart as you have the imagination to create—from heart-warming winter dishes such as Steak and Kidney Pie to the delicate, multilayered puff pastry confections that are Summer Fruit Millefeuilles.

Not only is there a pie for all occasions, but there are also pies for every type of cook. Whether you are just starting out on the road to culinary expertise or have been traveling down it for years, you will find recipes in this book to excite and stimulate you.

Many home cooks are unnecessarily put off by making pastry and pie dough—they often think that it is more difficult than it actually is. Pastry-making traditionally requires cool hands (pastry hands, as my grandmother used to call them) and a cool, logical head. Follow a few simple rules and it's hard to go wrong: dough should be handled as little as possible, to keep it from becoming dry and overworked. It should be chilled or rested before use, since this helps the glutens in the flour to relax and stops the cooked crust from shrinking away from the pan. Most pies and tarts turn out better if blind-baked first, and try to bake pie dough in metal pans—the metal conducts heat well and quickly, which helps to prevent the common problem of a soggy crust.

There are a few shortcuts that can help you to make the perfect pie dough. I often make my pie dough in a food processor, since this saves both time and effort. If you are worried about overmixing the dough, try just using the food processor to rub together the fat and flour, then continue by hand. There are also many store-bought products on the market that are indistinguishable from homemade dough. If time is short, there is nothing wrong with taking a shortcut and using a good-quality store-bought dough or pastry. The important thing is to produce a pie that looks and tastes delicious.

Caroline

INTRODUCTION

Pies: Sweet and Savory draws together recipes for pies and tarts from all over the world. From the lightest, most delicate layered fruit strudels to the heartiest steak pies, all types of the most delicious and diverse recipes are gathered together in one place. Pies and tarts can be as varied as the pastry and fillings they contain, and here there are recipes for every different type of pastry and dough imaginable. Potato- or crumble-topped pies also feature, and some recipes use bread or cobbler dough as a delicious base or a tempting topping.

In *Pies*, you will find an enormous variety of pies and tarts—from the classic en croûtes, made with beef and salmon, to the more unusual pastillas of North Africa stuffed with a heady mixture of game, herbs, and spices.

If you're in the mood to bake a sweet pie, you have a multitude of choices. You'll find classic American pies, such as Pumpkin Pie and Shoo Fly Pie, as well as British standards like Yorkshire Curd Tart. This book is **truly international**, featuring "pielike" dishes such as the Italian *Torta della Nonna*, a simple, ricotta-based tart, and the crispy *Baklava* of the Middle East, stuffed with nuts and spices and dripping with a honey syrup.

Also included is an array of mini pies and hand pies, galettes, turnovers, tartlets, and pasties. These fun, individual pies are loved by adults and children alike, whatever the occasion. They can be put together in a flash, and eaten hot or cold, making them ideal to take on a picnic, pack in a lunchbox, or serve at a party.

Despite the wealth of choice in *Pies*, it is simple to follow. The illustrated **Recipe Planners** guide you toward a particular dish by listing each recipe by pie type, so you can pick between **Cobblers and Crumbles** or **Double-crust Pies,** and everything in between, to match your mood and occasion beautifully.

The recipes in each chapter are **organized by key ingredient**, such as chicken, spinach, or apple, to help you decide what you want to cook. Each recipe is presented clearly and simply in a few method steps, accompanied by helpful "at-a-glance" icons that tell you the serving size, prep and cook times, and freezing information. Fabulous photography and clear instructions throughout will help you to produce mouthwatering results every time.

For those who really want to master the art of pastry making in all its forms, the **In Praise of Pie Dough** chapter contains precise, detailed step-by-step instructions for making perfect dough. Whether it's a time-consuming strudel dough or a handy quick puff-pastry recipe, the visual step-by-steps are there to guide you at every stage.

So whether you want to whip up a quick midweek supper and are seeking fresh inspiration, or wanting to succeed in making the perfect apple pie, there is something for everyone in this book. Ideal for novice home cooks to experienced chefs, this book contains a mixture of both old favorites and new classics for all.

I hope that *Pies* will become a much-loved and well-trusted reference book for every kind of pie and tart for years to come.

TOP-CRUST PIES

A top crust is particularly suited to those pies that require little more than a lid of homemade or store-bought pie dough, and where the filling is already at least partially cooked or requires little cooking time.

RABBIT AND CORN PIE WITH A HERB CRUST
COOK 1¾ HRS
page 65

SAVORY

CHICKEN POT PIES
COOK 40 MINS
page 74

STEAK AND WILD MUSHROOM PIE
COOK 2½–3 HRS
page 30

DOUBLE-CRUST PIES

A double crust suits pies that have rich, thick juices that can be soaked up by the bottom layer of pie crust. These pies need a slightly longer cooking time to crisp up both the base and the pie lid.

CHERRY LATTICE PIE
COOK 40–45 MINS
page 274

SAVORY

STEAK AND KIDNEY DOUBLE-CRUST PIE
COOK 2¾–3¼ HRS
page 33

LAMB AND POTATO PIE
COOK 1 HR 20 MINS
page 48

SAUSAGE, BACON, AND EGG PIE
COOK 50 MINS
page 51

PORK AND APPLE PICNIC PIE
COOK 1 HR
page 55

AUVERGNE TOURTE
COOK 1¼ HRS
page 59

CHICKEN AND HAM RAISED PIE
COOK 1½ HRS
page 77

CHICKEN PIE WITH CHEESE
COOK 35–40 MINS
page 82

CHICKEN AND HEART OF PALM PIE
COOK 35–40 MINS
page 85

KALAKUKKO
COOK 6½ HRS
page 142

STARGAZY PIE
COOK 40–50 MINS
page 153

CHEESE AND ONION PIE
COOK 40 MINS
page 178

FLAMICHE
COOK 40–45 MINS
page 208

CHESTNUT AND MUSHROOM PIE
COOK 35–40 MINS
page 210

SWEET

APPLE PIE
COOK 50–55 MINS
page 218

PEAR PIE WITH WALNUT CRUST
COOK 35–40 MINS
page 231

PEACH PIE
COOK 40–45 MINS
page 246

CROSTATA DI MARMELLATA
COOK 50 MINS
page 258

RHUBARB AND STRAWBERRY PIE
COOK 50–55 MINS
page 261

CHERRY PIE
COOK 50 MINS–1 HR
page 270

CROSTATA DI RICOTTA
COOK 1–1¼ HRS
page 316

GALETTE DES ROIS
COOK 30 MINS
page 325

COBBLERS AND CRUMBLES

A cobbler topping resembles a cross between a scone and a dumpling. It suits hearty fall stews and desserts. A crumble topping is quick and easy to make and traditionally works well to top sweet fruit fillings.

BEEF, FENNEL, AND MUSHROOM COBBLER
COOK 2½ HRS
page 35

SWEET

OATY BLACKBERRY AND APPLE CRUMBLE
COOK 45 MINS
page 225

APPLE AND BLACKBERRY COBBLER WITH CINNAMON
COOK 30 MINS
page 229

APPLE BROWN BETTY
COOK 35–45 MINS
page 230

PLUM AND CINNAMON COBBLER
COOK 30 MINS
page 240

PLUM CRUMBLE
COOK 30–40 MINS
page 242

PEACH COBBLER
COOK 30–35 MINS
page 244

RHUBARB SMULPAJ
COOK 30 MINS
page 264

BLUEBERRY COBBLER
COOK 30 MINS
page 267

CHERRY CRUMBLE
COOK 35–40 MINS
page 272

SAVORY

BEEF AND RED WINE COBBLER
COOK 2½–3½ HRS
page 37

CHICKEN COBBLER
COOK 2¼ HRS
page 89

FISH CRUMBLE
COOK 35–40 MINS
page 143

INDIVIDUAL PIES AND TARTS

Whether you're feeding a crowd or making a picnic, individual tarts and pies are the way to go. Folded turnovers or pasties make ideal portable food, and tartlets are a pretty addition to any table.

SWEET POTATO, RED ONION, AND THYME GALETTES WITH CHILE
COOK 50 MINS
page 192

SAVORY

ROAST CHICKEN HAND PIES
COOK 40 MINS
page 81

INDIVIDUAL CURRIED MUSSEL PIES
COOK 40–45 MINS
page 156

CONTINUED ....➤

SMOKED TROUT TARTLETS
COOK 30 MINS
page 148

RASPBERRY TARTLETS WITH CRÈME PÂTISSIÈRE

SWEET

QUICHES AND SAVORY TARTS

A savory quiche is traditionally deeper than a tart and has a higher ratio of eggs to cream in the filling. Both are ideal when you want to serve a more substantial dish for a light lunch or buffet.

SALMON AND SPINACH QUICHE
COOK 1 HR 10 MINS–1¼ HRS
page 138

SWEET TARTS

The starting point for a sweet tart is a good pie crust, made from either savory or sweet pastry. The crust can then hold a whole variety of fillings, with or without a custard to bind them.

NORMANDY PEAR TART
COOK 35–45 MINS
page 233

RHUBARB AND CUSTARD TART
COOK 1 HR 35 MINS
page 262

DOUBLE CHOCOLATE RASPBERRY TART
COOK 5–10 MINS
page 296

CONTINUED....➤

TARTE AU CITRON
COOK 45 MINS
page 281

BLUEBERRY CREAM CHEESE TART
COOK 45–50 MINS
page 268

EN CROÛTES AND LAYERED PIES

Light, delicate pastries such as puff pastry or rich pie doughs make good vehicles for en croûtes or layered pies. For a quick dessert, sandwich buttery puff pastry layers together with cream and fruit.

HERB FETA FILO PIE
COOK 1 HR
page 198

SAVORY

BOEUF EN CROÛTE
COOK 45 MINS–1 HR
page 42

FILO PIE WITH SPICY KALE AND SAUSAGE
COOK 1–1¼ HRS
page 53

VENISON WELLINGTONS
COOK 35 MINS
page 66

SQUAB BREASTS EN CROÛTE
COOK 30–35 MINS
page 69

CRISPY CHICKEN AND SPINACH PIE
COOK 35–40 MINS
page 78

STUFFED CHICKEN BREASTS EN CROÛTE
COOK 40–55 MINS
page 84

CHICKEN JALOUSIE
COOK 35 MINS
page 88

MIDDLE-EASTERN GUINEA HEN PIE
COOK 1½ HRS
page 99

SALMON COULIBIAC
COOK 55 MINS–1 HR
page 144

TARTE TATINS

Named after two French sisters who earned a living by baking their father's favorite apple tart, this is a true French classic. Other fruit works well, too, or use vegetables to give this dish a savory twist.

BEET TARTE TATIN
COOK 35–45 MINS
page 176

SAVORY

CARAMELIZED SHALLOT TARTE TATIN
COOK 45 MINS
page 180

SWEET

APPLE TARTE TATIN
COOK 35–50 MINS
page 224

PEAR TARTE TATIN
COOK 45–55 MINS
page 236

CARAMELIZED MANGO TARTLETS
COOK 30 MINS
page 249

CARAMEL BANANA TART
COOK 30–35 MINS
page 285

POTATO-TOPPED PIES

Potato toppings can be used with any type of vegetable, fish, or meat filling. An ideal way to use up leftover stews, the pies can be topped with fresh herbs, grated cheese, or mustard.

FRENCH BEEF AND HERB POTATO PIE
COOK 2–2½ HRS
page 45

LANCASHIRE HOTPOT
COOK 2½ HRS
page 47

SHEPHERD'S PIE
COOK 1 HR 20 MINS
page 49

VEGETABLE AND CHICKEN PIE
COOK 50 MINS
page 86

SALMON AND SHRIMP PIE
COOK 35 MINS
page 146

CHEESY POTATO-TOPPED TUNA PIE
COOK 35–40 MINS
page 151

SMOKED FISH PIE
COOK 50–55 MINS
page 152

HERRING, APPLE, AND ONION PIE
COOK 1 HR 10 MINS
page 155

SHEPHERDLESS PIE
COOK 50 MINS
page 172

KITCHEN GARDEN PIE
COOK 1¼–1½ HRS
page 205

FISHERMAN'S PIE
COOK 50 MINS–1 HR
page 135

MEAT PIES AND TARTS

A perfect dish for entertaining in the fall, this delicious steak pie is both homey and extravagant. If you can't find fresh wild mushrooms, use dried, or even cremini mushrooms instead.

STEAK AND WILD MUSHROOM PIE

SERVES 4–6 **PREP 50–55 MINS PLUS CHILLING** **COOK 2½–3 HRS** **FREEZE UP TO 1 MONTH**

EQUIPMENT
9½in (24cm) baking dish, pie funnel

INGREDIENTS

FOR THE FILLING
1lb 2oz (500g) mixed wild mushrooms, fresh, or 2½oz (75g) dried wild mushrooms, soaked for 30 minutes and drained
¼ cup all-purpose flour
salt and freshly ground black pepper
2¼lb (1kg) sirloin steak, cut into 1in (2.5cm) cubes
4 shallots, finely chopped
3 cups beef stock or water, plus extra if needed
leaves from 6 sprigs of parsley, finely chopped

FOR THE PASTRY
(For visual step-by-step instructions, see puff pastry pp.110–113)
1⅓ cups all-purpose flour, plus extra for dusting
½ tsp fine salt
12 tbps unsalted butter, cubed
1 large egg, beaten, to glaze

1 Preheat the oven to 350°F (180°C). Slice the mushrooms. Make the filling by seasoning the flour with salt and pepper. Toss the steak in it to coat.

2 Put the meat, mushrooms, and shallots in a Dutch oven. Add the stock and heat, stirring well. Bring to a boil, stirring constantly. Cover and cook in the oven for 2–2¼ hours, until tender.

3 To make the pastry, sift the flour and salt into a bowl. Rub in one-third of the butter with your fingertips until the mixture resembles bread crumbs. Add ½ cup water and bring it together to form a dough. Chill for 15 minutes.

4 Roll out the dough on a lightly floured surface to a 6in x 15in (15cm x 38cm) rectangle. Dot the rest of the butter over two-thirds. Fold the unbuttered side over half the buttered side. Fold the dough again so the butter is completely enclosed in layers of dough. Turn it over and roll over the edges to seal. Wrap in plastic wrap and chill for 15 minutes. Roll to 6in x 18in (15cm x 45cm), fold in thirds, make a quarter turn. Seal. Chill for 15 minutes. Repeat three more times, chilling for 15 minutes between each turn.

5 Add the parsley to the meat and season. Spoon it into the dish. Increase the heat to 425°F (220°C). Roll out the dough on a floured surface. Cut a strip from the edge. Dampen the rim of the dish and press the strip onto it. Put the rolled-out dough over the pie and press firmly to seal. Brush with the beaten egg. Make a hole in the top and add a pie funnel to allow steam to escape. Chill for 15 minutes. Bake for 25–35 minutes until golden brown. If browning too quickly, cover with foil. The filling can be made 2–3 days ahead.

This hearty pie is a treasured winter classic. The use of brown ale not only imparts a rich flavor, but also tenderizes the meat as it cooks. Serve with the gravy and lots of mashed potatoes.

STEAK AND ALE PIE

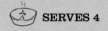 **SERVES 4**   **PREP 20 MINS PLUS COOLING**   **COOK 2¼ HRS**   **FREEZE UP TO 1 MONTH**

EQUIPMENT
9in (22cm) pie dish

INGREDIENTS

FOR THE FILLING
3 tbsp all-purpose flour
salt and freshly ground black pepper
1½lb (675g) beef stew meat,
cut into ¾in (2cm) pieces
3 tbsp sunflower oil
1 large onion, chopped
1 garlic clove, crushed
4oz (115g) button mushrooms, halved
⅔ cup beef stock
⅔ cup brown ale
1 bay leaf
½ tsp dried thyme
1 tbsp Worcestershire sauce
1 tbsp tomato paste

FOR THE DOUGH
12oz (350g) store-bought puff pie dough
(or to make your own, see pp.110–113)
flour, for dusting
1 egg, beaten, or milk, to glaze

1 To make the filling, season the flour to taste with salt and pepper. Toss the beef in the flour, shaking off any excess. Heat 2 tablespoons of the oil in a large saucepan and brown the beef in batches over high heat until browned on all sides. Remove beef to a plate and set aside.

2 Add remaining oil to the pan and fry the onion over medium heat for 5 minutes. Add the garlic and mushrooms and cook for 3-4 minutes until starting to brown, stirring frequently.

3 Add the stock, ale, bay leaf, thyme, Worcestershire sauce, tomato paste, and browned beef to the pan. Bring to a boil, scraping up any browned bits from the bottom. Reduce the heat, cover, and simmer gently for 1½ hours, or until the meat is tender.

4 With a slotted spoon, transfer the meat and vegetables to the pie dish. Reserve ⅔ cup of the gravy and pour the rest over the meat mixture. Cool.

5 Preheat the oven to 400°F (200°C). Roll out the dough on a lightly floured surface to a thickness of ⅛in (3mm), and 2in (5cm) larger than the dish. Cut a ¾in (2cm) strip, brush the dish rim with water, and place the strip on the rim. Brush with water. Place the dough over the dish, press the edges together to seal, trim off the excess dough, and crimp.

6 Decorate the top of the pie with the dough trimmings, then brush the dough with the beaten egg or milk, and cut a slit in the middle to allow steam to escape. Bake for 25 minutes, or until puffed and golden. Serve the pie hot with the reserved gravy. The filling can be made up to 24 hours ahead and kept, covered, in the refrigerator.

Although most pies tend to be single-crusted, a good old-fashioned pie like this steak and kidney one should always have a double crust to soak up the deliciously meaty, dark gravy.

STEAK AND KIDNEY DOUBLE-CRUST PIE

 SERVES 4   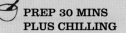 PREP 30 MINS PLUS CHILLING   COOK 2¾–3¼ HRS   FREEZE UNCOOKED, UP TO 2 MONTHS

1 Toss the steak in 2 tablespoons of seasoned flour. Heat half the olive oil in a large saucepan and brown the beef in batches over high heat on all sides. Transfer the meat as it cooks to a large plate. Lower heat to medium and add remaining oil to the saucepan. Add the onions, season with salt and pepper and cook for 5 minutes until soft, but not browned. Add mushrooms and cook for 3-4 minutes. Return steak to the pan, cover with stock, season, and add the thyme. Bring to a boil, reduce the heat to low, cover, and cook for 2–2½ hours, until tender.

2 To make the dough, rub the flour and lard together until the mixture resembles bread crumbs. Add the salt and enough cold water to form a soft dough. Wrap in plastic wrap and chill for 30 minutes.

3 Mash 2 tablespoons of all-purpose flour into the butter. Uncover the stew and increase the heat. When it boils, stir in the paste a little at a time. Reduce the heat and cook for 30 minutes until thick. Add the kidneys. Preheat the oven to 350°F (180°C).

4 Roll out the dough on a lightly floured surface to an 8in x 16in (20cm x 40cm) rectangle, ⅛–¼in (3–5mm) thick. Place the dish onto a short edge of the dough and cut a circle around it for the lid. Grease the dish, trim the remaining dough, and use to line the dish, allowing the sides to overhang. Fill with the filling and brush the edges with egg. Cover with the lid and seal. Brush with egg; cut 2 slits in the top. Bake for 40–45 minutes until golden brown. Cool for 5 minutes and eat the same day.

EQUIPMENT
7in (18cm) pie dish

INGREDIENTS

FOR THE FILLING
4 tbsp olive oil, plus extra for greasing
2 onions, finely chopped
4oz (100g) button mushrooms, wiped, halved or quartered, if necessary
1lb 5oz (600g) stewing steak, such as chuck, cut into 1¼in (3cm) chunks
¼ cup all-purpose flour
sea salt and freshly ground black pepper
2 cups beef stock
a large sprig of thyme
2 tbsp unsalted butter, softened
4 fresh lamb's kidneys, about 7oz (200g), trimmed, central core cut out, and cut into chunks

FOR THE DOUGH
(For visual step-by-step instructions see lard pie dough pp.106–107)
1½ cups self-rising flour, plus extra for dusting
⅔ cup lard or vegetable shortening
½ tsp salt
1 egg, beaten, to glaze

Most cobblers rise like scones when baked, however, if you use all-purpose flour they take on a different texture, resulting in a thinner, crisper cobbler topping. This topping will work well with any rich stew.

BEEF, FENNEL, AND MUSHROOM COBBLER

 SERVES 8   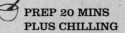 PREP 20 MINS PLUS CHILLING   🕐 COOK 2½ HRS   ❄ FREEZE STEW, UP TO 2 MONTHS

1 Preheat the oven to 350°F (180°C). Season the meat well, place in a large bowl, and toss with the flour and paprika so the pieces are evenly coated.

2 Heat half the olive oil in the pan, add the meat, and cook over medium heat, stirring frequently, for 8–10 minutes until evenly browned. Brown the meat in batches, since there will be too much to cook together. Remove with a slotted spoon and set aside.

3 Heat the remaining oil in the pan. Add the onions and cook for 6–8 minutes, until soft. Season well. Add the fennel and cook for 6 minutes, until beginning to soften slightly. Add the wine, increase the heat, and simmer for 1–2 minutes, until the alcohol evaporates. Return the meat to the pan, pour in the stock, and bring to a boil. Cover with a lid and bake for 1 hour.

4 To make the topping, rub the flour, cornmeal, a pinch of salt, and the butter together with your fingertips until the mixture resembles bread crumbs. Stir through enough milk to form a soft dough. Chill for 20 minutes, then roll out the dough on a floured surface and cut out 16 circles with the cookie cutter.

5 When the beef has been cooking for 1 hour, melt the butter in a frying pan. Add the mushrooms and oregano, and cook for 5 minutes, or until soft. Stir into the beef and fennel and cook for another 30 minutes. Increase the oven temperature to 400°F (200°C). Top the stew with the cobbler circles, overlapping them so there are few gaps where the filling can be seen. Brush them with the egg and bake for 30–40 minutes, until golden brown. Rest for 5 minutes before serving.

EQUIPMENT
large cast-iron pan,
2⅜in (6cm) round cookie cutter

INGREDIENTS

FOR THE FILLING
2½lb (1kg) beef stew meat,
  cut into bite-sized pieces
salt and freshly ground black pepper
1 tbsp all-purpose flour
2 tsp mild paprika
3 tbsp olive oil
2 onions, finely sliced
3 fennel bulbs, trimmed
  and cut into eighths
⅔ cup dry white wine
4 cups hot beef or vegetable stock
a pat of butter
1lb (450g) cremini mushrooms, quartered
a pinch of dried oregano

FOR THE COBBLER TOPPING
(For visual step-by-step instructions,
  see cobbler dough pp.118–119)
1 cup each all-purpose flour and cornmeal,
  plus extra for dusting
4 tbsp butter
⅓ cup milk
1 large egg yolk, beaten, to glaze

This classic pie is a good midweek standby when time is short. If you're serving a stew, make double quantities and serve half another day with this light, buttery crust for a quick and tasty meal.

HERB STEAK AND VEGETABLE PIE

SERVES 4   PREP 20 MINS   COOK 1½ HRS   FREEZE UP TO 1 MONTH

EQUIPMENT
1 quart pie dish

INGREDIENTS

FOR THE FILLING
1 potato, peeled and cut into bite-sized pieces
2 carrots, peeled and cut into bite-sized pieces
1 parsnip, peeled and cut into bite-sized pieces
salt and freshly ground black pepper
1½lb (675g) beef stew meat, chopped into bite-sized pieces
2 tbsp olive oil
1 onion, finely chopped
1 tbsp all-purpose flour
1 tbsp Worcestershire sauce
1¼ cups beef stock
⅔ cup red wine
2 tbsp finely chopped rosemary leaves
1 bay leaf

FOR THE DOUGH
10oz (300g) store-bought pie dough
(or to make your own, see pp.110–113)
flour, for dusting
1 large egg, lightly beaten, to glaze

1 Boil the potato, carrots, and parsnip chunks in a saucepan of salted water for 15 minutes, until soft. Drain and set aside. Put the meat in a large, nonstick frying pan with 1 tablespoon of the olive oil, and cook over high heat for 5–8 minutes, until browned all over. Remove with a slotted spoon and set aside.

2 Heat the remaining oil in the frying pan over low heat. Add the onion and a pinch of salt, and sweat gently for about 5 minutes, until soft and translucent. Stir in the flour, and continue to cook for another 2 minutes. Increase the heat a little, and add the Worcestershire sauce, stock, wine, rosemary, and bay leaf. Bring to a boil, reduce the heat slightly, and return the meat to the pan. Cover and simmer gently over low heat for about 30 minutes, stirring occasionally. Stir in the cooked vegetables and season well with salt and pepper.

3 Meanwhile, preheat the oven to 400°F (200°C). Remove the bay leaf from the meat and spoon it into the pie dish. Roll out the dough on a floured surface so that it is about 2in (5cm) larger all around than the top of the dish. Cut out a strip of dough about 1in (2.5cm) in from the edge to make a collar. Dampen the edge of the dish with a little water, fit the dough strip all the way around, and press down firmly.

4 Brush the dough collar with a little of the beaten egg, then top with the dough lid. Trim away the excess dough, then using your finger and thumb, pinch the edges of the dough together to seal. Brush the top of the pie with beaten egg, then cut 2 slits to allow steam to escape. Bake for 30 minutes, or until puffed up and golden brown. Serve hot.

A twist on a classic Boeuf Bourguignon, this hearty dish is topped with circles of dough flavored with horseradish. If you find horseradish too strong, try using your favorite mustard instead.

BEEF AND RED WINE COBBLER

SERVES 4   **PREP 40 MINS**   **COOK 2½–3½ HRS**   **FREEZE STEW, UP TO 2 MONTHS**

1 Toss the beef in 2 tablespoons seasoned flour. Heat half the olive oil in a large ovenproof Dutch oven over medium-high heat and fry the meat a few pieces at a time, until browned on all sides. Make sure not to overcrowd the pan or the meat will begin to steam rather than brown. Remove the meat as it cooks to a plate.

2 Heat the remaining oil in the pot and fry the onions and celery for 5 minutes, until soft but not brown. Add the mushrooms and fry for 3–4 minutes, until they begin to color in places.

3 Return the meat and vegetables to the Dutch oven and cover with the wine. Crumble in the bouillon cube, add 1¼ cups boiling water, the bouquet garni, sugar, and parsnips. Season and bring to a boil. Reduce the heat to its lowest setting, cover, and cook for 2–2½ hours, until the meat is tender. Check it from time to time, adding a little water if it is drying out.

4 Preheat the oven to 400°F (200°C). To make the cobbler topping, sift together the flour and salt. Rub in the butter with your fingertips until the mixture resembles fine bread crumbs. Add the parsley. Whisk the horseradish and milk, and mix with the dry ingredients to form a soft dough. Roll out the dough on a floured surface to ¾in (2cm) thick. Using the round cookie cutter, cut out circles. Re-roll the offcuts and cut again until the dough is used up. When the stew is cooked, remove the bouquet garni and top it with the dough disks, overlapping them slightly.

5 Brush the tops with egg and bake for 30–40 minutes, until puffed up and golden. Rest for 5 minutes before serving.

EQUIPMENT
large ovenproof Dutch oven, round cookie cutter

INGREDIENTS

FOR THE FILLING
1lb 5oz (600g) beef stew meat or chuck roast, cut into 1¼in (3cm) chunks
2 tbsp all-purpose flour
sea salt and freshly ground black pepper
4 tbsp olive oil
2 onions, finely chopped
2 celery stalks, finely cubed
6oz (150g) baby cremini mushrooms, wiped
2 cups red wine
1 beef bouillon cube
1 bouquet garni
1 tbsp sugar
2 parsnips, cut into ¾in (2cm) chunks

FOR THE COBBLER TOPPING
(For visual step-by-step instructions, see cobbler dough pp.118–119)
2¼ cups self-rising flour, plus extra for dusting
½ tsp salt
8 tbsp unsalted butter, chilled and cubed
1 tbsp finely chopped parsley
3 tbsp horseradish sauce or horseradish cream
2–4 tbsp milk
1 large egg, beaten, to glaze

These tasty meat and potato hand pies were originally created as a portable meal for field workers to carry with them. The thick-pleated crust was used as a handle for dirty hands and discarded after use.

CORNISH PASTIES

 MAKES 4   PREP 20 MINS PLUS CHILLING   COOK 40–45 MINS   FREEZE UP TO 1 MONTH

EQUIPMENT
baking sheet

INGREDIENTS

FOR THE DOUGH
(For visual step-by-step instructions see pie dough p.104)
½ cup lard, chilled and cubed
4 tbsp unsalted butter, chilled and cubed
1½ cups all-purpose flour, plus extra for dusting
½ tsp salt
1 large egg, beaten, to glaze

FOR THE FILLING
9oz (250g) skirt steak, trimmed and cut into ½in (1cm) cubes
3oz (80g) rutabaga, peeled and cut into ¼in (5mm) cubes
4oz (100g) red potatoes, peeled and cut into ¼in (5mm) cubes
1 large onion, finely chopped
splash of Worcestershire sauce
1 tsp all-purpose flour
sea salt and freshly ground black pepper

1 To make the dough, rub the lard and butter into the flour until the mixture resembles fine bread crumbs. Add the salt and enough cold water to bring the mixture together into a soft dough. On a lightly floured surface, knead the dough briefly, then wrap in plastic wrap and chill in the refrigerator for 30 minutes.

2 Preheat the oven to 375°F (190°C). Mix all the filling ingredients together and season well with salt and pepper.

3 Roll out the dough on a well-floured surface to ¼in (5mm) thick. Using a side plate, or saucer, cut 4 circles from the dough. Re-roll the offcuts. Fold the circles in half, then flatten them out, leaving a slight mark down the center. Pile one-quarter of the filling into each circle, leaving a ¾in (2cm) border all around.

4 Brush the border of the dough with a little beaten egg. Pull both edges up over the filling and press together to seal. Crimp the sealed edge with your fingers to form a decorative ridge along the top. Brush a little beaten egg all over the finished pasties.

5 Bake in the middle of the oven for 40–45 minutes until golden brown. Set the pasties aside to cool for at least 15 minutes before eating warm or cold. These will keep in the refrigerator for 2 days.

A classic flavor combination of beef and Stilton cheese is used in this rich, tasty pie. Make the pie dough for a luxurious topping, otherwise use store-bought pie dough for a speedier result.

BEEF AND STILTON PIE

SERVES 2   PREP 20 MINS   COOK 50 MINS – 1 HR   FREEZE UP TO 1 MONTH

EQUIPMENT
9in (22cm) pie dish

INGREDIENTS

FOR THE FILLING
1 tbsp olive oil
a pat of butter
2 onions, roughly chopped
12oz (350g) leftover roast beef, sliced
⅔ cup hot beef stock
salt and freshly ground black pepper
5oz (125g) blue cheese, such as Stilton

FOR THE DOUGH
9oz (250g) store-bought puff pie dough
(or to make your own, see pp.110–113)
all-purpose flour, for dusting
1 large egg, lightly beaten, to glaze

1 Preheat the oven to 400°F (200°C). To make the filling, heat the olive oil and butter in a saucepan over low heat. Add the onions and sweat very gently for 5–8 minutes, until soft and translucent.

2 Add the leftover beef to the onions and pour in the stock. Bring to a boil, then reduce the heat slightly, and simmer for about 10 minutes. Season with salt and black pepper. Set aside to cool slightly, then spoon the mixture into the pie dish, and crumble the the blue cheese over the top.

3 Roll out the dough on a lightly floured surface until it is a little larger than the pie dish. Cut out a strip of dough about 1in (2.5cm) from the edge to make a collar. Dampen the edge of the pie dish with a little water, fit the dough strip all the way around, and press down firmly. Brush the collar with a little beaten egg and top with the dough lid. Trim away the excess dough, then using your finger and thumb, pinch the edges of the dough together to seal.

4 Brush the top of the pie with the beaten egg to glaze, cut a slit in the top to allow the steam to escape, and bake for 30–40 minutes, until golden and puffed. Serve the pie hot.

Originating in Scotland, these delectable hand pies are a regional alternative to the Cornish Pasty. The simple steak and onion filling is complemented by the richness of traditional lard-based pie dough.

FORFAR BRIDIES

 MAKES 4    PREP 15 MINS
PLUS CHILLING   COOK 20–25 MINS   FREEZE UP TO
1 MONTH

1 To make the dough, rub the lard into the 2 types of flour until the mixture resembles bread crumbs. Add the salt and enough cold water to form a soft dough. Bring the dough together, wrap, and chill for 30 minutes. Preheat the oven to 400°F (200°C).

2 Mix the beef, onion, Worcestershire sauce, and salt and pepper together, then set aside. Roll out the dough on a floured surface to ¼in (5mm) thick. Using a side plate or saucer, cut 4 circles out of the dough. You may need to re-roll the offcuts to get all 4. If the dough cracks on rolling, gather it together and start again; the re-rolling will make it more robust. Fold the circles in half, trim the sides so that they are more rectangular in shape, then flatten them out again.

3 Pile one-quarter of the filling onto one-half of each dough circle, leaving a ¾in (2cm) border. Brush the border with a little beaten egg. Now fold the dough over and crimp the edges together. Brush the finished bridies with a little beaten egg, and cut a slit in the top of each one to allow the steam to escape.

4 Bake for 20–25 minutes, until golden brown. Set aside to cool for at least 10 minutes before eating. The bridies will keep in the refrigerator for 2 days.

EQUIPMENT
baking sheet

INGREDIENTS

FOR THE DOUGH
(For visual step-by-step instructions
  see pie dough p.104)
⅔ cup lard, chilled and cubed
1½ cups self-rising flour,
  plus extra for dusting
¾ all-purpose flour
½ tsp salt
1 large egg, beaten, to glaze

FOR THE FILLING
10oz (300g) finely chopped skirt steak
1 onion, finely chopped
splash of Worcestershire sauce
sea salt and freshly ground black pepper

Otherwise known as Beef Wellington, this impressive dish is perfect for entertaining. Cooking the puff pastry first, before laying the seared beef on top, helps to keep the pastry crisp.

BOEUF EN CROÛTE

SERVES 6   **PREP 45 MINS**   **COOK 45 MINS–1 HR**

EQUIPMENT
baking sheet

INGREDIENTS

FOR THE FILLING
2¼lb (1kg) beef tenderloin, cut from the thick end of the loin, trimmed of fat
salt and freshly ground black pepper
2 tbsp sunflower or olive oil
3 tbsp butter
2 shallots, finely chopped
1 garlic clove, crushed
9oz (250g) wild mushrooms, finely chopped
1 tbsp brandy or Madeira

FOR THE PASTRY
1lb 2oz (500g) store-bought puff pastry
(or to make your own, see pp.110–113)
all-purpose flour, for dusting
1 large egg, beaten, to glaze

1 Preheat the oven to 425°F (220°C). Season the meat with salt and pepper. Heat the oil in a large frying pan and fry the beef until browned all over. Place the beef in a roasting pan and roast for 10 minutes. Remove and set aside to cool.

2 Melt the butter in a saucepan. Fry the shallots and garlic for 2–3 minutes, stirring, until softened. Add the mushrooms, and cook, stirring constantly, for 4–5 minutes, until the juices evaporate. Add the brandy. Let it bubble for 30 seconds. Set aside to cool.

3 Roll out one-third of the pastry on a floured surface to a rectangle, 2in (5cm) larger than the beef. Place on a baking sheet, prick with a fork, then bake for 12–15 minutes, until crisp. Cool. Spread one-third of the mushroom mix on the center of the cooked pastry. Make the en croûte (see below). Brush the egg over the uncooked pastry crust. Slit the top to allow steam to escape. Bake 30 minutes for rare and 45 minutes for well done. If the pastry starts to brown too much, cover loosely with foil. Rest for 10 minutes before serving.

Making the en croûte

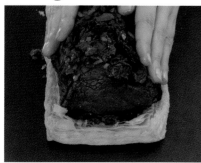

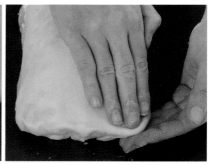

1 Place the beef on top of the cooked pastry and spread the remaining mushroom mixture over the meat.

2 Roll out the remaining pastry and place it over the beef, tucking in the edges.

3 Brush the beaten egg around the edges, and press down the raw pastry to seal.

These spicy little parcels are little more than an exotic adaptation of a Cornish Pasty, or a British version of a samosa and are perfect for any occasion. They are best served warm with a mixed salad.

SPICY BEEF HAND PIES

 **MAKES 8**   **PREP 20 MINS**   **COOK 50 MINS**   **FREEZE UP TO 1 MONTH**

1 Preheat the oven to 400°F (200°C). Season steak on all sides with salt and pepper. Heat 1 tablespoon of the olive oil in a large frying pan over medium-high heat. Add the steak and brown for about 3 minutes on each side to seal. Remove from the pan and set aside.

2 Heat the remaining oil in the same pan over low heat. Add the onions and a pinch of salt, and sweat for about 5 minutes, until soft and translucent. Add the garlic, chiles, ginger, coriander, and cumin and cook, stirring, for about 2 minutes, until fragrant. Add in the mushrooms, red bell pepper, and tomatoes and season with the cayenne pepper. Continue cooking over low heat for 5 minutes, until the mushrooms soften and begin to release their juices.

3 Slice the reserved steak into strips, and return to the pan along with 2 tablespoons water. Season and cook for about 2 minutes until the mixture is thick and moist, but not too runny.

4 Roll out the pastry on a floured surface, and cut into eight 7in (18cm) squares. Dampen each square around the edges with a little water. Divide the meat and onion filling into 8 equal portions, and spoon each one into the middle of a square. Bring together the opposite corners of each pastry square to form a parcel, pinching together to seal. Brush all over with the beaten egg and bake on the baking sheet for 20–30 minutes, until golden. Serve warm. The pies can be made a day ahead. Fill the pastry and make into parcels, then keep in the refrigerator until needed. Brush with the beaten egg, and bake as above.

EQUIPMENT
baking sheet

INGREDIENTS

FOR THE FILLING
1lb 2oz (500g) flank steak
2 tbsp olive oil
2 red onions, finely chopped
salt
2 garlic cloves, grated
  or finely chopped
2–3 medium-hot green chiles,
  seeded and finely chopped
3in (7.5cm) piece of ginger,
  finely chopped
1½ tsp coriander seeds, crushed
1½ tsp cumin seeds, crushed
5½oz (150g) mushrooms,
  finely chopped
1 red bell pepper, finely chopped
2 tomatoes, peeled, skinned, seeded,
  and finely chopped
½ tsp cayenne pepper

FOR THE DOUGH
1lb 5oz (600g) store-bought pie dough
  (or to make your own, see p.104)
all-purpose flour, for dusting
1 large egg, lightly beaten, to glaze

This classic French pie is like a continental version of the traditional British Cottage Pie. Originally designed to use up leftover roast beef, it is more commonly prepared using fresh ground beef.

FRENCH BEEF AND HERB POTATO PIE

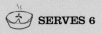 **SERVES 6**   **PREP 25–30 MINS**   **COOK 2–2½ HRS**

1 Finely chop 2 garlic cloves. Heat one-third of the olive oil in a sauté or frying pan. Add the onion and cook for 3–5 minutes, stirring, until soft but not brown. Add the chopped garlic, ground beef, salt and pepper, and tomatoes. Reduce the heat and cook gently, stirring occasionally, for 10–12 minutes, until the meat is brown. Stir in the stock and wine. Simmer over very low heat for 25–30 minutes, stirring occasionally, until most of the liquid has evaporated, but the meat is still moist. Do not cook the meat too fast or it will be tough.

2 To make the topping, place the potatoes in a saucepan with plenty of cold water and add salt. Cover and bring to a boil. Reduce the heat and simmer for 15–20 minutes, until tender when pierced with a knife. Pulse the basil, parsley leaves, and the rest of the garlic with the remaining oil in a food processor to form a purée, scraping the side of the bowl occasionally.

3 Drain the potatoes, return them to the pan and mash. Add the herb purée. Scald the milk in another pan. Gradually beat the milk into the potatoes over medium heat, and stir for 2–3 minutes, until the potatoes just hold a shape. Season to taste.

4 Preheat the oven to 375°F (190°C). Grease the baking dish with oil. Taste the meat for seasoning, then spoon it, with any of its liquid, into the dish. Spoon an even layer of the potatoes over the filling and smooth the top with the back of a spoon. Make a scalloped pattern on the potatoes. Bake until the top is golden brown, the edges bubbling with gravy, and the tip of a skewer inserted in the center for 30 seconds is hot to the touch when withdrawn; it should take 35–40 minutes. Cut the pie into 6 portions and serve.

EQUIPMENT
large shallow baking dish

INGREDIENTS

FOR THE FILLING
4 garlic cloves, peeled
⅓ cup olive oil,
   plus extra for greasing
1 large onion, diced
2¼lb (1kg) ground beef
salt and freshly ground black pepper
14oz can chopped tomatoes
1 cup beef stock
½ cup dry white wine

FOR THE TOPPING
2¼lb (1kg) potatoes, peeled
   and cut into 2–3 pieces
salt
1 bunch of basil, leaves only
1 bunch of parsley, leaves only
1 cup milk,
   plus extra if needed

The addition of pine nuts, dried apricots, and Middle Eastern spices turns this lamb pie into something special. Serve with a tossed salad garnished with finely sliced red onions and black olives.

FRUITY LAMB PIE

🍲 SERVES 4   🥣 PREP 15 MINS   ⏰ COOK 1¼ HRS   ❄ FREEZE UP TO 1 MONTH

EQUIPMENT
9in (23cm) deep dish

INGREDIENTS

FOR THE FILLING
1–2 tbsp olive oil
1 onion, finely chopped
salt and freshly ground black pepper
2 garlic cloves, grated or finely chopped
12oz (350g) boneless leg of lamb,
cut into bite-sized pieces
1 tsp ground turmeric
½ tsp ground allspice
1 tsp ground coriander
1 tsp ground cumin
2 tbsp all-purpose flour,
plus extra for dusting
3 cups hot lamb stock
2oz (50g) pine nuts
2oz (50g) dried apricots, roughly chopped
2oz (50g) raisins

FOR THE DOUGH
10oz (300g) store-bought pie dough
(or to make your own, see p.104)
1 large egg, lightly beaten, to glaze

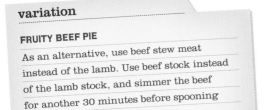

variation

FRUITY BEEF PIE
As an alternative, use beef stew meat instead of the lamb. Use beef stock instead of the lamb stock, and simmer the beef for another 30 minutes before spooning it into the pie dish.

1 Heat 1 tablespoon of the olive oil in a large Dutch oven over low heat. Add the onion and a pinch of salt, and sweat gently for about 5 minutes, until soft and translucent. Add the garlic, then increase the heat to medium, and add a little extra olive oil if needed. Add the lamb, and sprinkle over the spices. Cook, stirring occasionally, for 6–8 minutes, until the lamb is browned all over.

2 Remove from the heat, and stir in the flour and 1 tablespoon of the stock. Return to the heat, and pour in the remaining stock. Add the pine nuts, apricots, and raisins and season well with salt and pepper. Bring to a boil, reduce the heat to low, and simmer gently, stirring occasionally so that the mixture doesn't stick, for about 20 minutes, or until the sauce has thickened.

3 Meanwhile, preheat the oven to 400°F (200°C). Spoon the meat filling into the pie dish. Roll out the dough on a floured surface so that it is about 2in (5cm) larger than the top of the pie dish. Cut out a strip of dough about 1in (2.5cm) in from the edge to make a collar. Dampen the edge of the pie dish with a little water, fit the dough strip all the way around, and press down firmly. Brush the dough collar with a little of the beaten egg, then top with the dough lid. Trim away the excess dough, then, using your finger and thumb, pinch the edges of the dough together to seal. Decorate the top with any leftover dough, if liked.

4 Brush the top of the pie with the remaining beaten egg, then cut 2 slits in the top to allow steam to escape. Bake for 30–40 minutes, until cooked and golden brown all over. Serve hot.

Traditionally made with bone-in lamb chops, this hearty dish can also be made with cubed lamb. Although unusual, the addition of anchovies adds a piquancy, but by no means leaves a fishy taste.

LANCASHIRE HOTPOT

 SERVES 8   PREP 25 MINS   COOK 2½ HRS

1 Preheat the oven to 350°F (180°C). Heat a drizzle of the olive oil in a large frying pan, add the lamb chops, and cook over medium heat for 2 minutes on each side until lightly browned. You might need to do this in two batches if your pan is not that big.

2 Put a layer of the potatoes in the bottom of the dish, lay the chops on top, and season well with salt and pepper. Heat the remaining oil in the frying pan, add the onions, and cook over low heat, stirring frequently, for 10 minutes, or until beginning to soften. Stir in the anchovies. Spoon a layer of the onion mixture on top of the chops, then add the rest of the sliced potatoes and the onion mixture in alternating layers, finishing with a layer of sliced potatoes.

3 Pour in enough of the stock to come nearly up to the top of the potatoes. Dot the potatoes with butter, cover the dish tightly with foil, then bake for 2 hours, or until the potatoes are meltingly soft and the stock has been absorbed. Remove the foil for the last 20 minutes of cooking. Serve with pickled red cabbage.

EQUIPMENT
2 quart flameproof dish

INGREDIENTS
2 tbsp olive oil
8 large lamb chops, each about
   7oz (200g) in weight
2lb (900g) potatoes,
   cut into ¼in (5mm) slices
salt and freshly ground black pepper
4 onions, sliced
8 salted anchovies, finely chopped
2 cups hot vegetable stock
a pat of butter

A perfect supper for using up leftover roasted lamb and a very simple pie to put together if you use store-bought dough. The key flavors are brightened with fresh rosemary.

LAMB AND POTATO PIE

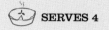 SERVES 4　　　　PREP 20 MINS　　　　COOK 1 HR 20 MINS

EQUIPMENT
7in (18cm) round pie pan

INGREDIENTS

FOR THE FILLING
1lb (450g) potatoes, peeled and quartered
salt and freshly ground black pepper
1 tbsp olive oil
1 onion, finely chopped
handful of rosemary sprigs, leaves picked and chopped
12oz (350g) leftover roasted lamb, roughly shredded or sliced
1 tbsp all-purpose flour, plus extra for dusting
1¼ cups hot vegetable stock
2–3 tsp mint sauce

FOR THE DOUGH
9oz (250g) store-bought pie dough (or to make your own, see p.104)
1 large egg, lightly beaten, to glaze

1 Preheat the oven to 400°F (200°C). Cook the potatoes in a saucepan of boiling salted water for 15 minutes until soft, then drain and set aside.

2 Heat the olive oil in another large pan over low heat. Add the onion and sweat gently for about 5 minutes, until soft and translucent. Stir in the rosemary and add the leftover lamb. Season well with salt and pepper.

3 Sprinkle in the flour and stir in, then pour in the stock. Keep stirring for about 10 minutes over medium heat, until the liquid begins to thicken, then add the reserved potatoes and stir in the mint sauce. Simmer for another 10 minutes, then cool slightly.

4 Divide the dough into 2 pieces, one a little larger than the other. Roll out the larger piece into a large circle on a floured surface and use to line the pie pan, allowing the dough to hang over the edge. Roll out the other piece to make the dough lid.

5 Spoon the lamb mixture into the crust, then place the dough lid on top. Using your finger and thumb, pinch the edges of the dough together to seal, and trim away the excess. Brush the top evenly with a little beaten egg and bake for 40–50 minutes, until the crust is cooked and golden. Set aside to cool in the pan for at least 15 minutes before serving.

There are many recipes for Shepherd's Pie, but the classic, creamy potato topping is a must. Add a little mustard, horseradish, or even Worcestershire sauce to the mashed potatoes for an individual twist.

SHEPHERD'S PIE

 SERVES 4   PREP 30 MINS   COOK 1 HR
20 MINS   FREEZE UP TO
6 MONTHS

1 Cook the potatoes in a large saucepan of boiling salted water for 15 minutes, or until soft. Drain, return to the pan, and mash well. Add the butter and mash again until creamy. Season with salt and pepper, then set aside.

2 Meanwhile, heat the olive oil in a large heavy-bottomed pan over medium heat. Add the onions and carrots and cook for 5 minutes, or until the onions are starting to soften. Add the lamb and cook, stirring constantly, for 10 minutes, or until no longer pink. Add the garlic and oregano and cook for 1 minute. Stir in the tomatoes and bring to a boil. Preheat the oven to 350°F (180°C).

3 Add the peas to the pan, and season well with salt and pepper. Bring to a boil, then reduce the heat and simmer for 20 minutes, stirring occasionally.

4 Pour a layer of the lamb and vegetable filling into a large dish, or the individual serving dishes, and top with the set-aside mashed potatoes. Bake for 25 minutes, or until brown on top and piping hot.

EQUIPMENT
large ovenproof dish,
or 4 individual serving dishes

INGREDIENTS

FOR THE TOPPING
1¼lb (500g) Russet potatoes
a pat of butter
salt and freshly ground black pepper

FOR THE FILLING
3 tbsp olive oil
1 large onion, cubed
2 large carrots, cubed
1¼lb (500g) ground lamb
3 garlic cloves, chopped
1½ tsp dried oregano
2 x 14oz cans chopped tomatoes
5oz (125g) frozen peas

When you have little more than a package of sausages and some tomatoes in the house, this is a fantastic alternative to sausage and mashed potatoes. Of course, fresh sausage meat can also be used.

CREOLE SAUSAGE AND TOMATO TART

SERVES 4   **PREP 15 MINS**   **COOK 1 HR 10 MINS**

EQUIPMENT
8in (20cm) square baking dish or fluted tart pan, baking beans

INGREDIENTS

FOR THE DOUGH
8oz (225g) ready-made pie dough
(or to make your own, see p.104)
all-purpose flour, for dusting
1 large egg, lightly beaten

FOR THE FILLING
½ tbsp olive oil
1 onion, finely chopped
salt and freshly ground black pepper
2 stalks celery, sliced
1 green bell pepper, finely sliced
½ tsp paprika
½ tsp cayenne pepper
½ tsp dried thyme
1 tsp dried oregano
14oz (400g) good-quality pork
sausages, casings removed
4 tomatoes, sliced

1 Preheat the oven to 400°F (200°C). Roll out the dough on a floured surface and use to line the baking dish or tart pan. Trim away any excess dough, line the crust with wax paper, and fill with baking beans. Bake for 15–20 minutes, until the edges are golden. Remove the beans and paper, brush the bottom of the crust with a little beaten egg, and return to the oven for 2–3 minutes to crisp. Remove from the oven, and set aside. Reduce the oven temperature to 350°F (180°C).

2 Meanwhile, for the filling, heat the olive oil in a large frying pan over low heat. Add the onion and a pinch of salt, and sweat gently for about 5 minutes, until soft and translucent. Add the celery and green bell pepper and cook for another 5 minutes. Add the paprika, cayenne, thyme, oregano, and ¼ teaspoon black pepper, and season well with salt. Add the sausage meat, breaking it up with a fork or the back of a spatula. Cook, stirring regularly, over low-medium heat for about 10 minutes, until no longer pink. Set aside to cool, then mix in the remaining egg.

3 Spoon the sausage mixture into the pie crust, then layer the tomatoes over the top. Bake for about 20 minutes, until lightly golden. Set aside to cool for about 10 minutes, then slice in the dish or pan. Serve with a crisp tossed salad.

The unusual addition of a little ketchup in the pastry here gives the crust extra flavor. This family-sized pie is perfect for those times when you want to prepare a special picnic or meal for a garden party.

SAUSAGE, BACON, AND EGG PIE

 SERVES 6–8   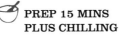 PREP 15 MINS PLUS CHILLING   COOK 50 MINS

1 To make the dough, place the flour and butter in a food processor and pulse until the mixture resembles bread crumbs. To make by hand, rub the butter into the flour with your fingertips until the mixture resembles bread crumbs. Season with salt and pepper, then add the ketchup and 5–6 tablespoons cold water, and pulse or mix again, until it comes together in a ball. Wrap the dough in plastic wrap and chill in the refrigerator for 30 minutes.

2 Preheat the oven to 400°F (200°C). Roll out half of the dough fairly thinly on a lightly floured surface and use to line the pie dish.

3 To make the filling, mix the sausage meat with the onion, nutmeg, mace, and mustard. Season to taste and spread evenly over the bottom of the pie crust. Place the bacon over the sausage mixture in lines and crack the eggs over the bacon, leaving them intact if possible, since it looks nice when slicing the pie.

4 Roll out the remaining pastry and use to cover the pie, then pinch the edges with your thumb and forefinger to seal. Lightly score a crisscross pattern on top and brush with a little milk.

5 Bake the pie for 20 minutes, then reduce the heat to 350°F (180°C), and bake for another 30 minutes. Cool before serving. You can make the pie dough the day before and chill until ready to use.

EQUIPMENT
8in (20cm) deep-dish pie pan

INGREDIENTS

FOR THE DOUGH
(For visual step-by-step instructions, see pie dough p.104)
2 cups all-purpose flour, plus extra for dusting
12 tbsp butter
salt and freshly ground black pepper
1½ tbsp ketchup

FOR THE FILLING
1lb (450g) sausage meat or good-quality pork sausages, casings removed
½ onion, finely chopped
a pinch of nutmeg
a pinch of mace
1 tbsp whole grain mustard
6 slices thick-cut bacon
4 large eggs
milk, to glaze

Making your own Sausage Rolls (especially using store-bought pie dough) is surprisingly easy. They can be prepared in advance then frozen, uncooked, making them perfect for entertaining.

SAUSAGE ROLLS

MAKES 24

PREP 30 MINS PLUS CHILLING

COOK 10–12 MINS

FREEZE UNCOOKED, UP TO 3 MONTHS

EQUIPMENT
baking sheet

INGREDIENTS

FOR THE DOUGH
14oz (400g) store-bought pie dough
(or to make your own, see pp.110–113)
all-purpose flour, for dusting
1 egg, beaten, to glaze

FOR THE FILLING
1½lb (675g) sausage meat
1 small onion, finely chopped
1 tbsp chopped thyme
1 tbsp grated lemon zest
1 tsp Dijon mustard
1 large egg yolk
salt and freshly ground black pepper

1 Preheat the oven to 400°F (200°C). Line a baking sheet with wax paper and chill.

2 Place the pie dough on a lightly floured surface and cut in half lengthwise. Roll out each piece to form a 12in x 6in (30cm x 15cm) rectangle, then cover with plastic wrap, and chill in the refrigerator.

3 Meanwhile, combine the sausage meat with the onion, thyme, lemon zest, mustard, and egg yolk, and season with salt and pepper.

4 Lay the dough on a floured surface. Form the sausage mixture into 2 thinly rolled tubes and place in the center of each piece of dough. Brush the inside of the dough with the beaten egg, then roll the dough over and press to seal. Cut each roll into 12 pieces.

5 Place the rolls on the chilled sheet, cut 2 snips in the top of each with scissors, then brush with beaten egg. Bake for 10–12 minutes, or until the dough is golden and flaky. Serve warm or transfer to a wire rack to cool completely before serving. These sausage rolls are good with a spicy mustard dipping sauce.

In their native Greece, filo pies are made with a mixture of wild bitter greens, but any greens work well, if they have a slightly bitter flavor. Use spring greens or spinach instead of kale, if preferrred.

FILO PIE WITH SPICY KALE AND SAUSAGE

SERVES 6   PREP 35–40 MINS   COOK 1–1¼ HRS   FREEZE UNCOOKED, UP TO 2 MONTHS

1 Heat 30g (1oz) of the butter in a sauté pan and cook the sausage meat, stirring, until it is crumbly and brown. Transfer to a bowl with a slotted spoon, leaving the fat behind. Add the onions to the pan and cook until soft. Add the kale, cover, and cook until the kale is wilted. Uncover and cook for 5 minutes, stirring, until the moisture has evaporated. Return the sausage meat to the pan with the allspice and stir into the kale. Season. Set aside to cool completely. Stir in the eggs.

2 Preheat the oven to 350°F (180°C). Melt the remaining butter in a saucepan and brush the pan with a little butter. Lay a folded damp dish towel on the work surface. Unroll the filo onto the towel. Using the pan as a guide, cut through the dough sheets to leave a 3in (7.5cm) border around the pan where possible. Cover the sheets with a second folded damp dish towel.

3 Place 1 filo sheet on top of a third damp towel and brush with butter. Transfer to the springform pan, pressing it well into the side. Butter another filo sheet and put it in the pan at a right angle to the first. Continue buttering and layering until half the filo is used, arranging alternate layers at right angles.

4 Spoon the filling into the crust. Butter another sheet of filo and cover the filling. Top with the remaining filo, brushing each, including the top one, with butter. Fold the overhanging filo over the top and drizzle with butter. Bake for 45–55 minutes, until golden brown. Let cool slightly, then serve hot or at room temperature. The pie can be made ahead up to the point of baking, wrapped in plastic wrap, and chilled for 2 days.

EQUIPMENT
11in (28cm) springform pan

INGREDIENTS

FOR THE FILLING
2 tbsp unsalted butter
9oz (250g) sausage meat
3 onions, finely chopped
1lb 10oz (750g) kale, washed, trimmed, and shredded
½ tsp ground allspice
sea salt and freshly ground black pepper
2 large eggs, beaten

FOR THE DOUGH
1lb 2oz (500g) filo dough
12 tbsp unsalted butter

This picnic pie makes a fabulous centerpiece for a summer buffet. Making it the old-fashioned way, using lard in the dough, helps keep the crust fresh for days, but sturdy enough to hold the filling.

PORK AND APPLE PICNIC PIE

SERVES 8   **PREP 30 MINS PLUS CHILLING**   **COOK 1 HR**

1 To make the dough, rub the flour, lard, and salt together until the mixture resembles bread crumbs. Add 6–8 tablespoons cold water, a little at a time, and bring together to form a dough. Add a little extra water, if needed. Wrap and chill for 30 minutes.

2 For the filling, heat the olive oil in a frying pan and fry the onion and pancetta for 5 minutes, until soft but not brown, then set aside to cool. Mix the ground pork, apples, apple juice, nutmeg, herbs, and lots of salt and pepper together in a large bowl with your hands. Finally, mix in the cooled onion mixture.

3 Preheat the oven to 375°F (190°C). Roll out the dough on a well-floured surface into a large circle about ¼in (7mm) thick, and use it to line the pan, making sure it overlaps the sides. Trim all but ½in (1cm) of the overhanging dough. Use your fingers to push the dough down into the corners of the pan.

4 Pile the filling into the tart crust, pressing it down firmly. Roll out the remaining piece of dough to make a circle large enough to cover the pie. Brush the edges with a little of the egg mixture, place the top on the pie, and press down firmly to seal. Crimp the edges. Brush the top with the remaining egg and poke 2 small holes in the top of the pie with a chopstick or skewer.

5 Place the pie on a baking sheet and bake for 1 hour, until golden brown. Set the pie aside to cool completely before serving. The pie can be stored in the refrigerator, well wrapped, for up to 3 days.

EQUIPMENT
9in (22cm) deep-sided, fluted tart pan with removable bottom

INGREDIENTS

FOR THE DOUGH
(For visual step-by-step instructions, see p.104)
2⅓ cups all-purpose flour, plus extra for dusting
1½ cups lard
1 tsp salt

FOR THE FILLING
1 tbsp olive oil
1 onion, finely chopped
3½oz (100g) pancetta, finely chopped
1lb 2oz (500g) ground pork
2 sweet apples, peeled, cored, and grated
2 tbsp apple juice
¼ tsp nutmeg, grated
1 tbsp sage or flat-leaf parsley, finely chopped
salt and freshly ground black pepper
1 large egg yolk, beaten with 1 tsp cold water, to glaze

A meaty pie with a crisp, buttery pastry top is always a welcome sight on the kitchen table. Using apple juice here sweetens and mellows the tasty filling to create a real winter classic.

PORK AND LEEK PIE

 **SERVES 4**   **PREP 25 MINS PLUS CHILLING**   **COOK 1 HR 10 MINS**   **FREEZE UP TO 1 MONTH**

EQUIPMENT
7in (18cm) round pie dish

INGREDIENTS

FOR THE FILLING
2 tbsp vegetable oil
1lb (450g) lean boneless pork chops,
cut into 1in (2.5cm) cubes
2 leeks, thickly sliced
6oz (150g) mushrooms, halved
1 tsp thyme leaves
⅔ cup chicken stock
1 tbsp cornstarch, mixed with 1 tbsp water
1 cup apple juice
2 tbsp tomato paste
salt and freshly ground black pepper

FOR THE DOUGH
all-purpose flour, for dusting
9oz (250g) store-bought pie dough
(or to make your own, see p.104)
1 large egg, beaten, to glaze

1 Heat the vegetable oil in a frying pan, add the pork and fry until browned, then remove from the pan and set aside. Add the leeks, mushrooms, and thyme to the pan and fry for 5 minutes. Add the stock, cornstarch, apple juice, and tomato paste, and bring to a boil, stirring until thickened. Return the pork to the pan, season to taste, and simmer for 25 minutes.

2 Transfer the pork and vegetables to the pie dish, reserving the sauce. On a lightly floured surface, roll out the dough and use to cover the dish, decorating the top with the dough trimmings. Cut a slit in the top of the pie to allow the steam to escape, then brush all over with the beaten egg. Chill for 30 minutes.

3 Preheat the oven to 400°F (200°C). Bake the pie for 35 minutes, or until the crust is golden, then serve with the reserved sauce.

There is something very satisfying about making your own Pork Pies, and it is not as difficult as it seems. Work fast with the hot-water pie dough, since it hardens quickly on cooling.

MINI PORK PIES

🍲 MAKES 12   🥣 PREP 45–50 MINS   ⏰ COOK 1 HR
                        PLUS CHILLING
                        AND COOLING

1 Preheat the oven to 400°F (200°C). Grind the pork, bacon, herbs, seasoning, and spices in a food processor until the meat is chopped, but not mushy. Or, cube the meat into ¼in (5mm) pieces and mix in the other ingredients.

2 To make the dough, place the flour and salt in a large bowl and make a well. Measure ⅔ cup boiling water into a bowl, add the lard, and stir until the fat has melted. Pour into the well and mix with a wooden spoon. Use your hands to bring the mixture together into a soft dough. Be careful, since it will be hot. Wrap one-quarter of the dough in a clean dish towel and put in a warm place.

3 Work quickly, since the dough hardens as it cools. Roll the dough out on a well-floured surface to ¼in (5mm) thick. Cut 12 circles big enough to line the pan, allowing the dough to overlap the edges slightly. Pack the filling into each crust and brush the edges with egg.

4 Roll out the set-aside dough and cut out 12 lids. Top the filling with the lids and press down to seal. Brush with egg. Make a hole in the top of each pie if filling with jelly, or cut 2 slits to allow the steam to escape. Bake for 30 minutes, then reduce the heat to 325°F (170°C) and cook for another 30 minutes, until golden brown. Cool in the pan for 10 minutes before turning out. Serve hot or cool and fill with jelly.

5 For the jelly, heat the stock and add the gelatin, stirring until it dissolves. Cool. Once the liquid starts to thicken, use the funnel to pour it into each pie, a little at a time. Each pie will need 2–3 tablespoons of liquid. Chill overnight before eating. The pies will keep for 3 days in an airtight container in the refrigerator.

EQUIPMENT
12-hole muffin pan,
small funnel (optional)

INGREDIENTS

FOR THE FILLING
7oz (200g) pork belly, trimmed of fat
    and skin, and cubed
7oz (200g) pork shoulder,
    trimmed and cubed
2oz (50g) thick-cut bacon, cubed
10 sage leaves, finely chopped
sea salt and freshly ground black pepper
¼ tsp nutmeg
¼ tsp allspice

FOR THE DOUGH
(For visual step-by-step instructions,
    see hot-water pie dough pp.108–109)
2 cups all-purpose flour,
    plus extra for dusting
½ tsp fine salt
⅔ cup lard, cubed
1 large egg, beaten, to glaze

FOR THE JELLY (OPTIONAL)
1 cup chicken stock
1½ tsp unflavored powdered gelatin,
    dissolved in ¼ cup cold water

A well-made Quiche Lorraine is undoubtedly one of the finest dishes to serve, either hot or cold on any occasion. Take the time to make your own rich pie dough for this—it deserves it.

QUICHE LORRAINE

SERVES 4–6   PREP 35 MINS   COOK 30–40 MINS   FREEZE UP TO
                    PLUS CHILLING   1 MONTH

EQUIPMENT
9in x 1½in (23cm x 4cm)
deep dish pie pan, baking beans

INGREDIENTS

FOR THE DOUGH
(For visual step-by-step instructions,
see pie dough p.104)
1½ cups all-purpose flour,
plus extra for dusting
8 tbsp butter, cubed
1 large egg yolk

FOR THE FILLING
7oz (200g) thick-cut bacon, chopped
1 onion, finely chopped
3oz (75g) Gruyère cheese, grated
4 large eggs, lightly beaten
⅔ cup heavy cream
⅔ cup milk
freshly ground black pepper

1 To make the dough, place the flour and butter in a food processor and blend until the mixture resembles fine bread crumbs. Add the egg yolk, and 3–4 tablespoons of chilled water to make a smooth dough. On a floured surface, knead the dough briefly. To make the dough by hand, rub the butter into the flour with your fingertips until the mixture resembles bread crumbs. Add the egg yolk and chilled water and mix to form a dough. Cover with plastic wrap and chill for 30 minutes.

2 Preheat the oven to 375°F (190°C). Roll out the dough on a lightly floured surface and use to line the pan, pressing the dough into the sides. Prick the bottom of the dough with a fork, then line with wax paper and baking beans. Bake for 12 minutes, then remove the paper and beans, and bake for another 10 minutes, or until lightly golden.

3 Meanwhile, heat a large frying pan over medium-low heat and dry-fry the chopped bacon for 10–15 minutes. Add the onion and fry for another 5–8 minutes, then spread the onions and bacon over the crust. Add the cheese.

4 Whisk together the eggs, cream, milk, and black pepper, and pour into the crust. Place the pan on a baking sheet and bake for 25–30 minutes, until golden and just set. Put aside to set, then slice and serve. Cook up to 48 hours in advance, cool, then chill. Reheat at 325°F (170°C) for 15–20 minutes.

This warming winter pie comes from the Auvergne region in France and is an ideal dish to prepare when it's cold outside. It tastes just as good served cold the following day.

AUVERGNE TOURTE

SERVES 8   PREP 30 MINS   COOK 1¼ HRS

1 Melt the butter in a large saucepan. Add the onion and cook over medium heat for 10 minutes. Add the garlic and chopped bacon and cook for another 5 minutes until the onion is soft, but not brown.

2 Preheat the oven to 350°F (180°C). Roll out the dough on a floured surface and, using the pie pan as a template, cut out a circle large enough to top the pie from one side. Use the rest of the dough to line the pan, leaving a ½in (1cm) overhang around the edges. Re-roll the dough if necessary after chilling the top.

3 Brush the inside of the crust, including the edges, with the egg wash. Set the remaining egg wash to one side.

4 Layer the crust with one-third of the finely sliced potatoes. Cover them with half the onion and bacon mixture and half the grated cheese. Scatter over half the parsley and season with salt and pepper.

5 Repeat the procedure and finish with a final layer of potatoes. Whisk together the half-and-half and the egg yolk, and pour it over the pie filling.

6 Top the pie with the precut circle of dough, pressing it down around the edges to seal. Crimp the edges. Brush the top of the pie with the remaining egg wash and cut 2 small slits in the top to allow steam to escape. Place the pie on a baking sheet and bake for 1 hour until well cooked, puffed up, and golden brown. Set aside to rest for 15–20 minutes before serving.

EQUIPMENT
9in (23cm) deep dish pie pan (metal) with sloping sides

INGREDIENTS

FOR THE FILLING
2 tbsp butter
1 large onion, finely sliced
1 garlic clove, finely chopped
4oz (100g) thick-cut bacon, chopped
1lb 6oz (650g) new potatoes, peeled and finely sliced
4oz (100g) Cantal cheese, grated or Wensleydale or mild Cheddar
1 heaping tbsp finely chopped flat-leaf parsley
salt and freshly ground black pepper
¾ cup half-and-half
1 large egg yolk

FOR THE DOUGH
1lb 2oz (500g) store-bought puff pie dough (or to make your own, see pp.110–113)
all-purpose flour, for dusting
1 large egg yolk, beaten with 1 tbsp cold water, to glaze

A traditional blind-baked pie crust can be filled with myriad different ingredients to create a delicious homemade tart. Omit the pancetta if you are cooking for vegetarians.

SPINACH, GOAT CHEESE, AND PANCETTA TART

 SERVES 6–8　　　PREP 20 MINS PLUS COOLING　　　COOK 40–45 MINS　　　FREEZE UP TO 2 MONTHS

EQUIPMENT
9in (22cm) tart pan with removable bottom, baking beans

INGREDIENTS

FOR THE FILLING
1 tbsp olive oil
6oz (150g) pancetta, cubed
6oz (150g) baby spinach, washed
4oz (100g) goat cheese
sea salt and freshly ground black pepper
1¼ cups heavy cream
2 eggs

FOR THE CRUST
store-bought prebaked pie crust
(or to make your own,
see p.104 and pp.122–123)

1 Heat the olive oil in a frying pan and fry the pancetta for 5 minutes, or until golden brown. Add the spinach and cook for a few minutes until it wilts. Drain off any water before using the filling and set aside to cool.

2 Spread the cooled spinach and pancetta mixture over the bottom of the pie crust. Cube or crumble the goat cheese, and spread it over the spinach. Season with a little salt (the pancetta is salty) and pepper.

3 Beat the cream and eggs together in a bowl. Place the pie crust on a baking sheet and, with the oven door open, rest it half on, half off the middle oven shelf. Hold the sheet with one hand and with the other pour the cream and egg mixture into the tart, then slide it into the oven.

4 Bake for 30–35 minutes, until puffed up and golden. Set aside to cool for 10 minutes, and remove the tart from the pan. It is best eaten warm from the oven but can be served cold. The pie crust can be made 2 days ahead, wrapped in plastic wrap, and chilled in the refrigerator until needed. The tart can be chilled overnight and gently reheated in a medium oven.

This dough is an unusual combination of whole wheat flour, cheese, and caraway seeds, which complements the earthy celery root and the salty bacon well. Serve with mashed potatoes and greens for a warming dinner.

CELERY ROOT AND SMOKED BACON SOUFFLÉ PIE

 SERVES 4   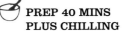 PREP 40 MINS
                           PLUS CHILLING   🕐 COOK 50 MINS   ❄ FREEZE PIE
                                                                           CRUST, UP TO
                                                                           1 MONTH

1 To make the dough, mix the flour and salt in a large bowl. Add the caraway seeds, then rub in the butter with your fingertips until the mixture resembles bread crumbs. Stir in the cheese. Mix 3 tablespoons cold water with the egg yolk and stir into the flour mixture to form a firm dough, adding more water if necessary. On a lightly floured surface, knead the dough gently, then wrap in plastic wrap and chill for 30 minutes. Reserve the egg white for the filling.

2 Cook the celery root in a saucepan of lightly salted boiling water until tender. Drain and return to the pan and dry out briefly over gentle heat. Mash with the butter and milk.

3 Dry-fry the bacon until cooked, but not crisp. Add to the celery root with any fat in the pan. Beat in the egg yolks and chopped chives and season well.

4 Preheat the oven to 400°F (200°C). Roll out the dough on a floured surface and use to line the pan. Line with foil or wax paper and baking beans. Bake for 10 minutes. Remove the foil or paper and beans and cook for another 5 minutes to dry out. Remove from the oven.

5 Beat all 3 egg whites until stiff. Add 1 tablespoon of the whites to the celery root mixture to slacken slightly, then fold in the remainder with a metal spoon. Spoon into the pie crust and bake for 25 minutes until risen, just set, and golden. Serve hot.

EQUIPMENT
8in (20cm) tart pan, baking beans

INGREDIENTS

FOR THE DOUGH
(For visual step-by-step instructions, see pie dough p.104)
1 cup whole wheat or spelt flour, plus extra for dusting
a good pinch of salt
1 tbsp caraway seeds
5 tbsp butter, chilled and cubed
3oz (85g) farmhouse Cheddar cheese, grated
1 large egg, separated

FOR THE FILLING
1 celery root, about 1lb (450g), peeled and cut into chunks
salt and freshly ground black pepper
4 tbsp butter
¼ cup milk
4 slices thick-cut bacon, cubed
2 large eggs, separated
2 tbsp chives, chopped

The crust of this traditional German tart is made from a classic pizza dough, rather than the usual pie dough, and topped with sweet, melting onions, sour cream, and caraway seeds.

ONION AND SOUR CREAM TART

 SERVES 8   PREP 30 MINS   COOK 1 HR –
                     PLUS RISING   1 HR 5 MINS
                     AND PROOFING

EQUIPMENT
10in x 13in (26cm x 32cm) baking sheet
with raised edges

INGREDIENTS

FOR THE DOUGH
3 tbsp olive oil, plus extra for greasing
4 tsp dried yeast, dissolved
in ¾ cup warm water
2¼ cups white bread flour,
plus extra for dusting
1 tsp salt

FOR THE FILLING
4 tbsp unsalted butter
2 tbsp olive oil
1lb 5oz (600g) onions, finely sliced
½ tsp caraway seeds
sea salt and freshly ground black pepper
⅔ cup sour cream
1⅔ cups crème fraîche
3 large eggs
1 tbsp all-purpose flour
3oz (75g) smoked thick-cut bacon, chopped

1 Add the olive oil to the dissolved yeast. Sift the flour and salt into a large bowl. Make a well in the middle and pour in the liquid ingredients, stirring constantly. Use your hands to bring the mixture together to form a soft dough. On a well-floured surface, knead the dough for 10 minutes until soft and elastic.

2 Place the dough in a large, lightly oiled bowl, cover with plastic wrap, and set aside to rise in a warm place for 1–2 hours, until doubled in size.

3 For the filling, heat the butter and olive oil in a large, heavy saucepan. Add the onions and caraway seeds, and season well. Cover and cook gently for 20 minutes, until they are soft but not brown. Uncover and cook for 5 minutes until any excess water evaporates.

4 In a separate bowl, whisk together the sour cream, crème fraîche, eggs, and all-purpose flour, and season well. Mix in the cooked onions and set aside to cool.

5 When the dough has risen, turn it out onto a floured surface and push it down gently with your knuckles to punch it down. Lightly grease the baking sheet. Roll the dough out to the size of the sheet and line it, making sure the pie has an upturned edge. Cover with lightly oiled plastic wrap, and set aside to rise in a warm place for 30 minutes, until puffy in places.

6 Preheat the oven to 400°F (200°C). Gently push down the dough (if it has risen too much) around the edges of the sheet. Spread the filling out over the dough and sprinkle the bacon on top. Bake on the top shelf of the oven for 35–40 minutes, until golden brown. Cool for 5 minutes before serving. Serve warm or cold. This dish can be covered and chilled overnight.

The rich, buttery crust is filled with salty bacon and creamy Brie to produce a mouthwatering tart. A classic recipe, perfect for a summer lunch or a picnic, served with salad.

BRIE AND BACON TART

SERVES 6–8   PREP 15 MINS   COOK 1¼ HRS   FREEZE UP TO 1 MONTH

1 Preheat the oven to 400°F (200°C). Roll out the dough on a floured surface and use to line the tart pan, allowing the dough to hang over the edges. Trim off the excess dough, then line the crust with wax paper and fill with baking beans. Bake for 20 minutes, or until the edges are golden. Remove the beans and paper, brush the bottom of the crust with a little beaten egg, and return to the oven for 1–2 minutes to crisp. Set aside. Reduce the oven temperature to 350°F (180°C).

2 Heat the olive oil in a large frying pan over low heat. Add the onion and a pinch of salt, and sweat gently for about 5 minutes, until soft and translucent. Increase the heat slightly, add the bacon, and cook for 5–8 minutes, until crisp and golden. Remove from the heat, and stir in the sun-dried tomatoes.

3 Spoon the onion and bacon mixture into the crust. Top evenly with the Brie strips, and sprinkle with the finely chopped chives.

4 Mix the cream and the 2 eggs together in a bowl. Add the garlic, and season well with salt and pepper. Carefully pour the tart filling over the top. Bake for 30–40 minutes until set, puffed, and lightly golden. Serve with a crisp tossed salad.

EQUIPMENT
7in x 12in (18cm x 30cm) rectangular fluted tart pan with removable bottom, baking beans

INGREDIENTS

FOR THE DOUGH
10oz (300g) store-bought pie dough
  (or to make your own, see p.104)
all-purpose flour, for dusting
1 large egg, lightly beaten, to glaze

FOR THE FILLING
1 tbsp olive oil
1 onion, finely chopped
salt and freshly ground black pepper
5oz (125g) thick-cut bacon,
  chopped into bite-sized pieces
8 sun-dried tomatoes
5oz (125g) Brie cheese,
  sliced into long strips
a small handful of chives,
  finely chopped
¾ cup heavy cream
2 large eggs
2 garlic cloves, grated or finely chopped

Mixing chopped fresh herbs into the dough is an easy way of varying the flavors of a dish to complement the pie filling. Use farmed rabbit if possible here, since wild rabbit needs a long, slow cooking time.

RABBIT AND CORN PIE WITH A HERB CRUST

 SERVES 4   PREP 40 MINS PLUS CHILLING   COOK 1¾ HRS   FREEZE UP TO 1 MONTH

1 To make the dough, sift 1¼ cups flour and ¼ teaspoon salt into a bowl. Add 4 tbsp of the butter and rub it in with your fingertips. Stir in the herbs. Add the remaining butter and ½ cup iced water and mix with a butter knife to form a lumpy dough. On a floured surface, knead the dough, then roll out to an oblong. Fold the bottom-third up and the top-third down over it and press the edges with the rolling pin. Quarter-turn the dough then roll, fold, and turn twice more. Wrap, and chill for 30 minutes.

2 For the filling, put the rabbit in a saucepan with the bacon and all the vegetables. Add the stock, bay leaf, and season with salt and pepper. Bring to a boil, reduce the heat, part-cover, and simmer gently for about 1 hour, until the rabbit is tender. Lift out the rabbit. Remove the meat and cut into pieces. Put in the pie dish on a baking sheet and discard the bay leaf.

3 Blend the sherry with remaining ¼ cup flour and 1 tablespoon water. Stir into the vegetables and stock, then bring to a boil, stirring. Add the cream and season. Stir into the rabbit. Cool.

4 Preheat the oven to 425°F (220°C). Roll and fold the dough once more, then roll out to slightly bigger than the pie dish. Cut off a strip all around. Dampen the rim of the dish and lay the strip on top. Dampen the strip and lay the dough on top. Press the edges together to seal. Trim, punch down, and flute with the back of a knife. Make leaves out of the trimmings and arrange on top. Cut a slit in the top and glaze with cream. Bake for 30 minutes, until golden. Serve hot.

EQUIPMENT
9in (23cm) deep dish

INGREDIENTS

FOR THE DOUGH
1½ cups flour, plus extra for dusting
salt and freshly ground black pepper
12 tbsp butter, chilled and cubed
2 tbsp chopped parsley
1 tbsp chopped thyme

FOR THE FILLING
1 oven-ready rabbit, cut into pieces
2oz (60g) smoked bacon, chopped
1 onion, chopped
2 carrots, sliced
1 potato, cubed
4 tomatoes, peeled and chopped
kernels from 2 corncobs
2 cups chicken stock
1 bay leaf
3 tbsp dry sherry
¼ heavy cream, plus extra to glaze

variation

HERB CRUST CHICKEN PIE
Wild rabbit tastes like free-range organic chicken, which you can use instead. Use 6oz canned or frozen corn instead of fresh corn, if you prefer.

An alternative to Beef Wellington, these individual parcels are both rich and luxurious. Perfect for entertaining, they can be prepared ahead up to the baking stage then finished at the last minute.

VENISON WELLINGTONS

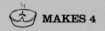 MAKES 4   PREP 40 MINS   COOK 35 MINS

EQUIPMENT
baking sheet

INGREDIENTS

FOR THE FILLING
¼oz (10g) dried wild mushrooms (optional)
2 tbsp olive oil
4 venison tenderloin steaks,
each 4–5½oz (120–150g)
salt and freshly ground black pepper
2 tbsp unsalted butter
2 shallots, finely chopped
1 garlic clove, finely chopped
7oz (200g) mixed mushrooms, including
wild mushrooms if possible
1 tbsp thyme leaves
1 tbsp brandy or Madeira

FOR THE PASTRY
1lb 2oz (500g) puff pastry
(or to make your own, see pp.110–113)
all-purpose flour, for dusting
1 large egg, beaten, to glaze

1 Preheat the oven to 400°F (200°C). If using dried mushrooms, put them in a bowl and cover with boiling water. Let stand for at least 15 minutes.

2 Heat the olive oil in a frying pan. Season the venison steaks on all sides with salt and pepper and fry them, two at a time, for 2 minutes on each side, until brown all over. Set aside to cool completely.

3 Melt the butter in the same pan. Add the shallots and cook for 5 minutes over medium heat, until soft. Add the garlic and cook for 1–2 minutes.

4 Coarsely chop the mushrooms and add them to the pan with the thyme. Season and cook for 5 minutes, until they are well softened and any juices have evaporated. Add the brandy and cook over high heat for 1 minute, until it evaporates. Remove and set aside to cool. If using dried mushrooms, drain them, chop coarsely, and add to the mushroom mixture.

5 Divide the pastry into 4 equal pieces and roll out rectangles about ¼in (5mm) thick, large enough to wrap around each steak on a floured surface. Pat the steaks dry with paper towels.

6 Place one-quarter of the mushroom filling in a rectangle roughly the same shape as the venison steak to one side of the pastry, leaving a clean edge of at least ¾in (2cm). Flatten the mushrooms and put a steak on top. Brush the edges of the pastry with beaten egg and fold the pastry over the meat. Press the edges down firmly to seal and crimp them. Repeat with the remaining steaks and pastry. Cut small slits in the top for the steam to escape, and brush the tops with more beaten egg. Bake the pastries on the baking sheet for 20–25 minutes, until puffed up and golden. Set aside to cool for 5 minutes before serving.

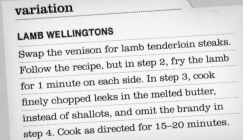

variation

LAMB WELLINGTONS
Swap the venison for lamb tenderloin steaks. Follow the recipe, but in step 2, fry the lamb for 1 minute on each side. In step 3, cook finely chopped leeks in the melted butter, instead of shallots, and omit the brandy in step 4. Cook as directed for 15–20 minutes.

For those on a low-fat diet, venison is a good alternative to beef.
A long, slow cooking time is needed to tenderize this wonderful,
gamey meat fully. If time is short, prepare the filling the day before.

VENISON PIE

SERVES 4–6   PREP 20 MINS   COOK 2–2¾ HRS   FREEZE UP TO
1 MONTH

1 Heat half the olive oil in a medium, heavy-bottomed
pan and gently fry the shallots, celery, and carrot
for 3 minutes. Add the garlic and cook for 2–3 minutes.
Remove with a slotted spoon and set aside.

2 Place the flour, nutmeg, and allspice in a large
plastic food bag, season well, and add the cubed
meat. Firmly hold the top of the bag to seal it, and
shake it to coat the meat in the seasoned flour.

3 Add the remaining olive oil to the pan and brown
the meat in 3 batches over medium heat, removing
each batch to a plate lined with paper towels.

4 Add the port and stir well to deglaze the bottom
of the pan. Add the cranberry sauce, orange zest
and juice, stock, and bay leaf to the pan, season and stir.

5 Return the vegetables and venison to the pan,
stir well, and bring to a boil. Cover, reduce the
heat, and simmer for 1½–2 hours, or until the venison
is tender. Remove the bay leaf.

6 Preheat the oven to 400°F (200°C). With a slotted
spoon, transfer the cooked venison and vegetables
to the pie dish. Bring the remaining cooking liquid in
the pan to a boil and cook over high heat for 5 minutes
to reduce. Carefully pour all the reduced sauce over
the meat in the dish.

7 Cut ¾in (2cm) wide strips from the edge of the
pastry to fit around the rim of the pie dish. Brush
the edge of the dish with water and place the strips
on the rim. Cover the pie with the remaining pastry,
trim, and press to seal. Brush with beaten egg and
cut a slit in the top to allow steam to escape. Bake
on a baking sheet for 15–20 minutes, until browned.

EQUIPMENT
9in (23cm) pie dish

INGREDIENTS

FOR THE FILLING
2 tbsp olive oil
4 shallots, halved
2 celery stalks, finely chopped
1 carrot, finely chopped
2 garlic cloves, finely chopped
2 tbsp all-purpose flour
½ tsp freshly grated nutmeg
½ tsp ground allspice
salt and freshly ground black pepper
1½lb (675g) shoulder of venison,
  cut into bite-sized chunks
⅔ cup port
¼ cup cranberry sauce
zest and juice of 1 orange
⅔ cup fresh beef stock
1 bay leaf

FOR THE PASTRY
7½oz (215g) sheet store-bought
  puff pastry (or to make your own,
  see pp.110–113)
1 large egg, beaten, to glaze

These fragrant parcels are a variation of the classic Moroccan pastilla, which is made with baby squab. It may look lengthy, but make the filling the day before, and then the recipe is quick to finish.

INDIVIDUAL QUAIL PASTILLA

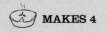 MAKES 4   PREP 50 MINS   COOK 55 MINS

EQUIPMENT
baking sheet

INGREDIENTS

FOR THE FILLING
4 prepared quails or squabs
2½ cups good-quality chicken stock
1 cinnamon stick, broken in half
1 jalapeño chile, halved and seeded
1 red onion, quartered
2 garlic cloves, peeled
¾in (2cm) piece fresh ginger, thickly sliced
⅓ cup sliced almonds, roasted and chopped
2 tbsp coriander, chopped
½ tsp ground cinnamon
freshly ground black pepper

FOR THE DOUGH
5 sheets store-bought filo dough
all-purpose flour, for dusting
3 tbsp olive oil

1 Place the quail in a saucepan. Add the stock, cinnamon stick, jalapeño chile, onion, garlic, and ginger, and bring to a boil. Reduce the heat and simmer for 30 minutes, until the quails are cooked. Strain the contents of the pan, reserving the liquid. Remove the quail, onion, and garlic and cool. Put the reserved liquid into the cleaned-out pan and simmer until it barely covers the bottom. Pull the meat off the bones in bite-sized shreds. Coarsely chop the onions and garlic and add them to the meat. Combine the meat mixture, almonds, and spices and season. Add the cooking liquid, so that the mixture is moist, but not too wet.

2 Preheat the oven to 400°F (200°C). Lay the filo sheets out on a floured surface and cut them into quarters. Make a pastilla (see below). Repeat 3 more times to make 4 filo bases. Divide the filling between the bases, heaping it in a circle in the center. Fold the edges in one at a time in a clockwise direction to cover the filling. Bake on the baking sheet for 20–25 minutes, until golden and crisp. Cool slightly before serving.

Making a pastilla

1 Brush 1 piece of filo with olive oil. Place a second piece at right angles across it, and brush with the oil.

2 Put a third piece diagonally across the filo, brush with oil. Put a fourth diagonally the other way and oil.

3 Brush 1 final piece with oil and fold in half. Trim to make a square, use to make a base in center of dough.

There are times in the fall when squabs are plump and plentiful. If you live near a supplier, stock up on them and use the breasts for this wonderful dish. The carcasses can be reserved for stock.

SQUAB BREASTS EN CROÛTE

 MAKES 4   PREP 15 MINS   COOK 30–35 MINS
                                 PLUS CHILLING
                                 AND MARINATING

1 Mix the red wine, balsamic vinegar, and zest and juice of 1 orange in a shallow nonmetallic dish. Add the squab breasts and season well. Coat evenly with the marinade, cover, and chill for at least 8 hours.

2 Remove the squab from the marinade and season with salt and pepper. Heat the olive oil in a frying pan and fry the shallots, bacon, and mushrooms over medium heat for 3–4 minutes, or until golden. Set aside. Preheat the oven to 400°F (200°C). Line the baking sheets with parchment paper.

3 Cut each pastry sheet into 4 to make 8 x 5in x 7in (11.5cm x 18.5cm) rectangles. Divide the shallot mixture between 4 of the pastry rectangles, leaving a 2in (5cm) border all around. Place 2 squab breasts on top of the shallot mixture in the center of each pastry rectangle. Brush the edges with water and top with the remaining rectangles. Press the pastry edges down firmly to seal, transfer to the baking sheets, and snip the top with scissors to make a hole for steam to escape. Brush each parcel with the beaten egg and bake for 25–30 minutes.

EQUIPMENT
2 baking sheets

INGREDIENTS

FOR THE FILLING
¼ cup red wine
2 tbsp balsamic vinegar
grated zest and juice of 1 orange
8 squab breasts
salt and freshly ground black pepper
1 tbsp olive oil
2 shallots, sliced
3½oz (100g) bacon, chopped
2oz (50g) cremini mushrooms,
  finely sliced

FOR THE PASTRY
2 x 11oz (320g) sheets store-bought puff
  pastry, each 9in x 15in (23cm x 37cm),
  (or to make your own, see pp.110–113)
1 large egg, beaten to glaze

These bite-sized puffs were inspired by a favorite dim sum dish of my family—Honey Puffs. Trying to re-create them at home, I came up with this surprisingly simple, yet delicious recipe.

CHINESE BARBECUE DUCK PUFFS

 MAKES 15   PREP 20 MINS
PLUS CHILLING   COOK 50 MINS   FREEZE UP TO
2 MONTHS

EQUIPMENT
baking sheet, 3¼in (8cm)
fluted round cookie cutter

INGREDIENTS

FOR THE PASTRY
(For visual step-by-step instructions,
see quick puff pastry pp.112–113)
1½ cups all-purpose flour,
plus extra for dusting
a pinch of salt
7 tbsp butter, frozen for 30 minutes
1 large egg yolk, beaten, plus 1 large egg,
beaten, to glaze
1 tbsp sesame seeds (optional)

FOR THE FILLING
½ Chinese barbecue-roasted duck
giving 7oz (200g) duck meat,
or 7oz (200g) Chinese-roasted pork
1 tbsp sunflower or vegetable oil
4 large scallions,
trimmed and finely sliced
1 garlic clove, crushed
1 tsp finely grated ginger
1 tbsp oyster sauce
1 tbsp Peking duck or hoisin sauce
1 tsp cornstarch

1 To make the pastry, put the flour and salt into a large bowl. Grate the butter into the flour, coating the grater with a little flour first to stop the butter from sticking. Work the butter and flour together with your hands, add the beaten egg yolk and 2 tablespoons cold water, and bring the mixture together to form a dough. Wrap in plastic wrap and chill for 30 minutes.

2 For the filling, finely chop the meat. If not using prepared duck, marinate 2 duck legs in 1 tablespoon hoisin sauce mixed with 1 tablespoon soy sauce for 30 minutes, then preheat the oven to 400°F (200°C) and roast for 30 minutes, until cooked. Cool and pull the meat off the bone before shredding it.

3 Heat the sunflower oil in a saucepan and fry the scallions and garlic for 2–3 minutes, until soft but not brown, then add the duck meat, ginger, and oyster and hoisin sauces. Mix the cornstarch with 4 tablespoons cold water and add to the pan. Cook briefly until thick, shiny, and any excess liquid has evaporated. Cool.

4 Preheat the oven to 400°F (200°C). Roll out the pastry on a well-floured surface and cut out 15 x 3¼in (8cm) circles with the round cookie cutter. Brush the edges with beaten egg. Place a heaping teaspoon of the filling into the center of the circles, then use your hands to crimp the edges and seal the pastries.

5 Place the pastries on the baking sheet and brush with beaten egg, and a sprinkle of sesame seeds, if using. Bake for 20 minutes, until shiny and golden brown. Set aside to cool for at least 5 minutes before serving. The filling can be chilled for up to 3 days. The pastry can be made and chilled overnight. The puffs can be frozen; defrost and reheat well.

Adding a puff-pastry lid to a hearty soup is a simple yet effective way of turning an appetizer-sized dish into a main course. Serve with a crusty country bread for mopping up all the juices.

PUFF-CRUSTED GAME SOUP

 SERVES 4   **PREP 20 MINS**   **COOK 1 HR 20 MINS**   **FREEZE FILLING, UP TO 3 MONTHS**

1 Melt the butter in a Dutch oven and fry the meat and onion for 5 minutes, stirring, until browned.

2 Blend in the flour and cook for 1 minute. Remove from the heat, gradually stir in the stock, add the red currant jelly, and bring to a boil, stirring. Add the mushrooms, sage, port, and some salt and pepper. Return to a boil, then reduce the heat, cover, and simmer very gently for 1 hour, stirring occasionally, until rich and very tender. Taste and adjust the seasoning if necessary.

3 Meanwhile, preheat the oven to 425°F (220°C). Cut 4 circles from the pastry slightly larger than the soup cups and brush with a little beaten egg. Stand the soup cups on a baking sheet. Brush the edges with a little more beaten egg. Ladle in the soup. Top with the circles of pastry, pressing down lightly with a fork around the edge to secure. Cut a small slit in the top of each pie lid to allow steam to escape. Bake for about 15 minutes, or until puffy, crisp, and golden brown. Set aside to cool for 3–5 minutes before serving.

EQUIPMENT
deep ovenproof soup cups

INGREDIENTS

FOR THE FILLING
a large pat of butter
6oz (175g) cubed game meat,
  cut into small pieces
1 red onion, chopped
2 tbsp all-purpose flour
3 cups beef stock
1 tbsp red currant jelly
3 cremini mushrooms,
  halved and sliced
1 tbsp sage, chopped
¼ cup ruby port
salt and freshly ground black pepper

FOR THE PASTRY
1 sheet store-bought puff pastry
  (or to make your own, see pp.110–113)
1 large egg, beaten, to glaze

POULTRY PIES
AND TARTS

When you need a simple yet sophisticated dish for entertaining, these individual pies are just the thing. Most fillings can be presented like this—just cut the lids to fit and bake until puffed up and golden.

CHICKEN POT PIES

MAKES 6

PREP 20 MINS PLUS CHILLING

COOK 40 MINS

FREEZE UP TO 1 MONTH

EQUIPMENT
6 x 3in (7.5cm) round pie dishes, 3in (7.5cm) round cookie cutter

INGREDIENTS

FOR THE DOUGH
(For visual step-by-step instructions, see pie dough p.104)
2 cups all-purpose flour, plus extra for dusting
12 tbsp butter, cubed
½ tsp salt
1 large egg, beaten, to glaze

FOR THE FILLING
3½ cups chicken stock
3 carrots, sliced
1lb 10oz (750g) large potatoes, cubed
3 celery stalks, thinly sliced
1¼ cups peas
1lb 2oz (500g) cooked, skinless, boneless chicken
4 tbsp unsalted butter
1 onion, chopped
3 tbsp all-purpose flour
⅔ cup heavy cream
whole nutmeg, for grating
sea salt and freshly ground black pepper
leaves from 1 small bunch of parsley, chopped

1 Preheat the oven to 400°F (200°C). To make the dough, rub the flour and butter together until the mixture resembles bread crumbs. Add the salt and enough cold water to bring the mixture together to form a soft dough. Wrap in plastic wrap and chill in the refrigerator for 30 minutes.

2 For the filling, boil the stock in a large saucepan. Add the carrots, potatoes, and celery, and simmer for 3 minutes. Add the peas and simmer for another 5 minutes, until all the vegetables are tender. Drain, reserving the stock. Cut the chicken into slivers and put in a bowl. Add the vegetables.

3 Melt the butter in a small pan over medium heat. Add the onion and cook for 3–5 minutes, until softened but not browned. Sprinkle the flour over the onions and cook for 1–2 minutes, stirring. Add 2 cups of the stock and heat, whisking, until the sauce comes to a boil and thickens. Reduce the heat and simmer for 2 minutes, then add the cream and a grating of nutmeg, then season. Pour the sauce over the chicken and vegetables, add the parsley, and mix gently. Divide the filling evenly among the dishes.

4 Roll the dough out on a well-floured surface to ¼in (7mm) thick. Cut out 6 rounds using the cookie cutter. Brush the edge of each pie dish with water and place the dough lids on top, pressing down firmly to secure in place. Place the pies on a baking sheet and brush with the beaten egg. Cut a slit in the top of each pie and bake for 15–20 minutes. The filling can be prepared 1 day ahead, covered, and stored in the refrigerator.

This rich, creamy Chicken Pie is topped with a glossy, golden brown dough lid that should shatter to the touch. Use homemade or store-bought pie dough for a family-pleasing, speedy midweek supper.

CHICKEN PIE

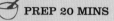

SERVES 4   PREP 20 MINS   COOK 40–45 MINS   FREEZE UP TO 1 MONTH

EQUIPMENT
7in (18cm) pie dish

INGREDIENTS

FOR THE FILLING
3 tbsp olive oil
1 onion, finely chopped
2oz (50g) pancetta, cubed
2 leeks, about 7oz (200g),
cut into ½in (1cm) slices
6oz (150g) button mushrooms, wiped,
halved or quartered, if necessary
2 large boneless, skinless chicken breasts,
about 14oz (400g), cut into
1in (2.5cm) chunks
1 heaping tbsp chopped thyme
1 heaping tbsp chopped flat-leaf parsley
1 tbsp all-purpose flour
1¼ cups half-and-half
1 tbsp Dijon mustard
salt and freshly ground black pepper

FOR THE PASTRY
9oz (250g) store-bought puff pastry
(or to make your own, see pp.110–113)
1 large egg, beaten, to glaze
flour, for dusting

1 Preheat the oven to 400°F (200°C). Heat 2 tablespoons of the olive oil in a saucepan, add the onion and fry for 5 minutes until softened, but not brown. Add the pancetta and cook for 2 minutes. Add the leeks and button mushrooms and cook for another 3–5 minutes until the pancetta is crisp.

2 Add the remaining olive oil to the pan and add the chicken and herbs. Fry over high heat for 3–4 minutes, until colored on all sides. Sprinkle the flour over the pie filling and stir it in well. Pour in the half-and-half, add the mustard and seasoning, and bring to a boil, stirring constantly. The mixture should thicken as it heats. Reduce the heat to low and cook for another 5 minutes, until the liquid has reduced. Transfer the filling to the pie dish.

3 Roll out the dough on a floured surface to a circle bigger than the pie dish and ⅛–¼in (3–5mm) thick. Cut a circle to fit the pie. Roll some of the trimmings out into long strips. Brush the rim of the dish with a little of the beaten egg and press the dough strips around the rim. Brush the edging with more beaten egg and top with the dough lid. Press down to seal the lid, then trim away any excess dough.

4 Brush the top of the pie with beaten egg, then cut 2 slits in the top to allow steam to escape. Bake for 20–25 minutes, until golden brown. Set aside to rest for 5 minutes before serving.

A homemade raised pie is wonderful, and this one is large enough to make a perfect buffet centerpiece. Make the pie ahead of time and chill for up to three days, but be sure to serve it at room temperature.

CHICKEN AND HAM RAISED PIE

SERVES 8–10   **PREP 1 HR PLUS CHILLING**   **COOK 1½ HRS**

1 To make the dough, sift the flour and 2 teaspoons of salt into a bowl. Rub in the fat until the mix resembles bread crumbs. Make a well, add ⅔ cup water, and cut in with a knife to form coarse bread crumbs. Form a dough and knead until smooth. Wrap and chill in the refrigerator for 30 minutes.

2 Cook 6 eggs in a saucepan of water for 7 minutes. Drain, cool, and peel. Cut 2 of the breasts and the pork into chunks. Grind coarsely in a food processor; place in a bowl; add lemon, herbs, nutmeg, and seasoning. Whisk 2 eggs, add to the ground meat, and beat until it pulls away from the sides. Cut the reserved chicken and ham into ¾in (2cm) cubes. Stir into the filling.

3 Preheat the oven to 400°F (200°C). Grease the pan. Shape three-quarters of the dough into a ball. Make the pie (see below). Make a hole in the lid and insert a foil roll for a chimney. Cut out leaves from the leftover dough, decorate, glaze, and bake for 1 hour. Reduce the heat to 350°F (180°C) and bake for 30 minutes.

EQUIPMENT
8–9in (20–23cm) springform pan

INGREDIENTS

FOR THE DOUGH
2½ cups all-purpose flour,
    plus extra for dusting
5 tbsp butter, chilled and cubed,
    plus extra for greasing
5 tbsp lard, chilled and cubed

FOR THE FILLING
9 large eggs
4 skinless, boneless chicken breasts,
    total weight 1lb 10oz (750g)
13oz (375g) lean boneless pork loin
finely grated zest of ½ lemon
1 tsp each dried thyme and sage
a large pinch of ground nutmeg
salt and freshly ground black pepper
13oz (375g) cooked lean ham

Constructing the pie

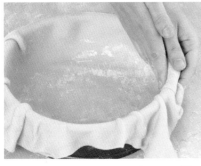

1 Roll out dough to size of pan, with a ¾in (2cm) overhang. Spread over half the filling; put the eggs on top.

2 Push in eggs; cover with the mix. Fold over dough overhang. Beat last egg with salt; use to brush edges.

3 Roll out the remaining dough ¼in (5mm) thick. Lay on top, press to seal, and trim.

This Greek-inspired pie is both pretty to look at and delicious to eat. Using filo dough like this means you don't have to worry too much about a perfect finish—the more crumpled the better!

CRISPY CHICKEN AND SPINACH PIE

 SERVES 6    PREP 20 MINS   ⏰ COOK 35–40 MINS   ❄ FREEZE UP TO 1 MONTH

EQUIPMENT
8in (20cm) cake pan with removable bottom

INGREDIENTS

FOR THE FILLING
9oz (250g) spinach
2 garlic cloves, finely chopped
3½oz (100g) feta cheese, coarsely chopped
½ tsp freshly grated nutmeg
7oz (200g) cooked chicken, shredded
2½oz (75g) drained Peppadew peppers, coarsely chopped
2 large eggs, beaten
salt and freshly ground black pepper

FOR THE DOUGH
6 sheets store-bought filo dough
4 tbsp butter, melted

1 Place the spinach in a colander and pour boiling water from a kettle over it to wilt it. Set aside to cool and drain.

2 Place the garlic, cheese, nutmeg, chicken, peppers, and eggs in a large bowl, season well, and stir to combine. Squeeze the liquid from the spinach, chop finely, and add to the bowl. Stir well and set aside. Preheat the oven to 400°F (200°C).

3 Place a sheet of filo dough in the bottom of the pan, so the edges are hanging over the sides. Brush it generously with butter and place another sheet of filo dough across the first, so they form a cross shape in the bottom. Brush with more butter. Repeat the dough layers until all the dough is used up and the bottom of the pan is completely covered.

4 Spoon the filling into the crust and carefully pull the overhanging layers of dough into the center to cover the filling. Brush the finished pie with the remaining melted butter. Place the pan on a baking sheet and bake for 35–40 minutes, until the crust is golden brown and crisp. Remove the outer ring of the pan and slice to serve. Serve hot or cold.

A lovely recipe to cook from scratch, this pie is also a great time-saver. Cook double the amount of chicken, then before you debone it, simply freeze what you don't need for a delicious stew for another day.

COQ AU VIN PIE

SERVES 4–6   PREP 25 MINS   COOK 55 MINS –   FREEZE UP TO
                  PLUS COOLING   1 HR 5 MINS   1 MONTH

1 Heat a medium, heavy-bottomed Dutch oven, add the bacon, and fry gently for 1 minute. Add the shallots and cook for 2 minutes. Add the garlic and mushrooms and cook for another 1–2 minutes.

2 Add the chicken, wine, bay leaf, and thyme to the pan, bring to a boil, season with salt and pepper, cover, and simmer gently for 25 minutes, or until the chicken is tender and cooked.

3 Place a colander over a large bowl or measuring cup and transfer the contents of the pan into the colander. Set aside for 10 minutes to allow all the juices to drain through and for the chicken to cool a little.

4 Remove the bay leaf from the colander. Place the chicken on a plate and spoon the bacon and mushroom mixture into the pie dish. Remove the meat from the chicken pieces and add to the dish. Sprinkle the parsley over the filling.

5 Return the drained cooking liquid to the pan, bring to a boil and cook over high heat for 5–10 minutes, to reduce and thicken. Pour the reduced sauce over the pie filling.

6 Preheat the oven to 400°F (200°C). Cut enough ¾in (2cm) wide strips from the edge of the pastry to fit around the rim of the pie dish. Brush the edge of the dish with water and place the strips on the rim. Cover the pie with the remaining pastry, trim, and press firmly to seal. Brush with beaten egg and cut a slit in the top to allow steam to escape. Bake on a baking sheet for 20–25 minutes, or until browned.

EQUIPMENT
9in (23cm) pie dish

INGREDIENTS

FOR THE FILLING
3½oz (100g) bacon, chopped
5 shallots, halved
2 garlic cloves, finely chopped
5½oz (150g) button mushrooms
4 chicken thighs
1¼ cups red wine
1 bay leaf
leaves from 4 sprigs of fresh thyme
  or ½ tsp dried thyme
salt and freshly ground black pepper
3 tbsp curly parsley, chopped

FOR THE PASTRY
7½oz (215g) sheet store-bought puff pastry
  (or to make your own, see pp.110–113)
1 large egg, beaten, to glaze

Pies are often the recipients of leftovers, brought together with a few added ingredients and a fresh, buttery pastry wrapping. Here, Sunday's leftovers become Monday's dinner.

ROAST CHICKEN HAND PIES

MAKES 10   **PREP 20 MINS**   **COOK 40 MINS**   **FREEZE UP TO 1 MONTH**

1 Preheat the oven to 400°F (200°C). Drizzle the pumpkin or squash with olive oil, scatter with the thyme, season with salt and pepper, and place in a roasting pan. Roast for 15–20 minutes, or until just softened and turning golden at the edges. Set aside to cool completely.

2 Mix the shredded chicken, roasted squash, scallions, and crème fraîche together in a bowl and season well. Roll out the pastry on a well-floured surface into a large sheet about ¼in (5mm) thick. Cut 20 x 4in (10cm) circles out of the pastry, gathering it up and re-rolling it if necessary.

3 Place 10 of the pastry circles onto 2 baking sheets, and brush the edges with a little beaten egg. Pile a heaping tablespoon of the filling mixture into the center of each and flatten it down with the back of the spoon, making sure to leave a ½in (1cm) border around the edge.

4 Top with the remaining 10 circles of pastry. These should be lightly rolled a little larger after cutting, since they will need to cover the mounded filling. Press down around the edges of the pies firmly, crimping the edges if desired to finish. Brush the tops with a little more beaten egg.

5 Use a chopstick to poke a small hole in the center of each pie and bake for 20 minutes, until well puffed up and golden brown. Remove from the oven and set aside to cool on a wire rack before serving warm or cold for a picnic. Chill the pies for up to 2 days. If freezing, reheat before serving.

EQUIPMENT
2 baking sheets

INGREDIENTS

FOR THE FILLING
7oz (200g) pumpkin or butternut squash, peeled and cut into cubes
olive oil, for drizzling
1 tsp finely chopped thyme
salt and freshly ground black pepper
6oz (150g) cold roast chicken, finely cubed or shredded
2 scallions, trimmed and finely sliced
3 tbsp crème fraîche

FOR THE PASTRY
1lb 2oz (500g) store-bought puff pastry (or to make your own, see pp.110–113)
all-purpose flour, for dusting
1 large egg yolk, beaten with 1 tsp cold water, to glaze

A Brazilian favorite, this simple chicken pie uses cream cheese, instead of a more usual flour-based sauce to bring the ingredients together and gives the filling a wonderfully creamy texture.

CHICKEN PIE WITH CHEESE

 **SERVES 6**   **PREP 35 MINS PLUS CHILLING**   **COOK 35–40 MINS**   **FREEZE UP TO 1 MONTH**

EQUIPMENT
9in (23cm) pie dish

INGREDIENTS

FOR THE DOUGH
(For visual step-by-step instructions, see p.104)
1⅓ cups all-purpose flour, plus extra for dusting
a pinch of salt
7 tbsp butter, cubed, plus extra for greasing
2 large eggs, beaten, plus 1 large egg, beaten, to glaze
½ cup heavy cream

FOR THE FILLING
2 tbsp olive oil
1 large onion, chopped
2 chicken breasts, finely sliced
2 tomatoes, peeled, seeded, and chopped
3½oz (100g) cremini mushrooms, sliced
2 tbsp parsley, chopped
14oz (400g) cream cheese
salt and freshly ground black pepper

1 Grease and flour the pie dish. To make the dough, rub the flour, salt, and butter together with your fingertips until the mixture resembles bread crumbs. Add the 2 beaten eggs and cream and bring the mixture together to form a dough. Wrap in plastic wrap and chill for 1 hour.

2 Meanwhile, for the filling, heat the olive oil in a medium nonstick frying pan and fry the onion until soft. Add the chicken, and cook for 5 minutes. Add the tomatoes and mushrooms, and cook for another 5 minutes. Remove from the heat, stir in the parsley and cream cheese, and season well with salt and black pepper. Set aside to cool.

3 Preheat the oven to 400°F (200°C). Roll half the dough out on a floured surface to a circle large enough to line the pie dish. Place the dough in the dish and trim around the edges. Add the filling and brush the edge with a little of the remaining beaten egg.

4 Roll out the remaining dough to a circle large enough to top the pie. Cover the pie with the remaining dough, trim, and press firmly to seal. Brush with the rest of the beaten egg and cut a slit in the top to allow steam to escape. Place on a baking sheet and bake for 20–25 minutes, until browned. Serve immediately or set aside to cool, and chill in the refrigerator for up to 2 days.

This quick and easy pie makes a tasty meal for children. Most children like corn, and extra cubed vegetables, such as mushrooms, celery, or carrots, can also be added to the filling.

CHICKEN AND SWEET CORN PIE

SERVES 4   PREP 15 MINS   COOK 1 HR

1 Preheat the oven to 400°F (200°C). Heat 1 tablespoon of olive oil in a large frying pan over medium-high heat. Season the chicken with salt and pepper. Add to the pan and cook, stirring, for about 10 minutes, until golden brown all over. Remove from the pan and set aside.

2 Heat the remaining olive oil in the same pan over low heat. Add the onion and a pinch of salt and sweat gently for about 5 minutes, until soft and translucent. Remove from the heat and stir in the flour and a little of the cream. Return the pan to low heat and add the remaining cream and the stock, stirring constantly for 5–8 minutes, until the mixture thickens. Stir in the corn and parsley and season well with salt and pepper.

3 Spoon the mixture into the pie dish or dishes. Roll out the pastry on a floured surface so that it is 2in (5cm) larger all around than the top of the pie dish. Cut a strip of pastry about 1in (2.5cm) in from the edge to make a collar. Dampen the edge of the dish with a little water; fit the pastry strip all the way around and press down firmly. Brush the pastry collar with a little of the beaten egg, then top with the pastry lid. Pinch the edges together with your fingers to seal.

4 Brush the top with the remaining beaten egg and cut 2 slits in the top to allow steam to escape. Bake for 30–40 minutes, until the pastry is puffed and golden. Serve hot.

EQUIPMENT
1 quart pie dish
or 4 individual pie dishes

INGREDIENTS

FOR THE FILLING
2 tbsp olive oil
3 skinless, boneless chicken breast fillets,
   cut into chunks
salt and freshly ground black pepper
1 onion, finely chopped
1 tbsp all-purpose flour,
   plus extra for dusting
⅔ cup heavy cream
1¼ cups hot vegetable stock
12oz can sweet corn kernels, drained
handful of flat-leaf parsley,
   finely chopped

FOR THE PASTRY
10oz (300) store-bought puff pastry
   (or to make your own, see pp.110–113)
1 large egg, lightly beaten, to glaze

Entertaining is often easier if you serve individual portions to ensure that there will be enough to go around. This dish has the added advantage of being easy to prepare in advance and bake as needed.

STUFFED CHICKEN BREASTS EN CROÛTE

 MAKES 4   PREP 25 MINS   COOK 40–55 MINS   FREEZE UP TO 1 MONTH

EQUIPMENT
2 baking sheets

INGREDIENTS

FOR THE FILLING
1 tbsp oil from a jar of sun-dried tomatoes
½ red onion, finely chopped
2 garlic cloves, finely chopped
1 red bell pepper, finely sliced
salt and freshly ground black pepper
4 sun-dried tomatoes in oil, drained
4 boneless, skinless chicken breasts
2½oz (75g) mozzarella,
sliced into 4
16 basil leaves
8 slices proscuitto

FOR THE PASTRY
2 x 11oz (320g) sheets store-bought puff
pastry, each 9in x 15in (23cm x 37cm)
(or to make your own, see pp.110–113)
1 large egg, beaten, to glaze

1 Preheat the oven to 400°F (200°C). Line the baking sheets with parchment paper.

2 For the filling, heat the oil in a nonstick frying pan and gently fry the onion for 3 minutes. Add the garlic, red bell pepper, and plenty of seasoning, and cook for 5 minutes, until the peppers are tender. Transfer to a medium high-sided bowl and add the sun-dried tomatoes. Purée the vegetables using a handheld electric blender to form a rough paste.

3 To stuff the chicken breast, make a lengthwise split down the side of each chicken breast with a very sharp knife. Place a slice of mozzarella and a quarter of the vegetable mixture into each pocket.

4 Place 4 basil leaves on top of each stuffed breast and season well with salt and pepper. Wrap 2 slices of proscuitto around each breast, as this will help to keep the stuffing in place.

5 Cut each pastry sheet into 4, to make 8 x 4½in x 7½in (11.5cm x 18.5cm) rectangles. Place a stuffed chicken breast on the center of a pastry rectangle, brush the edges with water, and top with another rectangle. Press the pastry edges down firmly to seal and transfer to the baking sheet. Repeat to wrap the remaining chicken. Brush each parcel with the beaten egg and bake for 35–40 minutes.

A version of the popular Brazilian pie, this pie is unusual in that it uses plain yogurt, rather than water, to bring the dough together. This gives the finished dough a more crumbly, flaky texture.

CHICKEN AND HEART OF PALM PIE

SERVES 6   **PREP 25 MINS PLUS CHILLING**   **COOK 35–40 MINS**

1 Grease and flour the pie dish. To make the dough, rub the flour, salt, and fat together with your fingertips until the mixture resembles bread crumbs. Add the egg and yogurt and bring the mixture together to form a soft dough. Wrap in plastic wrap and chill in the refrigerator for 1 hour.

2 For the filling, heat the olive oil in a medium nonstick frying pan over medium heat and fry the onion for 3 minutes. Add the garlic and chicken and fry for 10 minutes. Add the hearts of palm, tomatoes, and cream, season well, and stir to combine. Remove from the heat and set aside.

3 Preheat the oven to 400°F (200°C). Roll out half the dough on a floured surface to a circle large enough to line the pie dish. Place the dough in the dish and trim off the excess. Add the filling and brush the edge with a little of the beaten egg.

4 Roll out the remaining dough to a circle large enough to top the pie, then use to cover the pie. Trim off the excess dough, then, using your thumbs and forefingers, press firmly to seal. Brush with the remaining beaten egg, then cut a hole in the top to allow steam to escape. Place on a baking sheet and bake for 20–25 minutes, until brown.

EQUIPMENT
9in (23cm) pie dish

INGREDIENTS

FOR THE DOUGH
(For visual step-by-step instructions, see p.104)
1¾ cups all-purpose flour, plus extra for dusting
a pinch of salt
1 cup vegetable shortening, cubed, plus extra for greasing
1 large egg, plus 1 extra, beaten, to glaze
½ cup (100ml) plain yogurt

FOR THE FILLING
1 tbsp olive oil
1 onion, finely chopped
2 garlic cloves, finely chopped
2 boneless, skinless chicken breasts, chopped into bite-sized chunks
14oz can hearts of palm, chopped into bite-sized chunks
2 tomatoes, peeled, seeded, and finely chopped
½ cup heavy cream
salt and freshly ground black pepper

This tangy chicken pie is a pleasant change from a traditional crust-based pie. Gently flavoring the filling with turmeric turns this midweek meal into something special.

VEGETABLE AND CHICKEN PIE

 SERVES 2   PREP 20 MINS   COOK 50 MINS

EQUIPMENT
small ovenproof dish

INGREDIENTS

FOR THE TOPPING
1lb (450g) large potatoes, peeled
and cut into large chunks
salt and freshly ground black pepper
a large pat of butter
4–5 tbsp milk

FOR THE FILLING
3 tbsp butter
1 red bell pepper, thinly sliced
1 leek, sliced
¼ tsp ground turmeric
¼ cup all-purpose flour
1 cup milk
¾ cup crème fraîche
6oz (150g) green beans, cut into ¾in (2cm)
pieces and blanched
8oz (225g) cooked chicken, sliced
(or 2–3 chicken thigh fillets, cooked)

1 Preheat the oven to 400°F (200°C). Cook the potatoes in a large saucepan of boiling salted water for 15 minutes, or until tender. Drain, return the potatoes to the pan, and mash with the butter and enough milk to make thick mashed potatoes. Season with salt and set aside.

2 For the filling, melt the butter in a large pan. Add the red bell pepper and leek, and cook for 3–4 minutes, until soft. Stir in the turmeric, cook for a minute, then add the flour and cook for another 2–3 minutes. Pour in the milk slowly, while stirring constantly, and cook for 4–5 minutes, until thickened. Add the crème fraîche, green beans, and cooked chicken, and mix well.

3 Season well with salt and pepper and pour the filling into the dish. Cover with the mashed potatoes, then cook in the oven for 25 minutes, until golden and piping hot.

A fantastic dish for entertaining, this meal is prepared in handy individual servings. Use a good-quality pie dough and leftover or store-bought cooked chicken to achieve an impressive result in minutes.

CHICKEN JALOUSIE

 SERVES 4   PREP 25 MINS   COOK 35 MINS   FREEZE UP TO 1 MONTH

EQUIPMENT
baking sheet

INGREDIENTS

FOR THE FILLING
2 tbsp butter
2 leeks, thinly sliced
1 tsp chopped fresh thyme
or ½ tsp dried thyme
1 tsp all-purpose flour,
plus extra for dusting
⅓ cup chicken stock
1 tsp lemon juice
10oz (300g) skinless, boneless
cooked chicken, chopped
salt and freshly ground black pepper

FOR THE DOUGH
all-purpose flour, for dusting
1lb 2oz (500g) puff pie dough
(or to make your own, see pp.110–113)
1 large egg, beaten, to glaze

1 Melt the butter in a saucepan. Add the leeks and cook over low heat, stirring frequently, for 5 minutes, or until fairly soft. Stir in the thyme, then sprinkle over the flour and stir in. Gradually blend in the stock and bring to a boil, stirring until thickened. Remove from the heat, stir in the lemon juice, and set aside to cool.

2 Preheat the oven to 425°F (220°C). On a lightly floured surface, roll out just under half of the dough to a 10in x 6in (25cm x 15cm) rectangle and lay the dough on a large dampened baking sheet. Roll out the remaining dough to a 10in x 7in (25cm x 18cm) rectangle, lightly dust with flour, then fold in half lengthwise. Make cuts ½in (1cm) apart along the folded edge to within 1in (2.5cm) of the outer edge.

3 Stir the chopped chicken into the leek mixture and season generously with salt and pepper. Spoon evenly over the pie dough, leaving a 1in (2.5cm) border. Dampen the edges of the dough with water. Place the second piece of dough on top and press the edges together to seal, then trim off the excess dough. Brush the top with beaten egg and bake for 25 minutes, or until golden brown and crisp. Set aside to cool for 2–3 minutes before serving.

Although often used to top sweet dishes, a cobbler topping can also be used to turn a stew or casserole into a one-pot meal. Add mustard, chopped herbs, or even horseradish to complement the filling.

CHICKEN COBBLER

SERVES 4   **PREP 20 MINS**   **COOK 2¼ HRS**

1 Preheat the oven to 300°F (150°C). Heat 1 tablespoon of the olive oil in the casserole dish over medium heat. Add the onion and cook for 3–4 minutes, until soft. Season with salt and pepper, then stir in the garlic and parsnips, and cook for another 2–3 minutes, until the parsnips take on some color. Remove the vegetables and set aside. Heat the remaining oil in the casserole dish over a higher heat.

2 Toss the chicken in the flour and cook, skin-side down, for 8–10 minutes, or until golden all over. Pour in the Marsala and bring to a boil, then return the onion and parsnips to the casserole dish, add the tarragon, and pour in the stock. Bring to a boil, reduce to a simmer, cover with the lid, and put in the oven for 2 hours. Check occasionally to make sure it's not drying out, adding a little hot water if needed.

3 To make the cobbler topping, put the sifted flour into a bowl, season, then rub in the butter until the mixture resembles fine bread crumbs. Stir in the cheese and add the buttermilk to form a dough. Roll out the dough on a lightly floured surface to 1in (2.5cm) thick and cut out 10 x 2in (5cm) diameter circles. For the last 30 minutes of cooking, place them around the edge of the stew and return to the oven, uncovered.

EQUIPMENT
large flameproof casserole dish

INGREDIENTS

FOR THE FILLING
3 tbsp olive oil
1 onion, finely chopped
salt and freshly ground black pepper
3 garlic cloves, finely chopped
3 parsnips, peeled and sliced
6 chicken thighs, with skin on
1 tbsp all-purpose flour, seasoned with salt
   and black pepper
½ cup Marsala wine, sherry,
   or white wine
a few tarragon leaves
about 1 cup hot chicken stock

FOR THE COBBLER TOPPING
(For visual step-by-step instructions,
   see cobbler dough pp.118–119)
1 cup all-purpose flour, sifted
salt and freshly ground black pepper
4 tbsp butter, softened
1oz (25g) Cheddar cheese, grated
3–4 tbsp buttermilk

A lighter alternative to the beef filling of the Cornish Pasty, these delicious chicken parcels are given an unusual twist with the use of a mixture of sweet potato and the more traditional white potato.

CHICKEN PASTIES

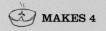 MAKES 4   PREP 30 MINS   COOK 35–40 MINS
                     PLUS CHILLING

EQUIPMENT
baking sheet

INGREDIENTS

FOR THE DOUGH
(For visual step-by-step instructions,
see pie dough p.104)
2 cups all-purpose flour,
plus extra for dusting
12 tbsp butter, chilled and cubed
2 large eggs
oil, for greasing

FOR THE FILLING
4oz (115g) cream cheese
6 scallions, sliced
2 tbsp parsley, chopped
salt and freshly ground black pepper
2–3 chicken breasts, about 12oz (350g),
cut into ¾in (2cm) chunks
1 potato, about 5½oz (150g),
cut into ½in (1cm) cubes
1 sweet potato, about 5½oz (150g),
cut into ½in (1cm) cubes

1 To make the dough, sift the flour into a bowl, then rub in the butter with your fingertips until the mixture resembles fine bread crumbs. In another bowl, beat the eggs and 3 tablespoons cold water together. Set aside 1 tablespoon of the mixture for glazing, then pour the rest over the dry ingredients and mix to form a dough. Wrap the dough in oiled plastic wrap and chill in the refrigerator for 30 minutes.

2 Meanwhile, for the filling, mix the cream cheese, scallions, and parsley together in a bowl, and season to taste with salt and pepper. Stir in the chicken, potato, and sweet potato.

3 Preheat the oven to 400°F (200°C). Divide the dough into 4 pieces. Roll out each piece on a floured surface and, using a small plate as a guide, cut into an 8in (20cm) circle. Spoon a quarter of the filling into the center of each circle. Brush the edges with water and bring together to seal, then crimp.

4 Place the pasties on a baking sheet and brush with the reserved egg mixture. Cut a slit in the tops and bake for 10 minutes, then reduce the heat to 350°F (180°C) and cook for 25–30 minutes, until a thin knife comes out clean when inserted into the center. Serve the pasties hot or cold.

A quick supper dish is given a Spanish makeover with this delicious pie. Try to find smoked paprika, since it will add a layer of sweet, smoky spice to the dish. Serve with any lightly steamed green vegetable.

SPANISH CHICKEN PIE

SERVES 4 　　　 PREP 15 MINS 　　　 COOK 45–50 MINS 　　　 FREEZE UP TO 1 MONTH

1 Heat the olive oil in a medium frying pan, add the chicken strips, and fry for 5 minutes over medium heat. Remove the chicken from the pan using a slotted spoon and transfer to a plate lined with paper towels.

2 Add the red onion to the pan and fry gently for 5 minutes. Add the paprika, garlic, peppers, and chorizo and cook for 5 minutes.

3 Stir in the tomatoes, olives, and rosemary, season well, bring to a boil, then reduce to a simmer. Cook for 15 minutes, or until the sauce has thickened. Preheat the oven to 400°F (200°C).

4 Stir the chicken strips into the tomato and chorizo mixture and place in the pie dish.

5 Cut enough ¾in (2cm) wide strips from the edge of the pastry to fit around the rim of the dish. Brush the edge of the dish with water and place the strips on the rim. Cover the pie with the remaining pastry, trim, and press firmly to seal. Brush with the beaten egg and cut a hole in the top to allow the steam to escape. Place on a baking sheet and bake for 15–20 minutes, until browned.

EQUIPMENT
9in (23cm) pie dish

INGREDIENTS

FOR THE FILLING
1 tbsp olive oil
3 boneless, skinless chicken thighs, cut into strips
1 red onion, finely sliced
1 tsp paprika (preferably smoked)
2 garlic cloves, finely chopped
½ red bell pepper, finely sliced
½ yellow bell pepper, finely sliced
3oz (85g) dry Spanish chorizo, sliced into bite-sized pieces
14oz can chopped tomatoes
1oz (30g) pitted green olives
2 tbsp rosemary leaves, chopped
salt and freshly ground black pepper

FOR THE PASTRY
7½oz (215g) store bought puff pastry (or to make your own, see pp.110–113)
1 large egg, beaten, to glaze

For people who cook a lot, finding a new ingredient is often a great inspiration. This smoked chicken is a great alternative to regular roast chicken, and it inspired these tasty little parcels.

SMOKED CHICKEN AND ARUGULA FILO PARCELS

 **MAKES 12**   **PREP 25 MINS**   **COOK 20 MINS**   **FREEZE UNCOOKED, UP TO 1 MONTH**

EQUIPMENT
baking sheet

INGREDIENTS

FOR THE FILLING
8oz (225g) arugula
4 scallions, finely chopped
4oz (115g) smoked chicken
⅓ cup crème fraîche
2oz (60g) pine nuts, roasted
2 tbsp sun-dried tomato pesto
grated zest of 1 lemon
freshly ground black pepper
1oz (30g) Parmesan cheese,
finely grated

FOR THE DOUGH
7oz (200g) filo dough
4 tbsp butter, melted

1 Preheat the oven to 350°F (180°C). Line the baking sheet with parchment paper. Wash the arugula and remove any tough stems. Place in a food processor with the scallions, smoked chicken, and crème fraîche, then process for a slightly chunky texture. The mixture should not be totally smooth. Add the pine nuts, pesto, and lemon zest. Season to taste with freshly ground black pepper.

2 Lay the filo dough out on a clean surface. Cover with a clean, damp dish towel to stop the dough from drying out. Brush one strip of filo dough with melted butter, then place another layer on top and brush with more butter. Cut the dough into 3in (7.5cm) strips, and place 1 heaping teaspoon of the arugula mixture near the top. Take the right corner and fold diagonally to the left to form a triangle over the filling. Fold along the crease of the triangle and repeat until you reach the end of the strip. Brush with butter once finished and scatter with grated Parmesan cheese. Place the parcels on the lined baking sheet.

3 Repeat with the rest of the dough and filling to make 12 parcels. Bake for 20 minutes. Remove from the baking sheet and put on a wire rack to cool. The dough parcels can be made the day before and chilled in the refrigerator until ready to cook.

These lovely little Latin American pies make great party or picnic food, and are good served hot or cold. Unusually the dough is fried rather than baked, giving a deliciously crisp finish to the dish.

CHICKEN AND CHEESE EMPANADAS

 **MAKES 10–12**   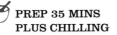 **PREP 35 MINS PLUS CHILLING**   **COOK 30 MINS**

1 To make the dough, melt the butter in a small saucepan, then add the lemon juice and ½ cup water. Add the flour and salt, and stir well to make a paste. On a floured surface, knead the dough well, then chill.

2 Meanwhile, for the filling, grind the chicken in a food processor. Heat the olive oil in a frying pan, add the onion, and cook over medium heat for 5 minutes. Add the ground chicken and cook for another 5 minutes, stirring occasionally. Add the wine, garlic, tomato paste, cayenne, and finely chopped parsley, and season well with salt and pepper. Mix well and cook for 10 minutes, then set aside to cool for 5 minutes. Stir in the grated cheeses.

3 Meanwhile, roll out the dough on a lightly floured surface to ¼in (5mm) thick. Using the cutter, cut out 10–12 circles. Place 1 tablespoon of the chicken and cheese mixture in the middle of each and fold in half. Dampen the edges a little with some cold water, then crimp together with your fingers.

4 Heat the sunflower oil in a deep-sided frying pan until hot, then fry the empanadas in batches over medium heat, turning them occasionally for 3–5 minutes, or until golden brown. Serve with aioli and a tomato and basil salad.

EQUIPMENT
4in (10cm) round cookie cutter

INGREDIENTS

FOR THE DOUGH
7 tbsp butter
juice of 1 lemon
1 ½ cups all-purpose flour,
   plus extra for dusting

FOR THE FILLING
5oz (125g) boneless, skinless
   chicken breast
2 tbsp olive oil
1 onion, finely chopped
3 tbsp dry white wine
3 garlic cloves, crushed
1 tbsp tomato paste
1 tsp cayenne pepper
1 tbsp finely chopped flat-leaf parsley
salt and freshly ground black pepper
3oz (75g) mozzarella, grated
1oz (25g) Parmesan, grated
1 cup sunflower or vegetable oil

Blind bake a tart crust and you have the basis of many tasty meals. Fill it with new season's asparagus, tender chicken, and fresh tarragon, and you have the taste of spring on a plate.

CHICKEN, ASPARAGUS, AND TARRAGON SPRING TART

SERVES 6–8

PREP 20 MINS PLUS CHILLING

COOK 1 HR 10 MINS–1¼ HRS

FREEZE PIE CRUST, UP TO 1 MONTH

EQUIPMENT
9in (22cm) deep-sided fluted tart pan with removable bottom, baking beans

INGREDIENTS

FOR THE DOUGH
(For visual step-by-step instructions, see pie dough p.104)
1½ cups all-purpose flour, plus extra for dusting
7 tbsp unsalted butter, softened
½ tsp salt

FOR THE FILLING
3½oz (100g) asparagus, trimmed and cut into 1¼in (3cm) pieces
salt and freshly ground black pepper
1 cup half-and-half
2 large eggs, plus 1 egg yolk
1 heaping tbsp tarragon, chopped
grated rind of ½ lemon
9oz (250g) cold, cooked chicken

1 To make the dough, rub the flour, butter, and salt together with your fingertips until the mixture resembles bread crumbs. Add 4–6 tablespoons cold water, a little at a time, and bring the mixture together to form a soft dough. Add a little extra water if needed. Wrap in plastic wrap and chill for 30 minutes. Preheat the oven to 350°F (180°C).

2 Roll out the dough on a well-floured surface to a large circle about ¼in (5mm) thick, and use to line the tart pan, making sure it overlaps the sides. Trim all but ½in (1cm) of the overhanging dough. Prick the bottom with a fork, line with wax paper, and fill with baking beans. Place it on a baking sheet and bake for 20–25 minutes, until the dough is lightly cooked. Remove the beans and paper and bake for another 5 minutes to crisp. Trim off any ragged edges from the tart crust while it is still warm.

3 Blanch the asparagus pieces in a saucepan of boiling salted water for 1 minute, then plunge them into a bowl of cold water. Whisk together the half-and-half, eggs, egg yolk, tarragon, and lemon rind, and season.

4 Distribute the chicken and asparagus evenly in the bottom of the crust, not packing the filling down too much. Place the tart on a baking sheet and carefully pour the half-and-half mixture over the filling.

5 Bake for 40–45 minutes, until it is cooked through and browning in places. Set aside to rest for at least 20 minutes before serving warm or cold. Best eaten the same day, but can be chilled overnight.

Sometimes simple entertaining dishes are what's required, but it's nice to spend a little more time producing something special. These tiny pies are a bit tricky, but they make wonderful Christmas canapés.

CHICKEN AND VEGETABLE PIELETS

 MAKES 24   PREP 15 MINS   COOK 50 MINS – 1 HR 5 MINS

EQUIPMENT
24-hole mini muffin pan,
2½in (6cm) round cookie cutter

INGREDIENTS
2 tbsp olive oil, plus extra for greasing
4 tbsp butter
1 small carrot, finely chopped
1 celery stalk, finely chopped
1 leek, white part only,
finely chopped
1 garlic clove, grated
or finely chopped
7oz (200g) cremini mushrooms, cubed
1lb 2oz (500g) skinless, boneless chicken
breast, cubed
1 tbsp thyme leaves, chopped
grated zest of 1 lemon
¼ cup dry white wine
1 cup heavy cream
salt and freshly ground black pepper

FOR THE PASTRY
3 sheets store-bought puff pastry
(or to make your own, see pp.110–113)
2 large eggs, lightly beaten, to glaze

1 Heat the olive oil and butter in a large frying pan over low heat. Add the carrot and celery, and gently sweat for about 5 minutes, until soft. Add the leek and sweat for another 2–3 minutes, until softened. Stir in the garlic and cook for 30 seconds before adding the cubed mushrooms. Cook, stirring occasionally, for 5 more minutes.

2 Increase the heat slightly and add the cubed chicken, thyme, lemon zest, and white wine. Cook, stirring occasionally, for 15–20 minutes. Pour in the cream, and season with salt and pepper. Cook for another 5 minutes, until thickened slightly. Remove the pan from the heat and set aside to cool.

3 Preheat the oven to 400°F (200°C). Lightly oil the muffin pan. Cut out 24 x 2½in (6cm) circles from the puff pastry with a round cookie cutter and use to line the holes in the prepared muffin pan. Spoon the chicken mixture into the pastry crusts.

4 Cut out 24 x 2in (5cm) circles from the remaining puff pastry and use to cover each of the chicken pies. Gently press the edges together with your fingers to seal. Brush the tops with the beaten eggs and bake for 15–20 minutes, until the pastry is golden brown. Serve the pielets hot with a salad of mixed greens and a dollop or two of tomato relish.

After a festive meal there are sometimes more leftovers than you know what to do with. These little parcels make use of some of those leftovers and are a good standby to serve unexpected guests.

ROAST TURKEY AND CRANBERRY TURNOVERS

 MAKES 4   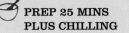 PREP 25 MINS PLUS CHILLING   🕐 COOK 25–30 MINS   ❄ FREEZE UP TO 1 MONTH

1 To make the dough, rub the flour and butter together with your fingertips until the mixture resembles bread crumbs. Add the salt and enough cold water to bring the mixture together to form a soft dough. Wrap in plastic wrap and chill for 30 minutes.

2 For the filling, heat the olive oil in a medium nonstick frying pan. Add the onion and cook over medium heat for 3 minutes, then add the garlic and cook for another 2 minutes. Remove from the heat and stir in the crème fraîche, cranberry sauce, turkey, and oregano. Season generously, stir well, and set aside.

3 Preheat the oven to 375°F (190°C). Line the baking sheets with parchment paper. Roll out the dough on a well-floured surface to ¼in (5mm) thick. Using a small plate (about 8in/20cm in diameter) cut out 4 circles from the dough, re-rolling the dough if necessary. Arrange one-quarter of the filling on half of each circle, leaving a ½in (1cm) border around the edge. Brush the edges with beaten egg, then bring them together to seal and crimp for a decorative finish.

4 Place the turnovers on the prepared baking sheets and brush with the remaining beaten egg. Cut a slit in the top of each turnover to allow steam to escape and bake for 20–25 minutes, until golden brown.

EQUIPMENT
2 baking sheets

INGREDIENTS

FOR THE DOUGH
(For visual step-by-step instructions, see pie dough p.104)
1¾ cups all-purpose flour, plus extra for dusting
11 tbsp butter, chilled and cubed
½ tsp salt
1 large egg, beaten, to glaze

FOR THE FILLING
1 tbsp olive oil
1 red onion, finely chopped
2 garlic cloves, finely chopped
⅓ cup low-fat crème fraîche or sour cream
3 tbsp cranberry sauce
7oz (200g) roast turkey, roughly chopped
2 tbsp fresh, chopped or 1 tsp dried oregano
salt and freshly ground black pepper

Traditionally, both a turkey and a ham are served on or around Christmas day, which can leave you with a lot of meaty leftovers. This simple, classic pie is always a good solution.

TURKEY AND HAM PIE

 SERVES 4   PREP 20 MINS   COOK 35–40 MINS   FREEZE UP TO
                     PLUS CHILLING   1 MONTH

EQUIPMENT
9in (23cm) pie dish

INGREDIENTS

FOR THE FILLING
3 tbsp butter
¼ cup all-purpose flour
1½–2 cups whole milk
1 heaping tsp Dijon mustard
salt and freshly ground black pepper
4 sprigs of thyme, leaves picked
or 1 tsp dried thyme
8oz (225g) cooked turkey, shredded
8oz (225g) cooked ham, shredded

FOR THE PASTRY
7½oz (215g) store-bought puff pastry
(or to make your own, see pp.110–113)
1 large egg, beaten, to glaze

1 Preheat the oven to 400°F (200°C). Melt the butter in a medium saucepan. Stir in the flour and cook for 2–3 minutes over medium heat, stirring constantly with a wooden spoon, until a smooth paste is formed. Gradually add the milk, stirring constantly, then bring to a boil. Reduce the heat and simmer for 3 minutes to make a white sauce. Stir in the mustard and season well with salt and pepper.

2 Add the thyme, turkey, and ham to the sauce, season well and stir to combine. Spoon the mixture into the pie dish.

3 Cut enough ¾in (2cm) wide strips from the edge of the pastry to fit around the rim of the pie dish. Brush the edge of the dish with water and place the strips on the rim. Cover the pie with the remaining pastry, trim the edges, and press firmly with your thumb and forefinger to seal. Brush with the beaten egg and cut a slit in the top to allow steam to escape. Chill in the refrigerator for 10 minutes to firm up the pastry.

4 Place the pie on a baking sheet and bake for 25–30 minutes, or until puffed up and golden brown on top.

This is an interpretation of the classic Moroccan pastilla, but here a large family-sized pie is served, which tastes even better cold the next day. You can make and chill the filling three days ahead.

MIDDLE-EASTERN GUINEA HEN PIE

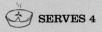 SERVES 4   PREP 1½ HRS   COOK 1½ HRS   FREEZE FILLING, UP TO 1 MONTH

1 If using a guinea hen, remove the breasts and set aside to use in another dish. Take the legs and wings off the body and chop the carcass coarsely. Put the guinea hen or chicken legs and the rest of the guinea hen (if using) in a large saucepan. Add the onions, garlic, ginger, and cinnamon stick and cover with the stock. Bring to a boil, reduce the heat to low and simmer, uncovered, for 45 minutes, until the legs are cooked through. Set aside to cool, then strain through a colander, reserving the liquid. Clean out the pan, add the reserved liquid and bring to a simmer until it barely covers the bottom of the pan.

2 Pull the guinea hen meat off the bones, leaving it in bite-sized shreds. Remove the onions and garlic, coarsely chop, add them to the meat, and return to the pan. Mix in the pomegranate molasses and honey and cook over medium heat until the mixture looks wet. Add the eggs and cilantro and cook for 2 minutes, until the mixture comes together. Season and cool.

3 Combine the walnuts, apricots, and cinnamon. Preheat the oven to 375°F (190°C). Brush the bottom of the pan with a little olive oil. Put a layer of filo into the bottom of the pan. Brush with more oil and layer a filo sheet on top, angling it slightly off center to the first piece. Continue until you have used 6 layers. Spread half the walnut mix over the base. Cover with half the meat. Top with remaining nut mix and finish with meat. Fold any ragged edges over the top, cut the remaining filo in half, and repeat the layering process. Brush with oil. Bake for 30–40 minutes, until brown. Cool for 5 minutes; dust with confectioners' sugar, if liked.

EQUIPMENT
8in (20cm) cake pan with removable bottom

INGREDIENTS

FOR THE FILLING
1 small guinea hen,
  or 2 large chicken legs
2 onions, quartered
4 garlic cloves, peeled
¾in (2cm) piece of ginger,
  thickly sliced
1 cinnamon stick
4 cups good-quality
  chicken stock
2 tbsp pomegranate molasses
1 tbsp honey
2 large eggs, lightly beaten
2–3 heaping tbsp cilantro, chopped
salt and freshly ground black pepper
4oz (100g) walnut pieces, roasted
  and coarsely chopped
2oz (50g) dried apricots,
  finely chopped
½ tsp ground cinnamon

FOR THE DOUGH
3 tbsp olive oil
9 sheets store-bought filo dough
confectioners' sugar (optional)

A sophisticated pairing of wild mushrooms and cream perfectly complements the subtle gamey flavor of the guinea hen. Serve with greens and plenty of mashed potatoes for a homey fall treat.

CREAMY WILD MUSHROOM AND GUINEA HEN PIE

 SERVES 6–8   PREP 25 MINS   COOK 30–35 MINS   FREEZE UP TO 1 MONTH

1 Preheat the oven to 400°F (200°C). Place the porcini mushrooms in a small bowl and cover with boiling water. Set aside for 10 minutes, then drain and squeeze any moisture out of the mushrooms.

2 Heat the olive oil in a medium nonstick frying pan and gently fry the shallots for 3 minutes. Add the garlic and cook for 1–2 minutes.

3 Add the guinea hen to the pan and cook for 3–4 minutes, until lightly browned. Add the cremini mushrooms, porcini mushrooms, Madeira, thyme, nutmeg, and seasoning and cook gently for 5 minutes. Add the cream, stir well, and transfer to the pie dish.

4 Cut enough ¾in (2cm) wide strips from the edge of the pastry to fit around the rim of the pie dish. Brush the edge of the dish with water and place the strips on the rim. Cover the pie with the remaining pastry, trim off the excess, and press firmly to seal. Brush with the beaten egg and cut a hole in the lid to allow steam to escape. Place on a baking sheet and bake for 15–20 minutes, until browned.

EQUIPMENT
9in (23cm) pie dish

INGREDIENTS

FOR THE FILLING
1oz (25g) dried porcini mushrooms
1 tbsp olive oil
4 shallots, halved
2 garlic cloves, finely chopped
14oz (400g) guinea hen breasts,
   cut into bite-sized pieces
7oz (200g) cremini mushrooms, halved
2 tbsp Madeira
leaves from 1 bunch fresh thyme
   or 1 tsp dried thyme
¼ tsp freshly grated nutmeg
salt and freshly ground black pepper
2 tbsp heavy cream

FOR THE PASTRY
7½oz (215g) sheet store-bought puff pastry
   (or to make your own, see pp.110–113)
1 large egg, beaten, to glaze

variation

CREAMY WILD MUSHROOM AND CHICKEN PIE

Try using chicken or turkey breast instead of the guinea hen in step 3, and follow the recipe as directed.

IN PRAISE OF PIE DOUGH

PIE DOUGH

A good pie dough is light, crisp, and suits all types of pies and tarts. Use the following quantities: 1 cup all-purpose flour, 5 tbsp unsalted butter, or follow the quantities in the recipe you are using.

1 Rub the all-purpose flour and the chilled and cubed unsalted butter together with your fingertips until the mixture resembles fine bread crumbs. Work swiftly, handling the dough as little as possible to keep the gluten in the flour from heating up. Try working in a cool room. To make a richer dough, add 1 lightly beaten egg yolk at this stage.

2 Add 3–4 tablespoons of water and a pinch of salt to the crumbs and bring together to form a soft dough. (If you are making a rich pie dough and have added an egg yolk at step 1, add just enough cold water to the crumbs, 1 tablespoon at a time, to form a soft dough.) Handle the dough gently and be careful not to overwork it; just work it until the texture is smooth. Add extra water if it is too dry. Wrap in plastic wrap and chill for 30 minutes. You can substitute the butter for lard or use half lard and half butter for some traditional recipes.

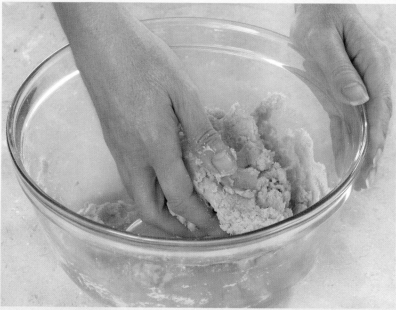

SWEET PIE DOUGH

The classic pie dough (see opposite) can be turned into something sweeter. Just substitute 1 tablespoon of the flour for granulated sugar, or follow the quantities in the recipe you are using.

1 Rub the all-purpose flour and the chilled and cubed unsalted butter together with your fingertips until the mixture resembles fine bread crumbs. Work swiftly, handling the dough as little as possible to keep the gluten in the flour from heating up. Try working in a cool room. Stir in the granulated sugar. To make a richer dough, add 1 lightly beaten egg yolk to the flour mixture.

2 Add 3–4 tablespoons of cold water and bring together to form a soft dough. (If you are making a rich pie dough and have added an egg yolk at step 1, add just enough cold water to the crumbs, 1 tablespoon at a time, to form a soft dough.) Handle the dough gently and be careful not to overwork it; just work it until the texture is smooth. Wrap in plastic wrap and chill for 30 minutes. If you need to scale up pie dough quantities, add extra water instead of more egg.

LARD-BASED PIE DOUGH

For this classic pie dough, which is great for a steak and kidney pie, use these quantities: 1³/₄ cups self-rising flour, ¹/₂ teaspoon of salt, 10 tbsp lard, or follow the quantities in the recipe you are using.

1 Sift the self-rising flour into a large bowl and add the salt. Combine these ingredients by mixing briefly with a wooden spoon.

2 Chop the lard or vegetable shortening into small ¹/₂in (1cm) cubes, then add the cubed lard to the flour in the bowl and stir in slightly.

3 Rub the cubed lard into the flour with your fingertips until the mixture resembles rough bread crumbs. Work swiftly, handling the dough as little as possible to keep the gluten in the flour from heating up. Try working in a cool room.

4 Add 3 tablespoons of cold water and mix to start to bring the mixture together, first with a wooden spoon, and then using your hands.

5 Use your fingertips to bring the mixture together to form a soft dough. Handle the dough gently and be careful not to overwork it; just work it until the texture is smooth. Add more water if the dough is too dry.

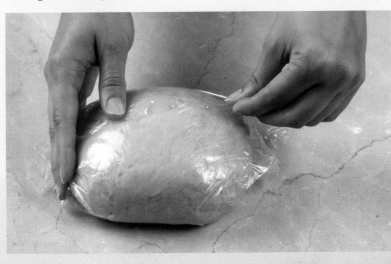

6 Wrap the dough in plastic wrap and chill in the refrigerator for at least 30 minutes before using.

HOT-WATER PIE DOUGH

This dough is best for pork pies. Use 2¼ cups all-purpose flour, ½ teaspoon of fine salt, ⅔ cup boiling water, 10 tbsp cubed lard, or follow the quantities in the recipe you are using.

1 Sift the flour into a large bowl and add the salt. Using a wooden spoon, mix, and then make a well in the middle of the flour mixture.

2 Measure the boiling water into a liquid measuring cup and add the cubed lard. Stir the mixture with a metal spoon until the fat has melted.

3 Carefully pour the hot melted fat mixture into the well in the center of the flour.

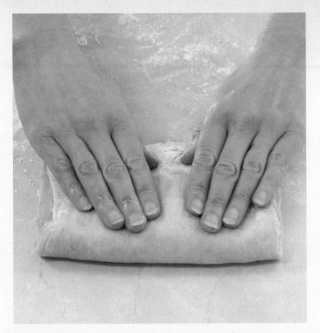

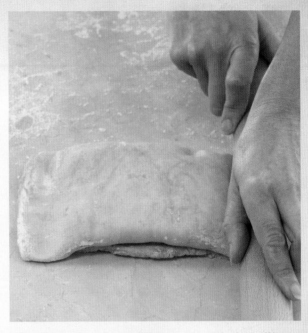

5 Fold the dough over again so the butter is completely enclosed in the layers of dough, then turn the dough over.

6 Roll over the edges of the dough with the rolling pin to seal. Wrap in plastic wrap and chill in the refrigerator for 15 minutes.

7 Lightly flour the surface again. Repeat the rolling and folding process of step 4, but without adding the butter. Seal, wrap, and chill for 15 minutes.

8 Repeat step 7 three more times, chilling the dough for 15 minutes between each turn. The dough is now ready to use as required.

QUICK PUFF PASTRY

This pastry is much quicker to make than the classic puff pastry.
Use 18 tbsp semifrozen butter, 1¹/₂ cups all-purpose flour, and
1 teaspoon of salt, or follow the quantities in the recipe you are using.

1 Freeze the butter for 30 minutes. Coarsely grate it into a bowl. Sift over the flour and the salt and rub together until well-combined and crumbly.

2 Pour in ¹/₃–¹/₂ cup water. Use a fork to start mixing, then use your fingertips to form a rough dough. If it is too dry, add more water.

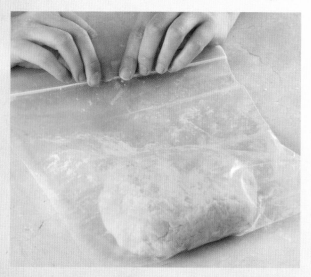

3 Shape the dough into a ball, then place in a clean plastic bag. Seal the bag and set aside to chill in the refrigerator for 20 minutes.

4 Thinly roll out the dough on a lightly floured surface to a long rectangle with short sides, about 10in (25cm). Keep the edges straight and even.

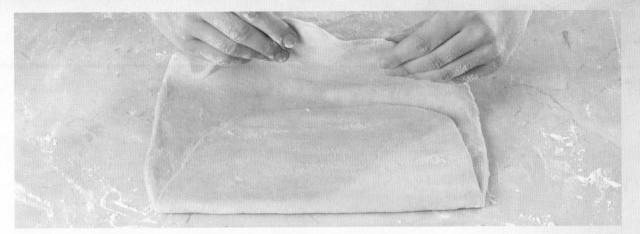

5 Take one-third of the pastry and fold it into the middle of the rectangle, then fold the remaining third over to make 3 layers. The rolling and folding process incorporates air into the pastry, making it puff up on baking.

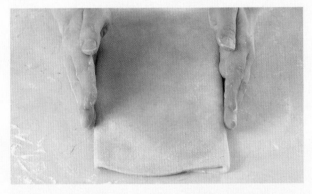

6 Turn the dough over so the seams are easily sealed when it is rolled out again. Make a quarter turn so that the folded edges are at the sides.

7 Roll out the dough again to a similar size as the original rectangle. Make sure to keep the short sides even in size.

8 Repeat the folding, turning, and rolling. Put the dough back in the plastic bag and chill in the refrigerator for 20 minutes.

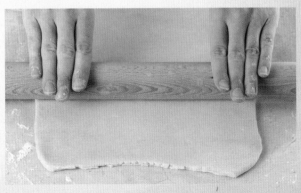

9 Roll, fold, and turn the pastry twice more, then chill in the refrigerator for a final 20 minutes. The dough is now ready to use as required.

STRUDEL PASTRY

To make a light, delicate strudel pastry, use: 1¹/₂ cups all-purpose flour, 1 egg, ¹/₂ teaspoon of lemon juice, and a pinch of salt, or follow the quantities in the recipe you are using.

1 Sift the all-purpose flour into a mound onto a clean work surface. Then, using your fingers, make a well in the center of the flour.

2 Beat the egg with ¹/₂ cup water, lemon juice, and salt together in a large bowl, then pour the mixture into the well.

3 Work the ingredients in the well with your fingertips, gradually drawing in the flour to combine into a dough.

4 Knead just enough flour into the other ingredients so that the dough forms a ball; it should be fairly soft.

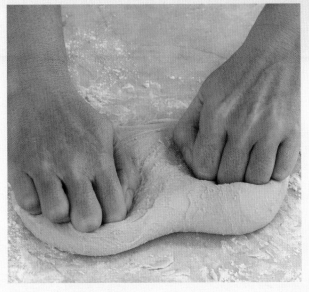

5 Knead the dough on a floured surface for 10 minutes, until it is shiny, smooth, and elastic; add more flour as necessary. Shape it into a ball.

6 On the floured surface, cover the ball of dough with another large clean bowl, and set aside to rest for 30 minutes.

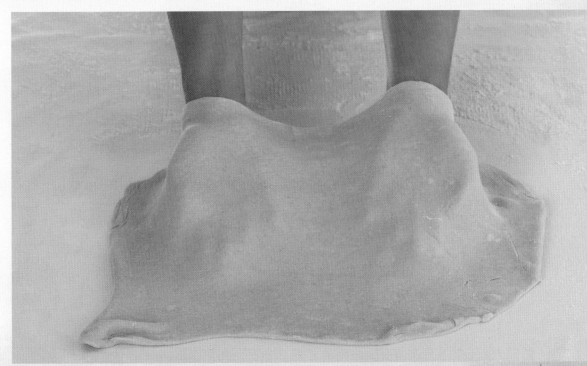

7 Flour your hands and stretch the dough, starting at the center and working outward. Continue to work outward until the dough is as thin as possible; it should be translucent. The dough is now ready to use as required.

GLUTEN-FREE PIE DOUGH

Ideal for people with a gluten intolerance. Use 1³/₄ cups gluten-free all-purpose flour, 1 teaspoon xanthan gum, a pinch of salt, 7 tbsp butter, and 1 egg, or follow the quantities in the recipe you are using.

1 Sift the flour, xanthan gum, and salt into a large bowl and mix together to combine. For sweet pie dough, add 2 tablespoons confectioners' sugar with the flour.

2 Add the cold, cubed butter and rub it in with your fingertips until the mixture resembles bread crumbs. Alternatively, pulse in a food processor.

3 Beat the egg, then add to the mixture and stir it in with a palette knife or a butter knife until the mixture clumps together.

4 Add 1–2 tablespoons of cold water, gradually, a few drops at a time, mixing after each addition. Repeat until it comes together to form a dough.

5 On a floured surface, knead the dough lightly until smooth. Shape the dough into a ball, then wrap in plastic wrap.

6 Chill the dough in the refrigerator for 10 minutes, until firm. This will make rolling out the dough easier. Use the dough as required.

COBBLER DOUGH

Use these quantities: 1¼ cups self-rising flour, ⅓ cup granulated sugar, a pinch of salt, 5 tbsp butter, ½ cup buttermilk, and 1 egg, or follow the recipe you are using.

1 For a cobbler topping, sift the flour, granulated sugar (omit for a savory cobbler), and a pinch of salt into a large bowl.

2 Add the chilled and cubed unsalted butter and mix with your fingertips until the mixture resembles bread crumbs.

3 Beat together the buttermilk and egg, then add to the dry ingredients, and mix to form a dough.

4 Put the filling into a baking dish. Place walnut-sized spoonfuls of the dough over the filling; leave space for the mix to spread.

5 Lightly press down on the balls of mixture to help them combine with the filling and bake. If you like, add chopped herbs or spices to the basic mix to complement the filling.

COOKIE CRUST

These simple sweet crusts are an ideal alternative to pie dough.
Use 9oz (250g) vanilla wafers, ¼ cup granulated sugar, and 8 tbsp
unsalted butter, or follow the quantities in the recipe you are using.

1 Preheat the oven to 350°F (180°C). Crush the cookies in a plastic bag with a rolling pin or use a food processor; you want 2½ cups crushed cookies.

2 Mix the vanilla wafers and granulated sugar with the melted and cooled butter in a large bowl until it resembles wet sand.

3 Pour the cookie mixture into your chosen tart or cake pan and press it firmly into the bottom and sides of the pan. Make sure the filling is packed as firmly as possible and that there is a good side to the crust so that the filling can be contained, unlike a cheesecake crust. Place the tart crust on a baking sheet and bake for 10 minutes. Set aside to cool. Once cold, store the tart crust in the refrigerator until needed.

CRUMBLE TOPPING

To make a traditional sweet crumble topping use: 1 cup all-purpose flour, 1/3 cup granulated sugar, and 6 tbsp unsalted butter, or follow the quantities in the recipe you are using.

1 Sift the flour into a large bowl. Add the granulated sugar and mix to combine. Use light brown sugar instead of granulated, if liked.

2 Chop the cold butter into ½in (1cm) cubes with a sharp knife, then add the cubed butter to the flour mixture.

3 Rub the butter into the flour and sugar mixture with your fingertips until the mixture resembles coarse bread crumbs. Do not make the mixture too fine or uniform; any larger lumps of butter will melt into the crumble topping and give a nicer taste and texture to the finished dish.

LINING A TART PAN

Follow these steps to line any tart pan perfectly every time.
Use the tart pan as a template before lining it with the dough,
and take care not to overstretch it or it may shrink when baked.

1 Roll out the dough on a lightly floured surface
to a large circle, about ⅛in (3mm) thick. Don't use
too much flour, since it may make the dough dry.

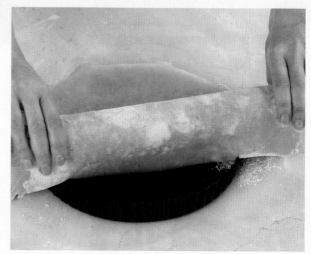

2 Roll the dough up carefully using the rolling pin,
then unroll it over the tart pan, making sure it
overlaps on all sides.

3 Push the dough in with your
fingers, gently pressing it into
the bottom and sides of the pan.
It should overlap the sides by
at least ¾in (2cm).

BAKING BLIND

To achieve a crisp pie crust, bake the unfilled pie crust either partially or completely before adding the filling, depending on the recipe. Use dried beans as an alternative to baking beans.

1 Prick the bottom of the dough all over with a fork to keep it from puffing up, and line with a piece of parchment or wax paper.

2 Weigh the parchment paper down with baking beans. Place the pie crust on a baking sheet—this supports the sides of the dough until cooked.

3 Bake blind in the center of a preheated oven for 20–25 minutes, until the sides of the dough are cooked. Remove the beans and paper.

4 Return the crust to the oven and bake for 5 more minutes to crisp the bottom. Set aside to cool, trimming the edges with a knife while warm.

DECORATIVE EDGES

There's nothing like a homemade pie or tart. For an individual finishing touch, don't just stop at neatly trimming the edges, try one of these ideas to make your baked goods look as special as they taste.

Crimped
Pinch the pastry edge with the forefinger and thumb of your right hand and make even indentations in the top edge with the forefinger of your left hand.

Fork-crimped
A quick and simple finishing touch that also helps to seal the pastry lid—especially useful if the filling is quite wet. Press down all around the edges of the pie using the tines of a fork.

Feathered

Using kitchen scissors, snip 1in (2cm) cuts, ½in (1cm) apart, into the edge of the pie dough. With your fingertips, fold every alternate flap of dough back, diagonally, along the edge of the pie. Leave the next flap lying on the edge of the dish. This creates an elegant, feathered effect.

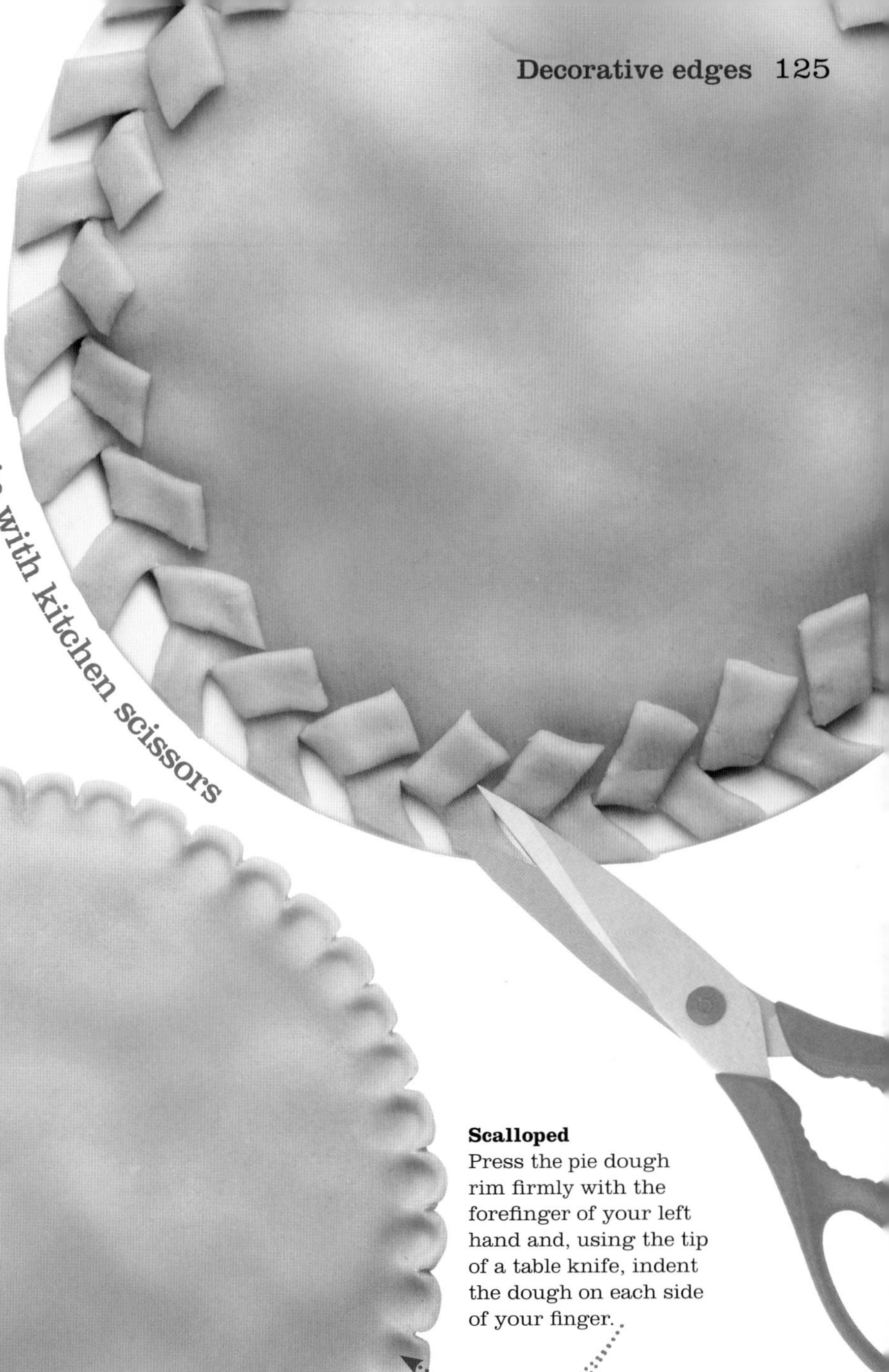

Snip with kitchen scissors

Scalloped

Press the pie dough rim firmly with the forefinger of your left hand and, using the tip of a table knife, indent the dough on each side of your finger.

Use the tip of a knife

Arrowhead
Cut a 1in (2cm) wide
strip, from leftover
pastry, long enough to
go around the edge of
the pie. Cut the strip into
equal-sized triangles.
Moisten the edge of the
pie lid with water and
position the triangles all
the way around, slightly
overlapping each other.

Work at an angle to achieve this impressive finish

Fluted
Pinch the dough edge
with the forefinger
and thumb of your
right hand, and make
indentations at a slight
angle, in the edge,
with the forefinger
of your left hand.

Cornish pasty edges
Pinch the sealed pasty
edge together with the
forefinger and thumb of
your right hand, and make
even indentations in the
edge with the forefinger
of your left hand, to give
an even, crimped finish.

Braided
Cut out 3 x ½in (1cm) wide
pastry strips, long enough
to go around the pie edge.
On a floured work surface,
braid the strips together.
Moisten the edge of the pie
with water and position the
braid, pressing down on it
lightly to secure it in place.

Knocking up
Place a sharp knife
horizontally next to the trimmed
edge of a double puff-pastry crust.
Tap the knife into the pastry edge, to
form layers, gently pressing the pastry
lid down so it does not move. This
technique opens up the layers in the
pastry, allowing air in between them,
which makes them puff up and separate
on baking for a delicious crust.

DECORATIVE TOPS

The top of a covered pie can be decorated in a variety
of ways with leftover dough trimmings. You can also
make a feature of the steam hole in a pie—it looks great
and stops the dough from becoming soggy.

Decorative shapes
Roll out any leftover dough
and design your own shapes,
such as leaves, and cut them
out using a sharp knife.
Or use a small cutter in the
shape of a heart, flower,
star, numbers, or letters to
personalize the pie.

Dough shapes personalize your pie

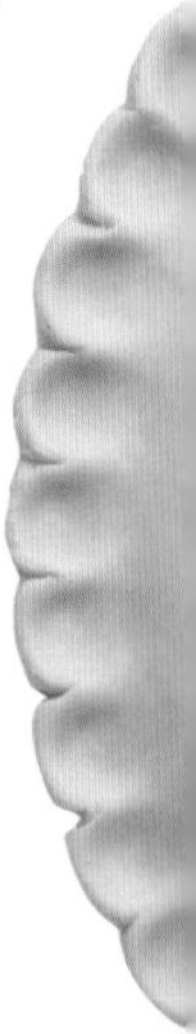

Twisted ribbon
Cut a 1in (2cm) wide dough
strip, long enough to go around
the pie. Hold the strip at one end
and twist it from the other end.
Moisten the edge of the pie with
water and secure the dough strip
in place. Seal the edges together.

Cutouts
Cut several holes in the center of the pie lid, using a small cutter in the shape of your choice, such as a leaf, before positioning it on the pie. You can also cut a cross in the lid when it's in position and pull back the point of each triangle to create a decorative steam hole.

Dough rose
Cut out 4 x 3in (7.5cm) dough squares and stack them up. Place the squares on one forefinger and pull the corners down to form a ball. Cut a cross halfway through the ball, and open out the layers to create petals.

A pretty finishing touch

Lattice top
Roll out any leftover dough and using a fluted dough wheel, cut it into ½in (1.5cm) wide strips, long enough to go across the tart. Moisten the tart edges with water and arrange the strips across the filling. Trim to fit all around the outer edge.

FISH PIES
AND TARTS

This simple dish is quick and easy to make, but always goes down a treat. Substitute the white wine for fish stock when cooking for children and serve with a green vegetable, such as peas.

FISH AND SWEET CORN PIE

SERVES 4   PREP 15 MINS   COOK 55 MINS   FREEZE UP TO 1 MONTH

EQUIPMENT
1 quart pie dish

INGREDIENTS

FOR THE FILLING
1 tbsp olive oil
1 onion, finely chopped
salt and freshly ground black pepper
6 slices thick-cut bacon, finely chopped
1 tsp all-purpose flour
⅔ cup dry white wine
handful of flat-leaf parsley, finely chopped
⅔ cup heavy cream
7oz can sweet corn, drained
1½lb (675g) raw white fish, such as haddock or pollack, cut into chunks

FOR THE PASTRY
10oz (300g) store-bought puff pastry (or to make your own, see pp.110–113)
all-purpose flour, for dusting
1 large egg, lightly beaten, to glaze

1 Preheat the oven to 400°F (200°C). Heat the olive oil in a large frying pan over low heat. Add the onion and a pinch of salt and sweat gently for about 5–10 minutes, until soft and translucent. Add the bacon and cook for another 5 minutes. Remove from the heat, stir in the flour, and add a little of the wine. Return to the heat, pour in the remaining wine, and cook for 5–8 minutes, until thickened.

2 Stir in the parsley, cream, and corn, and spoon the mixture into the pie dish with the fish. Combine gently, and season well with salt and pepper.

3 Roll out the pastry on a floured surface so it is about 2in (5cm) larger all around than the pie dish. Cut out a strip of pastry about 1in (2.5cm) from the edge to make a collar. Dampen the edge of the pie dish with a little water, fit the pastry strip all the way around, and press down firmly. Brush the collar with a little beaten egg and top with the pastry lid. Trim away the excess pastry, then, using your thumb and finger, pinch the edges of the pastry together to seal. Cut 2 slits in the top of the pie to allow steam to escape.

4 Brush the top of the pie all over with the remaining beaten egg and bake for 20–30 minutes, until the pastry is puffed and golden. Serve hot.

Here a traditional fish pie mix is topped with a buttery pastry lid.
Use any mixture of fresh and smoked fish in the filling, and for
variety, add a couple of hard-boiled eggs, cut into quarters.

CLASSIC FISH PIE

SERVES 4   PREP 20 MINS   COOK 20–25 MINS   FREEZE UP TO
                                                                1 MONTH

1 Preheat the oven to 400°F (200°C). Poach
the salmon and haddock in a saucepan of lightly
simmering water for 5 minutes, until just cooked.
Drain and set aside to cool. Melt the butter in another
pan, then remove from the heat and whisk in the flour
until a thick paste is formed. Add the milk a little at
a time, whisking to avoid any lumps. Season with
salt and pepper, and add the nutmeg. Bring the sauce
to a boil, stirring constantly, then reduce the heat
and cook for another 5 minutes, stirring.

2 Flake the fish into a bowl and add the shrimp.
Spread the spinach over the top and pour the sauce
over it. Season to taste. When the spinach is wilted, mix
the filling together and transfer to the pie dish.

3 Roll out the pastry on a floured surface to a circle
bigger than the pie dish and ⅛–¼in (3–5mm) thick.
Cut a circle to fit the pie. Roll some of the trimmings
out into long strips. Brush the rim of the dish with
beaten egg and press the pastry strips around the rim.
Brush the edge with more egg and top with the pastry
lid. Press the edges down to seal, then trim away any
excess pastry. Brush the top of the pie with the
remaining egg and cut 2 slits to allow steam to escape.

4 Bake for 20–25 minutes, until golden. Set aside
to rest for 5 minutes before serving. Best eaten the
same day, the pie can be chilled overnight and reheated.

EQUIPMENT
7in (18cm) pie dish

INGREDIENTS

FOR THE FILLING
10oz (300g) skinless salmon
   fillet, pin-boned
7oz (200g) skinless smoked
   haddock fillet, pin-boned
4 tbsp unsalted butter
5 tbsp all-purpose flour
1½ cups milk
salt and freshly ground black pepper
a pinch of freshly grated nutmeg
7oz (200g) shrimp, peeled and deveined
4oz (100g) baby spinach, washed

FOR THE PASTRY
9oz (250g) store-bought puff pastry
   (or to make your own, see pp.110–113)
all-purpose flour, for dusting
1 large egg, beaten, to glaze

Haddock is the fish of choice in this traditional family dish, but you can use your favorite white fish if you like. Serve the pie with steamed broccoli or fresh peas for a healthy midweek supper.

FISHERMAN'S PIE

 **SERVES 6**   **PREP 20–30 MINS PLUS INFUSING**   **COOK 50 MINS – 1 HR**

1 Cook the potatoes in a saucepan of boiling, salted water for 15–20 minutes, until tender. Drain thoroughly, then put back into the pan and mash. Heat the milk in a small pan, add the butter, salt and pepper, and stir until mixed. Pour the mixture into the potatoes, and beat over medium heat for 2–3 minutes, until fluffy. Taste for seasoning. Set aside.

2 For the filling, pour the milk into a sauté pan, then add the peppercorns, bay leaves, and onion. Bring to a boil, then remove, cover, and leave in a warm place to infuse for about 10 minutes.

3 Add the fish to the milk, cover, and simmer for 5–10 minutes, depending on thickness; it should flake easily when tested with a fork. Transfer the fish to a large plate, using a slotted spoon; reserve the cooking liquid. Let the fish cool, then flake with a fork.

4 Melt the butter in a pan over medium heat. Whisk in the flour and cook for 30 seconds–1 minute, until foaming. Remove from the heat. Pour the fish cooking liquid through a sieve into the butter mixture. Whisk the liquid into the sauce, then return to the heat and cook, whisking, until the sauce boils and thickens. Season and simmer for 2 minutes. Stir in the parsley.

5 Preheat the oven to 350°F (180°C). Melt some butter and use to brush the pie dish. Ladle one-third of the sauce into the bottom of the dish. Spoon the flaked fish on top, in an even layer. Cover with the remaining sauce, then distribute the shrimp evenly on top. Sprinkle the chopped eggs over the shrimp.

6 Spread the mashed potatoes on top to cover the filling completely. Bake for 20–30 minutes, until the topping is brown and the sauce bubbles.

EQUIPMENT
2 quart baking dish

INGREDIENTS

FOR THE TOPPING
1lb 6oz (625g) potatoes, washed, peeled, and cut into pieces
salt and freshly ground black pepper
¼ cup milk
4 tbsp butter

FOR THE FILLING
3½ cups milk
10 peppercorns
2 bay leaves
1 small onion, peeled and quartered
1lb 10oz (750g) skinned haddock fillets, cut into pieces
6 tbsp butter, plus extra for greasing
¼ cup all-purpose flour
leaves from 5–7 parsley sprigs, chopped
4½oz (125g) shrimp, peeled, deveined, and cooked
3 large eggs, hard-boiled, coarsely chopped

Slow cooking the onions gives them a gentle, sweet taste, perfect when paired with strong, salty anchovies. If freezing the tart, add the anchovy garnish after it is defrosted.

ONION AND ANCHOVY TART

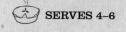 **SERVES 4–6**　　**PREP 15 MINS PLUS CHILLING**　　**COOK 1¼ HRS**　　**FREEZE UP TO 3 MONTHS**

EQUIPMENT
8in (20cm) fluted tart pan with removable bottom, baking beans

INGREDIENTS

FOR THE DOUGH
12oz (350g) store-bought pie dough
(or to make your own, see p.104)
all-purpose flour, for dusting

FOR THE FILLING
2 tbsp olive oil
2 tbsp butter
1lb (450g) onions, thinly sliced
1lb 10oz (750g) cottage cheese
½ cup milk
2 large eggs
1 tsp cumin seeds or caraway
seeds, crushed (optional)
salt and freshly ground
black pepper
2oz (60g) anchovy fillets,
halved lengthwise

1 Roll out the dough thinly on a lightly floured surface, and use it to line the pan. Chill for 30 minutes.

2 Heat the olive oil and butter in a frying pan, add the onions, cover, and cook over low heat, stirring occasionally, for 20 minutes, or until the onions are soft, but not browned. Uncover and cook for another 4–5 minutes until golden. Set aside to cool.

3 Preheat the oven to 400°F (200°C). Line the dough crust with wax paper and fill with baking beans. Bake for 15 minutes, then remove the beans and paper and bake for another 10 minutes.

4 Reduce the heat to 350°F (180°C). Spoon the onions into the crust, spreading them in an even layer. Beat the cottage cheese, milk, eggs, and cumin or caraway, if using, together in a bowl. Season to taste with salt and pepper, then pour into the crust. Lay the anchovy fillets in a lattice pattern on top and bake for 25 minutes, or until the dough is golden and the filling is set. Serve warm. The tart can be cooked up to 1 day in advance, covered, and chilled. Reheat in a hot oven for 10 minutes, or until warmed through.

All the tastes of a Mediterranean summer come together in these quick and easy tartlets. If you are short on time, buy store-bought puff pastry. Serve as an appetizer or light lunch with a tossed salad.

ANCHOVY, PEPPER, AND THYME TARTLETS

 **MAKES 4**   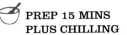 **PREP 15 MINS PLUS CHILLING**   ⏰ **COOK 25–30 MINS**

1 Preheat the oven to 400°F (200°C). Lightly brush or spray the muffin pan with oil.

2 Cut the pastry into 4 squares on a lightly floured surface and use to line the holes in the prepared muffin pan, pushing the pastry down gently into the corners. Chill in the refrigerator for 1 hour.

3 To make the filling, combine the eggs, cream, and Parmesan in a liquid measuring cup, and season to taste with salt and pepper. Mix well.

4 Place an anchovy in each of the prepared puff pastry crusts. Divide and arrange the peppers, thyme, and mozzarella evenly between the 4 crusts. Top each tart with a slice of tomato. Pour the egg and cream mixture over the filling, into the crusts, and grind a little black pepper over the top. Bake the tarts for 25–30 minutes, until golden on top. Serve warm.

EQUIPMENT
4-hole muffin pan

INGREDIENTS

FOR THE PASTRY
oil, for greasing
1 sheet store-bought puff pastry
   (preferably made with butter)
   (or to make your own, see pp.110–113)
all-purpose flour, for dusting

FOR THE FILLING
2 large eggs
¾ cup cream
2 tbsp freshly grated Parmesan cheese
salt and freshly ground black pepper
4 anchovy fillets in olive oil, drained
½ x 10oz jar roasted mixed peppers, drained
   and chopped
leaves from 4 sprigs of thyme
2½ oz (75g) mozzarella, grated
1 plum tomato, sliced into 4 rounds

Baking a pie crust blind helps to ensure that the crust does not become soggy once the filling is introduced and baked. However, spinach produces a lot of water, so be sure to drain it well before use.

SALMON AND SPINACH QUICHE

 **SERVES 6–8** **PREP 20 MINS PLUS CHILLING** **COOK 1 HR 10 MINS–1¼ HRS** **FREEZE PIE CRUST, UP TO 1 MONTH**

EQUIPMENT
9in (22cm) deep-sided, fluted tart pan with removable bottom, baking beans

INGREDIENTS

FOR THE DOUGH
(For visual step-by-step instructions, see pie dough p.104)
1½ cups all-purpose flour, plus extra for dusting
7 tbsp unsalted butter, softened
½ tsp salt

FOR THE FILLING
7oz (200g) baby spinach
2 tbsp olive oil
1 garlic clove, crushed
salt and freshly ground black pepper
4oz (100g) cooked salmon, broken into pieces
1 cup half-and-half
2 large eggs, plus 1 egg yolk
1 tsp grated lemon rind

1 For the dough, rub the flour, butter, and salt together with your fingertips until the mixture resembles fine bread crumbs. Add enough cold water, a little at a time, to bring the mixture together to form a soft dough. Add a little more water if the mixture is too dry. Wrap in plastic wrap and chill for 30 minutes.

2 Preheat the oven to 400°F (180°C). Roll out the dough on a well-floured surface to a large circle about ¼in (5mm) thick and use to line the tart pan, making sure it overlaps the sides, then trim all but ½in (1cm) off the overhanging dough with a pair of scissors. Push the dough down into the corners of the pan making sure it clings to the sides well.

3 Prick the bottom of the pie crust with a fork, line with wax paper and fill with baking beans. Place on a baking sheet and bake 20–25 minutes, until the dough is lightly cooked. Remove the beans and paper and bake for another 5 minutes to crisp. Trim off any ragged edges while it is still warm.

4 For the filling, cook the baby spinach in a large frying pan with the olive oil and garlic for 2–3 minutes until soft. Season well. Place the spinach in a sieve and press out any excess water. Set aside to cool.

5 Spread the cooled spinach evenly over the bottom of the tart. Spread the salmon out alongside the spinach. Whisk together the half-and-half, eggs, yolk, lemon rind, and seasoning. Place the tart crust on a baking sheet and pour the cream mixture over the filling.

6 Bake for 45 minutes until just set. Cool for 30 minutes before eating warm or cold. Best eaten on the day it is made, but can be chilled overnight.

Baking salmon "en croûte" (wrapped in a puff-pastry crust before baking) helps keep this delicate fish moist and succulent. The watercress cream also adds a layer of flavor to the finished dish.

SALMON EN CROÛTE

SERVES 4   **PREP 25 MINS**   **COOK 30 MINS**

EQUIPMENT
baking sheet

INGREDIENTS

FOR THE FILLING
oil, for greasing
3oz (85g) watercress,
coarse stems removed
4oz (115g) cream cheese
salt and freshly ground black pepper
1lb 5oz (600g) skinless salmon fillet

FOR THE PASTRY
14oz (400g) sheet store-bought puff pastry
(or to make your own, see pp110–113)
all-purpose flour, for dusting
1 large egg, beaten, or milk, to glaze

1 Preheat the oven to 400°F (200°C). Lightly grease the baking sheet. Chop the watercress very finely, place in a bowl, add the cream cheese, season generously with salt and pepper, and mix well.

2 Cut the salmon fillet into 2 pieces. Roll out the pastry on a lightly floured surface to ⅛in (3mm) thick. It should be roughly 3in (7.5cm) longer than the salmon pieces and just over twice as wide. Trim the edges straight, then transfer to the baking sheet.

3 Place 1 piece of salmon in the middle of the pastry. Spread the top with the watercress cream and place the other piece of salmon on top. Lightly brush the pastry edges with water, then fold the 2 ends over the salmon. Fold in the sides so they overlap slightly and press together to seal. Re-roll the trimmings and use to decorate the top of the pastry, if liked. Brush with beaten egg, and make 2 or 3 holes with a skewer to allow steam to escape.

4 Bake for 30 minutes, or until the pastry is well risen and golden brown. Test if the salmon is cooked by pushing a skewer halfway through the thickest part and leaving for 4–5 seconds; when removed, it should feel hot.

5 Remove from the oven and set aside to cool for 2–3 minutes, then slice and serve. The whole dish can be made up to 12 hours before baking. Cover with plastic wrap and chill until ready to cook.

Fish and fennel work wonderfully together. This sophisticated version of a fish pie will become an all-time favorite with friends and family. Use other varieties of fish if you like, such as haddock or pollack.

SALMON, FENNEL, AND WHITE WINE PIE

 **SERVES 6**   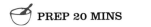 **PREP 20 MINS**   ⏰ **COOK 1¼–1½ HRS**

1 Preheat the oven to 400°F (200°C). Arrange the fennel slices in the bottom of the ovenproof dish, pour the wine over the top, season well, and cover tightly with foil. Bake for 35–45 minutes, until tender. Pour the cooking liquid out of the dish and set aside, leaving the fennel in the dish. Reduce the oven temperature to 350°F (180°C).

2 Melt the butter in a medium saucepan. Stir in the flour and cook for 2–3 minutes over medium heat, stirring with a wooden spoon, until a smooth paste is formed. Gradually add the milk and the reserved cooking liquid, stirring constantly, to make a white sauce. Stir in the parsley, dill, and lemon zest and juice, and season well.

3 Place the salmon in the dish with the fennel, then pour the sauce over the top and stir well.

4 Cut an 11in x 8in (28cm x 20cm) rectangle from the pastry. Cut enough ¾in (2cm) wide strips from the remaining pastry to fit around the edges of the filling. Place the strips around the edge of the dish, directly on the filling. Brush the strips with a little of the beaten egg and cover the pie with the pastry rectangle. Brush with the remaining beaten egg and cut a hole in the top to allow steam to escape. Place on a baking sheet and bake for 40–45 minutes, until browned.

EQUIPMENT
11in x 8in x 2in (28cm x 20cm x 5cm) ovenproof dish

INGREDIENTS

FOR THE FILLING
1 fennel bulb, about
    9oz (250g), thinly sliced
1 cup dry white wine
salt and freshly ground black pepper
3 tbsp butter
3 tbsp all-purpose flour
1½ cups whole milk
2 tbsp flat-leaf parsley, chopped
2 tbsp dill, chopped
zest of 1 lemon
1 tbsp lemon juice
1lb 2oz (500g) salmon fillet, skinned
    and cut into bite-sized pieces

FOR THE PASTRY
12oz (320g) sheet store-bought puff pastry
    (or to make your own, see pp.110–113)
1 large egg, beaten to glaze

A twist on the traditional Finnish dish of fish, usually made with perch and baked slowly. Since perch can be difficult to find, salmon is used in this wonderfully unusual recipe.

KALAKUKKO

SERVES 6–8   **PREP 30 MINS**   **COOK 6½ HRS**

EQUIPMENT
baking sheet

INGREDIENTS

**FOR THE DOUGH
(For visual step-by-step,
instructions, see p.104)**
**2½ cups rye flour,
plus extra for dusting**
¾ cup all-purpose flour
½ tbsp salt
4 tbsp butter, cubed

FOR THE FILLING
**13oz (375g) salmon fillet, skinned
and cut into bite-sized pieces**
**4½oz (125g) bacon,
cut into bite-sized pieces**
salt and freshly ground black pepper
2 tbsp butter, melted

1 Preheat the oven to 400°F (200°C). Line a baking sheet with parchment paper. To make the dough, place the flours and salt in a bowl, then rub in the butter with your fingertips until the mixture resembles bread crumbs. Gradually add about 1¼–1¾ cups cold water to make a soft dough. Cut the dough into 2 equal portions.

2 Roll out half the dough on a lightly floured surface to form a circle about 11in (28cm) in diameter. Place the circle on a large baking sheet lined with parchment paper. Scatter some rye flour in the middle of the dough, then put alternate layers of salmon and bacon pieces in the center of the dough, seasoning with salt and pepper between the layers and leaving a ¾in (2cm) border around the edge. Brush the border of the dough with a little water.

3 Repeat to roll out the remaining dough, as before. Place the second circle of dough carefully over the salmon and bacon and press the edges firmly together to seal tightly. Crimp the edges to finish if required.

4 Brush the pie generously with melted butter and bake for 30 minutes, or until it starts to brown. Reduce the oven temperature to 225°F (110°C).

5 Remove the pie from the oven and carefully transfer it (still on the parchment paper) onto a large sheet of foil. Wrap it completely in foil, return to the oven, and cook for another 6 hours.

6 Remove from the oven and cover with a dish towel so that crust doesn't get too hard. To serve, slice the kalakukko like a cake. It can be served hot or cold.

To make a change from the more usual mashed potato-topped fish pies, try topping your fish with this tasty crumble mix. Steamed asparagus or green beans make the perfect accompaniment to this special dish.

FISH CRUMBLE

🍲 SERVES 4–6   🥣 PREP 30 MINS   ⏰ COOK 35–40 MINS

1 Preheat the oven to 350°F (180°C). To make the crumble topping, melt the butter in a large nonstick frying pan, add the sliced baby leeks, and fry gently over medium-low heat for 10 minutes. Remove the pan from the heat.

2 Place the bread, pine nuts, tarragon, and cheese in a food processor, and process until even-sized bread crumbs form. Transfer to the pan with the cooked leeks, add the oats, mustard, and plenty of salt and pepper, and stir well. Remove from the heat.

3 For the filling, grease the ovenproof dish and place the salmon, shrimp, and scallops in the dish. Pour over the wine and half-and-half, then sprinkle with lemon zest and parsley. Season well with salt and pepper.

4 Sprinkle the crumble mixture over the top and place the dish on a baking sheet. Bake for 25–30 minutes, or until the crumble starts to turn golden brown and the fish is cooked through.

EQUIPMENT
2 quart ovenproof dish

INGREDIENTS

FOR THE CRUMBLE TOPPING
2 tbsp butter
6 baby leeks, finely sliced
6oz (175g) fresh white bread, roughly torn
⅓ cup roasted pine nuts
3 tbsp tarragon leaves
2oz (60g) Grana Padano cheese, roughly chopped
¾ cup oats
1 tsp English mustard or mustard powder
salt and freshly ground black pepper

FOR THE FILLING
butter, for greasing
7oz (200g) salmon fillet, skinned and chopped into bite-sized pieces
7oz (200g) jumbo shrimp, peeled and deveined
7oz (200g) scallops, without the coral
½ cup dry white wine
½ cup half-and-half
zest of 1 lemon
3 tbsp parsley, chopped

This impressive dish is perfect for entertaining. It can be prepared and assembled, covered with plastic wrap, and chilled until needed. Remove it from the refrigerator 15 minutes before baking.

SALMON COULIBIAC

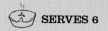 SERVES 6   PREP 30 MINS   COOK 55 MINS–1 HR

EQUIPMENT
baking sheet

INGREDIENTS

FOR THE FILLING
¼ cup long-grain white rice
⅔ cup fish stock
a pinch of turmeric
1 tbsp butter
1 shallot, finely chopped
4oz (115g) shrimp, peeled,
deveined, and cooked
3 tbsp mixed green herbs,
such as tarragon, dill, chives,
and flat-leaf parsley, chopped
zest of 1 lemon
1 tbsp lemon juice
salt and freshly ground black pepper
2oz (50g) arugula
14oz (400g) piece of salmon fillet
(approximately 4in x 5½in [10cm x 13 cm]),
skinned and pin-boned

FOR THE PASTRY
11oz (320g) sheet store-bought
puff pastry, 9in x 14in (23cm x 35cm)
(or to make your own, see pp.110–113)
all-purpose flour, for dusting
1 large egg, beaten to glaze

1 Place the rice, fish stock, and turmeric in a small saucepan. Bring to a boil, cover, reduce the heat and simmer for 15 minutes, or until the rice is cooked.

2 Melt the butter in a small pan over medium heat and fry the shallot for 3–5 minutes, until cooked. Preheat the oven to 350°F (180°C) and line the baking sheet with parchment paper.

3 Place the shrimp, herbs, lemon zest, and juice in a large bowl. Add the cooked rice and shallot, season well, and stir to combine.

4 Cut the pastry in half widthwise to get 2 x 9in x 7in (23cm x 17.5cm) rectangles. Place one half on the lined baking sheet. Roll out the second half of the pastry on a lightly floured surface until it measures 13in x 11in (33cm x 27.5cm). Set aside.

5 Place half the arugula on the smaller pastry rectangle, leaving a 2in (5cm) border all around, and top with half the rice mixture. Place the salmon on top and cover with the remaining rice and arugula.

6 Brush the pastry border with beaten egg and place the larger pastry rectangle over the salmon. Press the pastry edges together, seal, and trim to make a neat shape. Brush the pastry with beaten egg and bake for 30–35 minutes, until golden brown.

A gougère is a little choux pastry puff traditionally made in the Burgundy region of France. Here they are flavored with Gruyère cheese and smoked salmon for an elegant canapé or party dish.

CHEESE GOUGÈRES WITH SMOKED SALMON

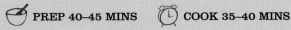

MAKES 8   PREP 40–45 MINS   COOK 35–40 MINS

1 Preheat the oven to 375°F (190°C). Grease the baking sheets. To make the pastry, melt the butter in a saucepan with 1 cup water and ¾ teaspoon of salt. Bring to a boil, then remove the pan from the heat, add the flour, and beat until smooth. Return the pan to the stovetop and beat over low heat for 30 seconds to dry.

2 Remove the pan from the heat. Add 4 eggs, 1 at a time, beating well. Beat the fifth egg, and add it gradually. Stir in half the cheese. Place 8 x 2½in (6cm) mounds of dough on the baking sheets. Beat the remaining egg and salt together, and brush over each of the puffs. Sprinkle with the remaining cheese. Bake for 30–35 minutes, until firm. Remove, and transfer to a wire rack. Slice the tops and set aside to cool.

3 Wilt the spinach in a pan of boiling, salted water for 1–2 minutes. Drain well and set the spinach aside to cool. When cool, squeeze to remove the water and chop. Melt the butter in a frying pan. Add the onion and cook until soft. Add the garlic, nutmeg, salt and pepper to taste, and the spinach. Cook, stirring, until all the liquid has evaporated. Add the cream cheese and stir until the mixture is thoroughly combined. Remove from the heat.

4 Add two-thirds of the smoked salmon, pour in the milk, and stir. Mound 2–3 tablespoons of filling into each cheese puff. Arrange the remaining smoked salmon on top. Rest the tops against the side of each filled puff and serve at once.

EQUIPMENT
2 baking sheets

INGREDIENTS

FOR THE PASTRY
5 tbsp unsalted butter,
 plus extra for greasing
1¼ tsp salt
1 cup all-purpose flour, sifted
5 large eggs, plus 1 extra, to glaze
5oz (125g) Gruyère cheese,
 coarsely grated

FOR THE FILLING
2¼lb (1kg) fresh spinach,
 trimmed and washed
salt and freshly ground black pepper
2 tbsp unsalted butter
1 onion, finely chopped
4 garlic cloves, finely chopped
a pinch of ground nutmeg
9oz (250g) cream cheese
6oz (175g) smoked salmon,
 sliced into strips
¼ cup milk

Here a traditional mashed potato-topped fish pie is given a grown-up twist with the use of succulent jumbo shrimp. The mustard should complement the filling, not overwhelm it, so taste as you go.

SALMON AND SHRIMP PIE

 SERVES 6　　　PREP 15 MINS　　　COOK 35 MINS

EQUIPMENT
8in x 12in (20cm x 30cm) ovenproof dish

INGREDIENTS

FOR THE TOPPING
2lb (900g) potatoes, peeled and quartered
salt and freshly ground black pepper
2 tbsp milk

FOR THE FILLING
12oz (350g) cooked salmon,
flaked into chunks
12oz (350g) hot-smoked salmon fillets,
flaked into chunks
7oz (200g) shrimp, cooked,
peeled, and deveined
salt and freshly ground black pepper
2 tbsp butter
¼ cup all-purpose flour
2 cups milk
2 tbsp chives, chopped
1 tbsp capers in brine,
rinsed and drained
2oz (60g) Cheddar cheese, grated
½ cup fresh white bread crumbs

1 Preheat the oven to 400°F (200°C). Cook the potatoes in a large saucepan of boiling salted water for 15 minutes, or until soft. Drain the potatoes, return to the pan and mash well with a potato masher until there are no lumps. Add the 2 tablespoons milk, mash again until smooth, then season to taste with salt and pepper. Set the potatoes aside.

2 Arrange the salmon and shrimp in the ovenproof dish so that they are evenly distributed. Season with salt and pepper, and set aside.

3 Gently melt the butter in a pan over low heat. Remove from the heat and stir in the flour with a wooden spoon. Add a little milk and beat until smooth. Return the pan to the heat, and continue adding the milk, a little at a time, stirring constantly, until the sauce has thickened. Whisk to get rid of any lumps, then stir in the chives and capers.

4 Pour the sauce over the shrimp and salmon and stir well. Cover with the mashed potatoes. Combine the cheese and bread crumbs, season well, and sprinkle evenly over the mashed potatoes. Bake for 15–20 minutes, until heated through and the topping is crisp and golden.

Using chopped fresh dill in the dough of this rich tart helps to complement the dill used in the filling. Smoked salmon is considered luxurious, but salmon trimmings are cheap and work well here.

SMOKED SALMON AND DILL TART

SERVES 4–6 | **PREP 25 MINS PLUS CHILLING** | **COOK 1 HR 5 MINS** | **FREEZE UP TO 1 MONTH**

1 To make the dough, rub the flour and butter together with your fingertips until the mixture resembles bread crumbs. Add the egg yolk and dill to the flour mixture, then add 1–2 tablespoons cold water and bring together to form a smooth dough. Wrap in plastic wrap and chill for 30 minutes.

2 Preheat the oven to 350°F (180°C). Roll out the dough on a floured surface to a circle large enough to line the tart pan. Place the dough in the pan, pressing it down well into the bottom and around the edges. Trim off any excess dough, then prick the bottom with a fork. Line with parchment paper and fill with baking beans. Place the pan on a baking sheet and bake for 20 minutes. Remove the beans and paper and return to the oven for another 5 minutes to crisp.

3 For the filling, arrange the salmon in the bottom of the crust. Place the sour cream, milk, the 2 eggs, Grana Padano cheese, and dill in a large liquid measuring cup, season generously with black pepper, and beat well. Pour over the salmon and bake for 35–40 minutes, or until golden and set in the middle. Serve hot or warm.

EQUIPMENT
8in (20cm) tart pan, baking beans

INGREDIENTS

FOR THE DOUGH
(For visual step-by-step instructions, see pie dough p.104)
1 cup all-purpose flour
4 tbsp butter, chilled and cubed
1 large egg yolk
2 tbsp dill, finely chopped

FOR THE FILLING
5oz (140g) smoked salmon trimmings
½ cup sour cream
4 tbsp milk
2 large eggs
¾oz (20g) Grana Padano cheese, grated
3 tbsp dill, chopped
freshly ground black pepper

Smoked trout often has a more delicate color and flavor than smoked salmon. Horseradish is hot, so if you don't like it fiery add a little and taste before adding any more. Serve with a tossed salad.

SMOKED TROUT TARTLETS

 MAKES 6   PREP 30 MINS
PLUS CHILLING   COOK 30 MINS   FREEZE UP TO
1 MONTH

EQUIPMENT
6 x 4in (10cm) tartlet pans,
baking beans

INGREDIENTS

FOR THE DOUGH
(For visual step-by-step instructions,
see pie dough p.104)
¾ cup all-purpose flour,
plus extra for dusting
3 tbsp butter, chilled and cubed
a pinch of salt
1 small egg

FOR THE FILLING
½ cup crème fraîche
1 tsp creamed horseradish
½ tsp lemon juice
grated zest of ½ lemon
1 tsp capers, rinsed and chopped
salt and freshly ground black pepper
4 large egg yolks, beaten
7oz (200g) smoked trout
bunch of dill, chopped

1 To make the dough, place the flour, butter, and salt in a food processor and process until the mixture resembles bread crumbs. Add the egg and mix until incorporated. To make by hand, rub the flour, butter, and salt together with your fingertips until the mixture resembles bread crumbs. Add the egg and mix to form a soft dough, adding a little water if necessary.

2 Roll out the dough on a lightly floured surface and use to line the tartlet pans. Line the crusts with wax paper and fill with baking beans. Chill in the refrigerator for 30 minutes.

3 Preheat the oven to 400°F (200°C). Bake the crusts for 10 minutes, then remove the beans and paper and bake for another 5 minutes.

4 To make the filling, mix the crème fraîche, horseradish, lemon juice and zest, and capers in a bowl, and season to taste with salt and pepper. Stir in the egg yolks, smoked trout, and dill.

5 Divide the filling evenly among the tartlet crusts and bake for 10–15 minutes, until the filling is set. Set aside to cool for 5 minutes before removing the tartlets from the pans and serving warm.

These traditional Spanish dough parcels are often served as tapas or an appetizer. They can be made quickly from a few pantry essentials, and make a great picnic dish or canapé.

EMPANADAS

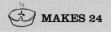 MAKES 24   PREP 45 MINS PLUS CHILLING   COOK 40–50 MINS   FREEZE UP TO 1 MONTH

EQUIPMENT
3½in (9cm) round cookie cutter,
baking sheet

INGREDIENTS

FOR THE DOUGH
(For visual step-by-step instructions,
see pie dough p.104)
2¼ cups all-purpose flour,
plus extra for dusting
½ tsp salt
6 tbsp butter, cubed
2 large eggs, beaten, plus 1 large egg,
beaten to glaze

FOR THE FILLING
1 tbsp olive oil, plus extra
for greasing
1 onion, finely chopped
5oz can tomatoes, drained
2 tsp tomato paste
7oz can tuna, drained
2 tbsp parsley, finely chopped
salt and freshly ground black pepper

1 To make the dough, sift the flour into a large bowl with the salt. Add the butter and rub it in with your fingertips until it resembles fine bread crumbs. Add the 2 beaten eggs with 4–6 tablespoons water and combine to form a dough. Cover with plastic wrap and chill in the refrigerator for 30 minutes.

2 Meanwhile, heat the olive oil in a frying pan, add the onion, and fry over medium heat, stirring frequently, for 5–8 minutes, until translucent. Add the tomatoes, tomato paste, tuna, and parsley, and season to taste with salt and pepper. Reduce the heat and simmer for 10–12 minutes, stirring occasionally.

3 Preheat the oven to 375°F (190°C). Roll out the dough on a lightly floured surface to ⅛in (3mm) thick and cut out 24 circles with the cookie cutter. Put 1 teaspoon of the filling on each circle, then brush the edges with water, fold over, and pinch together.

4 Grease a baking sheet, then place the empanadas on the baking sheet and brush with beaten egg. Bake for 25–30 minutes, until golden brown. Serve warm.

An all-time children's favorite, leave out the scallions for picky eaters, or add more vegetables for the more adventurous child. Use extra Cheddar for the topping, instead of the mozzarella if you like.

CHEESY POTATO-TOPPED TUNA PIE

 SERVES 4   PREP 15 MINS   COOK 35–40 MINS   FREEZE UP TO 1 MONTH

1 Cook the potatoes in a large saucepan of salted boiling water for 15 minutes, or until tender. Drain the potatoes, return to the pan and mash. Stir in the butter and the milk and mix well to combine. Season to taste with salt and pepper and set aside. Preheat the oven to 400°F (200°C).

2 For the filling, melt the butter in a medium pan. Stir in the flour and cook for 2–3 minutes over medium heat, stirring constantly with a wooden spoon, until a smooth paste is formed. Gradually add the milk, stirring constantly, to make a white sauce.

3 Stir in the Cheddar cheese, tuna, corn, peas, scallions, and parsley and season well. Transfer to the ovenproof dish. Top with the mashed potatoes, spreading it in an even layer, and sprinkle the grated mozzarella over the top. Place the dish on a baking sheet and bake for 15–20 minutes, or until golden brown.

EQUIPMENT
2 quart ovenproof dish

INGREDIENTS

FOR THE TOPPING
2¼lb (1kg) floury potatoes, such as Russet Burbanks, peeled and chopped into small chunks
salt and freshly ground black pepper
4 tbsp butter
¼ cup whole milk

FOR THE FILLING
4 tbsp butter
½ cup all-purpose flour
1¼ cups whole milk
4oz (115g) aged Cheddar cheese, grated
2 x 7oz cans tuna in spring water, drained
7oz can sweet corn, drained
1¼ cups frozen peas
4 scallions, finely chopped
2 tbsp parsley, finely chopped
salt and freshly ground black pepper
3½oz (100g) firm mozzarella, grated (or ready-grated mozzarella)

A mixture of smoked fish can be used as a filling for a fish pie when you want something a little different. Topped with cheesy mashed potatoes, this rich dish just needs a tossed salad as an accompaniment.

SMOKED FISH PIE

 SERVES 4–6   PREP 20 MINS   COOK 50–55 MINS   FREEZE UP TO 1 MONTH

EQUIPMENT
2 quart ovenproof dish

INGREDIENTS

FOR THE TOPPING
1¾lb (800g) floury potatoes, such as Russet Burbanks, peeled and chopped into small chunks
10oz (300g) sweet potatoes, peeled and chopped into small chunks
salt and freshly ground black pepper
3 tbsp butter
3 tbsp whole milk
1¾–2½oz (50–75g) Cheddar cheese, grated

FOR THE FILLING
3 tbsp butter, plus extra for greasing
¼ cup all-purpose flour
1½–2 cups whole milk
2oz (50g) Gruyère cheese, grated
2 tbsp parsley, chopped
grated zest of 1 lemon
juice of ½ lemon
3 tsp capers in brine, drained and rinsed
10oz (300g) undyed smoked haddock fillet, skinned and chopped into bite-sized pieces
10oz (300g) undyed smoked cod fillet, skinned and chopped into bite-sized pieces
4½oz (125g) smoked salmon trimmings

1 To make the topping, cook the floury and sweet potatoes in a large saucepan of salted boiling water for 15 minutes, or until tender. Drain the potatoes, return to the pan, and mash with a potato masher. Stir in the butter and milk, and mix well to combine. Season to taste with salt and black pepper and set aside. Preheat the oven to 350°F (180°C).

2 For the filling, melt the butter in a small nonstick pan over low heat. Stir in the flour and cook for 2–3 minutes over medium heat, stirring constantly with a wooden spoon, until a smooth paste is formed. Gradually add the milk, stirring constantly, to make a white sauce. Bring to a boil while stirring, then add the Gruyère, parsley, lemon zest and juice, and capers, and season well with black pepper. Stir until all the cheese has melted. Remove from the heat and set aside.

3 Grease the ovenproof dish and place all the fish in the dish. Pour in the sauce and stir well to coat the fish thoroughly. Top with the mashed potatoes and the grated Cheddar cheese. Place the dish on a baking sheet and bake for 25–30 minutes, or until golden brown and bubbling.

This fabled, whole fish pie heralds from Cornwall, England, where there is even a folk tale to explain the origins of the dish. Spectacular to look at, it is not as difficult to prepare as it seems. Eat on the day it is made.

STARGAZY PIE

SERVES 4–6   PREP 40 MINS   COOK 40–50 MINS

1 Preheat the oven to 400°F (200°C). Boil the eggs in a saucepan for 9 minutes, until they are hard-boiled. Set aside to cool, then slice into thin slices. Cook the potatoes in a large pan of boiling salted water for 5 minutes. Drain and rinse them under cold water.

2 Meanwhile, heat the olive oil in a pan and fry the pancetta and onion for 5 minutes, or until the pancetta is crisp and the onion is soft, but not brown.

3 Roll out the pastry on a floured surface and use to line the pie dish. Trim off the excess pastry, leaving a ½in (1cm) edge overhanging. Re-roll the remaining pastry into a disk big enough to cover the top.

4 Layer two-thirds of the cooked potatoes over the bottom of the dish, then cover with half the onion and pancetta mixture. Scatter with half the chopped parsley and season. Arrange the sliced egg over the filling in a single layer. Lay the sardines over the filling in a single layer, cut-side down, with the tails at the center and the heads at the edge of the pie. If the fish are too long, snip the ends off and use offcuts to fill in the spaces between the fish. Scatter over the remaining onion mix, parsley, and a final layer of potato.

5 Whisk the mustard into the half-and-half and pour over the filling. Brush the edges of the pie with beaten egg and lay the lid on top. Where you can see the fish heads poking up snip a little slit. Ease the fish heads through the slits, molding the pastry around them. Crimp the edges of the pie together to seal, and trim off any excess pastry. Use offcuts to make a few small pastry stars. Brush the top with egg and stick on the stars. Brush the stars with egg and bake the pie on a baking sheet for 30–40 minutes, until golden brown. Set aside to cool for 10–15 minutes before serving.

EQUIPMENT
9in (23cm) deep dish pie pan
with sloping sides

INGREDIENTS

FOR THE FILLING
2 large eggs
14oz (400g) waxy potatoes, such as
   Yukon Golds, peeled weight, cut into
   ¼in (5mm) slices
salt and freshly ground black pepper
2 tbsp olive oil
3½oz (100g) pancetta,
   chopped into ½in (1cm) strips
1 onion, finely sliced
1 heaping tbsp flat-leaf parsley,
   finely chopped
4 sardines, scaled and gutted with head
   still intact, rinsed and patted dry
1 tbsp Dijon mustard
⅔ cup half-and-half

FOR THE PASTRY
1lb 2oz (500g) store-bought puff pastry
   (or to make your own, see pp.110–113)
all-purpose flour, for dusting
1 large egg, lightly beaten, to glaze

A fabulous dinner party dish, this is more of a deconstructed pie. The layers of buttery puff pastry are made crisp and flat by sandwiching them in between two baking sheets halfway through cooking.

INDIVIDUAL HALIBUT AND SPINACH PIES

 SERVES 4   **PREP 10 MINS**   **COOK 25 MINS**

EQUIPMENT
2 baking sheets

INGREDIENTS

FOR THE PASTRY
10oz (300g) sheet store-bought puff pastry
(or to make your own, see pp.110–113)
all-purpose flour, for dusting
1 tbsp butter, for brushing

FOR THE FILLING
4 x 4½oz (125g) pieces of halibut fillets,
or salmon can be used
salt and freshly ground black pepper
a large pat unsalted butter
2 tbsp olive oil
1 garlic clove, crushed
7oz (200g) ready-washed
baby spinach leaves
1 small jar or ½ cup store-bought
hollandaise sauce
grated zest of ½ lemon

1 Preheat the oven to 375°F (190°C). Roll out the pastry on a floured surface to ¼in (5mm) thick. Using the fish fillets as a template, cut the pastry into 8 equal rectangles, about 5in x 2¾in (12cm x 7cm). They should be the same size as the fish. Gently score a diagonal stripe across the rectangles, taking care not to cut all the way through the pastry. Melt the tablespoon of butter and use it to brush the pastry pieces well.

2 Use a metal spatula to place the pastry pieces on a baking sheet, and bake for 5–7 minutes, until they start to color and puff up. Place a similarly sized baking sheet on top of the pastry, pushing down firmly, then bake for another 7–10 minutes, until the pastry is flat, crisp, and golden brown.

3 Season the fish fillets well on both sides. Fry them in 1 tablespoon butter and 1 tablespoon olive oil for 2–3 minutes each side, until they are just firm to the touch when gently pressed with a finger in the center.

4 Heat the remaining butter and olive oil in a large saucepan. Add the garlic and cook for 1–2 minutes, until it is soft. Add the spinach to the pan, season well, and cook for 2–3 minutes, stirring occasionally, until it has just broken down. Heat the hollandaise sauce in a small pan over gentle heat until warmed through. Watch over the pan, since there is a risk of it splitting. Add the lemon zest and season with black pepper.

5 Place 1 piece of pastry on each of the 4 serving plates. Cover the pastry with the spinach, then spread 1 tablespoon of hollandaise over the spinach and place a fish on top. Cover with another spoonful of hollandaise and top with the remaining pastry. Serve.

Herring and apple is a traditional British pairing, and here the strong taste of the fish is matched with a sweet, creamy filling. Best eaten on the day, but, if liked, chill overnight and eat cold the next day.

HERRING, APPLE, AND ONION PIE

SERVES 4–6   **PREP 20 MINS PLUS CHILLING**   **COOK 1 HR 10 MINS**   **FREEZE CRUST, UP TO 2 MONTHS**

1 To make the dough, rub the flour, salt, butter, and lard together with your fingertips until it resembles loose bread crumbs. Add 4–6 tablespoons cold water and bring the mixture together to form a dough. Wrap well in plastic wrap and chill for 30 minutes.

2 Preheat the oven to 350°F (180°C). Roll out the dough on a well-floured surface to ¼in (7mm) thick and use to line the pie pan, trimming the edges of all but ½in (1cm) overhang of dough. Prick the bottom with a fork, line with wax paper, and fill with baking beans. Place on a baking sheet and bake for 15–20 minutes, until the dough is lightly cooked. Remove the beans and paper and bake for another 5 minutes to crisp the bottom. Trim the edges.

3 Blanch the potato slices in a large saucepan of boiling, salted water for 2–3 minutes, until they begin to soften. Drain well. Lay half the fish over the bottom of the dough. Spread half the sliced apple and onion over the fish, then top with half the potato slices. Press down firmly to evenly distribute the filling in the dish. Place the last of the fish over the potatoes in a single layer, the remaining apple and onion, and top with the remaining potatoes, layered in an overlapping ring around the edge. Fill the center with another, smaller ring of potatoes, so that the top is covered.

4 Whisk the half-and-half, egg yolk, and mustard together and season well. Pour the mixture over the filling. Place on a baking sheet and bake for 40–45 minutes, until golden brown and the center yields easily when pierced with a skewer. Set aside to cool for 5 minutes.

EQUIPMENT
9in (23cm) deep-dish metal pie pan, baking beans

INGREDIENTS

FOR THE DOUGH
(For visual step-by-step instructions, see p.104)
1½ cups all-purpose flour, plus extra for dusting
a pinch of salt
5 tbsp butter, at room temperature
2 tbsp lard or vegetable shortening

FOR THE FILLING
1lb 2oz (500g) waxy potatoes such as Yukon Golds, peeled and very finely sliced
salt and freshly ground black pepper
4 small- or 5 medium-sized herring, scaled, gutted, and filleted, or sardines can be used
1 large sweet apple, peeled, cored, and finely sliced
1 onion, peeled, halved and finely sliced
¾ cup half-and-half
1 large egg yolk
1 heaping tsp Dijon mustard

The filling of this dish is based on a recipe for a "mouclade," a French dish where mussels are smothered in a mild, curry-flavored cream. Serving it as a mini, puff pastry-topped pie gives it a modern twist.

INDIVIDUAL CURRIED MUSSEL PIES

 MAKES 4   PREP 30 MINS
PLUS COOLING   COOK 40–45 MINS   FREEZE UP TO
1 MONTH

EQUIPMENT
4 x 4in (10cm) round pie dishes
(1¼in [3cm] deep)

INGREDIENTS

FOR THE FILLING
2¼lb (1kg) mussels, scrubbed
and beards removed
1 tbsp olive oil
1 onion, coarsely chopped
1 bunch parsley
½ cup dry white wine
2 tbsp butter
4 baby leeks, finely chopped
2 carrots, finely cubed
salt and freshly ground black pepper
1–2 tsp medium curry powder
¼ cup half-and-half
2 tbsp chopped cilantro

FOR THE PASTRY
7½oz (215g) sheet store-bought puff pastry
(or to make your own, see pp.110–113)
1 large egg, beaten, to glaze

1 Preheat the oven to 400°F (200°C). Discard any mussels that stay open when tapped sharply.

2 Heat the olive oil in a large saucepan and gently fry the onion for 5 minutes. Add the parsley, wine, mussels, and ½ cup water and bring to a boil. Cover and cook for 5 minutes. Discard any mussels that do not open. Strain the mussels through a sieve and reserve the cooking liquid.

3 Melt the butter in a medium pan over medium heat, add the leeks and carrots, season well, then cover with a lid and fry gently for 5 minutes, stirring occasionally. Add the curry powder and cook for 5 more minutes. Stir 1 cup of the reserved cooking liquid into the vegetable mixture and simmer for 5 minutes to reduce. Set aside to cool for 15 minutes.

4 Remove the cooked mussels from their shells and add to the creamy vegetable mixture. Stir in the half-and-half and cilantro, and season well. Divide the mussel mixture among the pie dishes.

5 Cut the pastry into 4 lids to fit the top of the pie dishes. Moisten the rim of each dish with water and press the lids on firmly to seal. Brush with the egg and cut a hole in the center of each lid to allow steam to escape. Place the pies on a baking sheet and bake for 15–20 minutes, until browned.

This light, delicate seafood pie is perfect for summer entertaining. Slice through the crunchy filo topping to reveal a rich, creamy, and luxurious filling. Serve with a tossed salad and baby new potatoes.

FILO-TOPPED SEAFOOD PIE

SERVES 4–6   **PREP 20 MINS**   **COOK 30–35 MINS**

EQUIPMENT
11 x 8in x 2in (28cm x 20 x 5cm) ovenproof dish

INGREDIENTS

FOR THE FILLING
4 tbsp butter, plus extra for greasing
5oz (140g) mixture of watercress, arugula, and spinach leaves
¼ cup all-purpose flour
⅔ cup half-and-half
1¼ cups dry white wine
3oz tub fresh brown crab meat
2 tbsp parsley, chopped
juice and zest of ½ lemon
freshly ground black pepper
6oz tub fresh cooked mussels, in brine (drained weight)
7oz (200g) scallops, coral removed
5½oz (150g) jumbo shrimp, peeled and deveined

FOR THE DOUGH
6oz (175g) store-bought filo dough
(4 x 10in x 16in/26cm x 44cm sheets)

1 Preheat the oven to 400°F (200°C). Grease the ovenproof dish.

2 Place the watercress, arugula, and spinach in a colander and pour boiling water from a kettle over the top to wilt. Set aside to cool and drain. Once cool, squeeze out the excess liquid and chop finely.

3 For the filling, melt 3 tbsp of the butter in a medium nonstick saucepan over low heat. Stir in the flour and cook for 2–3 minutes over medium heat, stirring constantly, until a smooth paste is formed. Gradually add the half-and-half and then the wine, then bring to a boil to thicken, stirring to make a creamy, smooth sauce. Stir in the chopped greens, crab, parsley, lemon juice and zest, and season well with black pepper. Set aside.

4 Drain and rinse the mussels and stir into the sauce. Add the scallops and shrimp and stir well to mix.

5 Spoon the seafood mixture into the prepared dish. Roughly tear the filo dough into strips and arrange half the strips over the seafood, folded and twisted to give texture. Drizzle or brush 1 tbsp melted butter over it, then top with the remaining filo strips and butter.

6 Place the dish on a baking sheet and bake for 20–25 minutes, or until the pastry is golden brown and crisp. Serve immediately.

A dish for a special occasion, the musky fragrance of the saffron gently flavors the delicate seafood filling. You can store the cooked crust, well wrapped, for up to 2 days before finishing.

CRAB AND SHRIMP SAFFRON TART

SERVES 2–4   PREP 20 MINS PLUS CHILLING   COOK 50 MINS – 1 HR 5 MINS   FREEZE UP TO 2 MONTHS

1 To make the dough, rub the flour and butter together with your fingertips until the mixture resembles bread crumbs. Add the egg yolk and 1 tablespoon cold water and bring the mixture together to form a soft dough. Add a little extra water if it is too dry. Wrap in plastic wrap and chill for 30 minutes.

2 Preheat the oven to 350°F (180°C). Roll out the dough on a floured surface to a large circle about ⅛in (3mm) thick, and use to line the tart pan, making sure it overlaps the sides. Trim off all but ¾in (2cm) of the overhanging dough. Use your fingers to push the dough down into the pan. Prick the bottom with a fork, line with parchment paper, and fill with baking beans. Place the crust on a baking sheet and bake for 20–25 minutes, until cooked. Remove the beans and paper and bake for another 5 minutes to crisp. Cool.

3 For the filling, splash 1 tablespoon of hot water over the saffron in a small bowl. Put the crab meat and shrimp into a sieve and press down well over a sink to remove any excess water. Mix the crab and shrimp together with your fingers, then scatter them over the surface of the tart.

4 Whisk together the cream and egg in a liquid measuring cup. Add the herbs, saffron and its soaking water, and seasoning, and mix well. Place the tart crust on the baking sheet and, with the oven door open, rest it half on, half off the middle oven shelf. Hold the sheet with one hand and with the other pour as much of the cream and egg mix as possible into the tart, then slide it into the oven. Bake for 30–35 minutes, until golden in places and puffed up. Set aside to cool for 10 minutes, then trim off the overhanging dough and remove the tart from the pan. Serve warm or cold.

EQUIPMENT
6in (15cm) tart pan with removable bottom, baking beans

INGREDIENTS

FOR THE DOUGH
(For visual step-by-step instructions, see pie dough p.104)
¾ cup all-purpose flour, plus extra for dusting
4 tbsp unsalted butter, chilled and cubed
1 large egg yolk

FOR THE FILLING
a pinch of saffron
4½oz (125g) white crab meat
3½oz (100g) small shrimp, peeled and deveined
¾ cup heavy cream
1 large egg
1 tbsp tarragon or chervil, finely chopped
sea salt and freshly ground black pepper

VEGETARIAN PIES AND TARTS

All the flavors of a warm summer's day resonate in the filling of these delicious tarts. If you can't find baby plum tomatoes, use any others, but make sure they are ripe to bring out their full flavor.

TOMATO AND PESTO TARTS

 **MAKES 4**   **PREP 25 MINS PLUS CHILLING**   **COOK 20–25 MINS**   **FREEZE UP TO 1 MONTH**

EQUIPMENT
4 x 5in (12cm) fluted tart pans with removable bottoms

INGREDIENTS

FOR THE DOUGH
(For visual step-by-step instructions, see pie dough p.104)
1½ cups all-purpose flour, plus extra for dusting
7 tbsp butter, cubed, plus extra for greasing
½ tsp salt

FOR THE FILLING
¼ cup sun-dried tomato pesto
handful of basil leaves, plus extra to garnish
6 sun-dried tomatoes in oil, drained and finely chopped
12–16 baby plum tomatoes, halved lengthwise
salt and freshly ground black pepper
1 large egg
½ cup half-and-half
2½oz (75g) mozzarella, grated

1 To make the dough, rub the flour and butter together in a bowl with your fingertips until the mixture resembles fine bread crumbs. Stir in the salt and add 3–4 tablespoons cold water to bring together to form a smooth dough. Wrap in plastic wrap and chill for 30 minutes. Lightly grease the tart pans.

2 Divide the dough equally into 4 portions. Roll out one-quarter of the dough on a well-floured surface to a circle large enough to line one of the pans. Place the dough in the pan and trim the edges. Prick the bottom with a fork and place on a baking sheet. Repeat using the remaining dough. Chill for 30 minutes.

3 Preheat the oven to 400°F (200°C). Line each tartlet crust with foil, pressing it down well. Bake for 5 minutes then remove the foil. Spread 1 tablespoon pesto over the bottom of each tart. Cover the pesto with one-quarter of the basil leaves and spoon one-quarter of the chopped sun-dried tomatoes into the center of each tart. Arrange 3 or 4 halved plum tomatoes around the edge of each tart and season to taste with black pepper.

4 Beat the egg and cream together in a liquid measuring cup, season well, and pour carefully over the tomatoes. Sprinkle the mozzarella over the top and bake for 15–20 minutes. Serve garnished with fresh basil leaves.

Nothing could be easier to make than this simple tomatoey tart, which takes only minutes to prepare. Serve with a tossed salad for an after-work dinner or an informal appetizer at a dinner party.

TOMATO AND HARISSA TART

 SERVES 6   **PREP 30 MINS**   **COOK 15 MINS**

1 Preheat the oven to 400°F (200°C). Roll out the pastry on a floured surface to a large rectangle or square. Lay on a baking sheet, then use a sharp knife to score a border about 2in (5cm) in from the edges all the way around, being careful not to cut all the way through the pastry. Using the back of the knife, score the pastry around the outer edges.

2 Working inside the border, smother the pastry with the tapenade. Arrange the plum and cherry tomatoes on top in an even pattern, cut-side up. Mix the harissa with the olive oil, and drizzle over the tomatoes. Scatter the thyme leaves over the top.

3 Bake for about 15 minutes, until the pastry is cooked and golden. Serve hot.

EQUIPMENT
baking sheet

INGREDIENTS

FOR THE PASTRY
14oz (400g) store-bought puff pastry
  (or to make your own, see pp.110–113)
all-purpose flour, for dusting

FOR THE FILLING
2 tbsp vegetarian tapenade or
  regular tapenade
3 plum tomatoes, halved
12 cherry tomatoes, halved
2–3 tbsp harissa paste
1 tbsp olive oil
4 sprigs of thyme, leaves only

This simple tart is ideal when tomatoes are in season and they are dark red, ripe, and plentiful. Here, a normal pie dough is given a lift with the addition of fresh Parmesan cheese and basil.

TOMATO AND DIJON TART WITH A PARMESAN AND BASIL CRUST

 **SERVES 6–8**   **PREP 20 MINS PLUS CHILLING AND COOLING**   **COOK 55 MINS**   **FREEZE CRUST, UP TO 2 MONTHS**

1 To make the dough, process the flour, Parmesan, butter, basil leaves, and salt together in a food processor until the mixture resembles fine green bread crumbs. Add the egg and 1 tablespoon cold water, and bring the mixture together to form a soft dough. Add a little extra water if needed. Wrap in plastic wrap and chill for 30 minutes. Preheat the oven to 400°F (200°C).

2 Roll out the dough on a well-floured surface to a large circle about ⅛in (3mm) thick and use to line the tart pan, making sure it overlaps the sides. Trim all but ½in (1cm) of the overhanging dough. Prick the bottom with a fork, line with wax paper, and fill with baking beans. Place it on a baking sheet and bake for 15 minutes, until the dough is lightly cooked. Remove the beans and paper, and bake for another 5 minutes to crisp. Trim off any ragged edges while still warm. Reduce the heat to 350°F (180°C).

3 For the filling, place the tomatoes in an overlapping circle around the edge of the tart. Fill the center with a smaller circle of tomato slices. Scatter the chopped parsley over the tomatoes. Whisk together the half-and-half, crème fraîche, eggs, mustard, salt and pepper in a large bowl. Place the tart back on a baking sheet and carefully pour the cream mixture over the tomatoes. Scatter the grated Parmesan cheese over the top.

4 Bake for 35 minutes, or until golden on top and the filling has just set. Set the tart aside to cool for at least 30 minutes before eating warm or cold. This is best eaten the day it is made.

EQUIPMENT
9in (22cm) tart pan with removable bottom, baking beans

INGREDIENTS

FOR THE DOUGH
(For visual step-by-step instructions, see pie dough p.104)
1 cup all-purpose flour, plus extra for dusting
¼ cup grated vegetarian-style Parmesan or regular Parmesan cheese
6 tbsp unsalted butter, softened
10 basil leaves
½ tsp salt
1 large egg

FOR THE FILLING
3–4 ripe, medium tomatoes, all of similar size and shape, thinly sliced
1 tbsp flat-leaf parsley, finely chopped
⅔ cup half-and-half
⅔ cup crème fraîche
2 large eggs
1 heaping tbsp Dijon mustard
salt and freshly ground black pepper
¼ cup grated vegetarian-style Parmesan or regular Parmesan cheese

These delicious individual slices make a light, tasty vegetarian alternative to meat pies. Good served warm or cold, they transport well and make a perfect picnic pie or lunchtime treat.

MEDITERRANEAN JALOUSIE

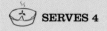 **SERVES 4**　　　　**PREP 20 MINS**　　　　**COOK 25 MINS**

EQUIPMENT
baking sheet

INGREDIENTS

FOR THE PASTRY
1lb 2oz (500g) store-bought puff pastry
(or to make your own, see pp.110–113)
all-purpose flour, for dusting
beaten egg or milk, to glaze

FOR THE FILLING
3 tbsp basil pesto
7oz (200g) mozzarella,
cut into ½in (1cm) cubes, or grated
5oz (140g) artichokes in oil, drained
5oz (140g) sun-dried tomatoes
in oil, drained
1oz (30g) pitted green olives
freshly ground black pepper

1 Preheat the oven to 425°F (220°C). Roll out just less than half the pastry on a lightly floured surface to a 12in x 6in (30cm x 15cm) rectangle, then place the pastry on a large dampened baking sheet. Roll out the remaining pastry to a 12in x 7in (30cm x 18cm) rectangle, lightly dust with flour, then fold in half lengthwise. Make cuts ½in (1cm) apart along the folded edge to within 1in (2.5cm) of the outer edge.

2 Spread the pesto over the pastry on the baking sheet to within 1in (2.5cm) of the edges, and top with half the cheese. Pat the artichokes and tomatoes with paper towels to remove any excess oil, and arrange on top of the cheese with the olives. Scatter with the remaining cheese and season to taste with black pepper.

3 Dampen the edges of the pastry with water. Carefully place the second piece of pastry on top and press the edges together to seal; trim away the excess. Brush the top with beaten egg and bake for 25 minutes, or until golden brown and crisp. Set aside to cool for a few minutes before slicing and serving. This is good served with a tossed salad.

This Italian-inspired tart is the perfect thing to serve on a hot summer's day. To make this easy tart even quicker, use some roasted red bell peppers from a jar or the deli counter.

ROASTED RED BELL PEPPER TART

SERVES 6–8   **PREP 15 MINS**   **COOK 1¼ HRS**

1 Preheat the oven to 400°F (200°C). Put the peppers on a baking sheet. Using your hands, smear each one with the olive oil. Roast in the oven for about 20 minutes, until lightly charred. Transfer to a plastic bag and set aside until cool enough to handle before skinning and seeding.

2 Meanwhile, roll out the dough on a floured surface, and use to line the tart pan. Trim away the excess dough. Line the crust with wax paper and fill with baking beans. Bake for 15–20 minutes, until the edges are golden. Remove the beans and paper, brush the bottom of the crust with beaten egg, and bake for another 2–3 minutes to crisp. Remove from the oven and set aside. Reduce the heat to 350°F (180°C).

3 Pulse the roasted bell peppers, eggs, mascarpone, and basil in a food processor until combined. Season with salt and pepper. Spread the pesto over the bottom of the crust, then pour in the pepper mixture. Bake for 25–35 minutes, until set. Set aside to cool for 10 minutes before garnishing with basil, and serving with an arugula and fennel salad.

EQUIPMENT
9in (23cm) square fluted tart pan with removable bottom, baking beans

INGREDIENTS

FOR THE FILLING
4 large red bell peppers
1 tbsp olive oil
2 large eggs
1 tbsp mascarpone
handful of basil leaves,
  plus extra to garnish
salt and freshly ground black pepper
1 tsp sun-dried tomato pesto

FOR THE DOUGH
10oz (300g) store-bought pie dough
  (or to make your own, see p.104)
all-purpose flour, for dusting
1 large egg, lightly beaten, to glaze

A jar of tapenade is a wonderful thing to keep in the pantry, here adding depth of flavor to a few basic ingredients. This tart is delicious served with an arugula salad dressed with a nutty vinaigrette.

OLIVE, ROSEMARY, AND RED ONION TART

 SERVES 4–6   PREP 15 MINS PLUS CHILLING   COOK 1¼ HRS   FREEZE UP TO 1 MONTH

EQUIPMENT
9in (22cm) fluted tart pan with removable bottom, baking beans

INGREDIENTS

FOR THE DOUGH
8 tbsp unsalted butter
3 tbsp milk
1 cup self-rising flour

FOR THE FILLING
3 tbsp olive oil
3 red onions, finely sliced
1 tsp granulated sugar
2 tbsp rosemary leaves, finely chopped
1 tsp salt
1 cup heavy cream
3 large eggs, beaten
freshly ground black pepper
1oz (30g) Parmesan cheese, finely grated
2 tbsp vegetarian black olive tapenade or regular tapenade
5–10 pitted green olives
5–10 pitted black olives

1 To make the dough, heat the butter and milk together in a saucepan until the butter is melted. Stir in the flour and mix until a ball forms. Set aside to cool. When cool enough to handle, press the dough into the tart pan and chill for 30 minutes.

2 Preheat the oven to 400°F (200°C). Line the pie crust with parchment paper, fill with baking beans, and bake for 15 minutes. Remove the paper and beans and return to the oven for another 5 minutes, or until firm to the touch and golden brown.

3 For the filling, heat the olive oil in a heavy-bottomed frying pan. Add the onions, and fry, stirring, over high heat for 5 minutes. Add the sugar, rosemary leaves, and salt. Reduce the heat and cook slowly, stirring occasionally, for 20 minutes, or until the onions are very soft and slightly caramelized. Meanwhile, whisk the cream, eggs, black pepper, and Parmesan cheese together in a bowl.

4 Reduce the heat to 375°F (190°C). Place the tart pan on a baking sheet and spread the tapenade over the bottom of the dough. Spread the onions on top, carefully pour in the cream filling, and arrange the olives on top. Bake for 25 minutes, or until just set and turning golden on top. Serve warm or cold.

This crispy filo pie is dense, yet incredibly hard to resist. No cream or eggs are used to bring together the filling, since the potatoes and cheese seem to work well on their own. Serve the pie hot or cold.

POTATO AND BLUE CHEESE FILO PIE

 SERVES 6   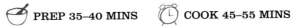 PREP 35–40 MINS   COOK 45–55 MINS

1 Preheat the oven to 350°F (180°C). Melt the butter in a saucepan, then brush the pan with a little of the butter. Lay a damp dish towel on a work surface and unroll the filo dough sheets onto the towel.

2 Using the pan as a guide, cut through the dough to leave a 3in (7.5cm) border around the pan. Cover with a second damp towel.

3 Put 1 filo sheet on a third damp towel and brush with butter, then press into the pan. Repeat with another sheet, putting it in the pan at a right angle to the first. Continue until half the filo dough is used.

4 Arrange half the potatoes in the pan. Sprinkle with half the cheese, shallots, herbs, salt, and black pepper. Repeat with the remaining filling ingredients. Cover the pie with the remaining filo, buttering and layering, then cut a 3in (7.5cm) hole from the center with a knife, so the filling shows.

5 Bake for 45–55 minutes, until golden brown. While still hot, spoon the sour cream into the center of the pie and serve in wedges. The pie can be prepared ahead up to the point of baking, wrapped in plastic wrap, and chilled in the refrigerator for 2 days.

EQUIPMENT
11in (28cm) springform cake pan

INGREDIENTS

FOR THE DOUGH
13 tbsp unsalted butter
1lb 2oz (500g) store-bought filo dough

FOR THE FILLING
2¼lb (1kg) potatoes, very thinly sliced
4½oz (125g) blue cheese, crumbled
4 shallots, finely chopped
4–5 sprigs each parsley, tarragon, and chervil, leaves finely chopped
salt and freshly ground black pepper
3–4 tbsp sour cream

A good vegetarian alternative to the chicken or tuna empanadas, these three fillings make for a nice party selection. Make them in advance and store in a container for up to two days.

CHEESE AND POTATO EMPANADAS

 **MAKES 24** **PREP 40 MINS** **COOK 55 MINS** **FREEZE UP TO 3 MONTHS**

EQUIPMENT
3in (7.5cm) round cookie cutter,
baking sheet

INGREDIENTS

FOR THE DOUGH
juice of 1 lemon
7 tbsp butter, cubed
1½ cups all-purpose flour, sifted, plus
extra for dredging and dusting
a pinch of salt

FOR THE FILLING
14oz (400g) potatoes, parboiled, peeled,
and cut into ½in (1cm) cubes
salt
1 tbsp olive oil
1 medium onion, finely chopped
1 tsp dried dill
1 tsp dried mint
⅔ cup dry white wine
4oz (125g) aged Cheddar cheese,
coarsely grated
oil, for greasing

1 To make the dough, place the lemon juice, butter, and ½ cup of water in a medium saucepan and heat gently for 2–3 minutes, until the butter melts. Put the mixture into a large bowl and cool for 2–3 minutes. Add the flour and salt, and mix well. On a floured surface, knead the dough, dredging 2–3 tablespoons more flour into the dough until it is smooth and no longer sticky. Wrap and chill for 30 minutes.

2 For the filling, place the potatoes in a medium-sized pan of salted boiling water, bring to a boil, then reduce the heat and simmer for about 5 minutes. Drain the potatoes and set aside.

3 Heat the olive oil in a large frying pan and fry the onion and a little salt gently for 15 minutes, until soft. Stir in the herbs, and add the wine. Increase the heat to high and cook for 2–3 minutes, until the wine has evaporated. Stir in the potatoes, reduce the heat to low and cook for 5–10 minutes, until the potatoes start to break up and are cooked. Transfer the mixture to a large bowl and set aside to cool for 10 minutes.

4 Roll out the dough on a well-floured surface to ¼in (5mm) thick. Cut out 16 circles with the cookie cutter and set aside. Re-roll the remaining dough and repeat until you have 24 circles. Set aside.

5 Add the cheese to the filling and season. Preheat the oven to 350°F (180°C). Oil the baking sheet. Divide the filling into 24 portions. Spoon a portion into the center of one of the dough circles, compressing it with the spoon. Brush water on the dough in a circle all around the filling. Fold the dough across the filling and crimp the edges. Bake for 20–25 minutes. Cool for 5 minutes, then cool completely on a wire rack.

A wonderful dish to take on a picnic, this crisp filo pie is good served cold or at room temperature when the rich, ripe flavors of the vegetable filling really come into their own.

MEDITERRANEAN FILO PIE

🍲 SERVES 6   🥣 PREP 20 MINS   ⏰ COOK 50–55 MINS

1 Heat the olive oil in a large nonstick frying pan. Add the onions and cook over medium heat for 5 minutes. Add the garlic, peppers, zucchini, and eggplant and stir well. Cook over medium-high heat for 15 minutes, or until all the vegetables are tender, stirring occasionally to stop them from sticking. Set aside.

2 Preheat the oven to 400°F (200°C). Place a sheet of filo dough in the bottom of the cake pan, so the edges are hanging over the sides. Brush it generously with melted butter and place another sheet of dough across the first, so they form a cross shape in the bottom. Brush with more butter. Repeat the filo layers until all the dough is used up and the bottom of the pan is completely covered.

3 Spoon half the vegetables into the crust, top with half the pesto, then half the basil leaves, and half the crumbled feta. Season well with black pepper. Repeat the layers once. Carefully pull the overhanging layers of dough into the center, to cover the filling. Brush the finished pie with the remaining melted butter. Place the pan on a baking sheet and bake for 35–40 minutes, or until the filo dough is golden brown and crisp. Remove the outer ring of the pan and leave the pie to rest for 15 minutes before slicing.

EQUIPMENT
8in (20cm) cake pan with removable bottom

INGREDIENTS

FOR THE FILLING
1 tbsp olive oil
2 red onions, finely sliced
2 garlic cloves, finely chopped
1 red bell pepper, finely sliced
1 yellow bell pepper, finely sliced
1 zucchini, sliced
1 small eggplant, sliced
¼ cup sun-dried tomato pesto
leaves from 1 bunch of basil
7oz (200g) feta cheese,
   coarsely crumbled
freshly ground black pepper

FOR THE DOUGH
9½oz (270g) store-bought filo dough
   (6 x 10½in x 17¼in/ 26cm x 44cm sheets)
2 tbsp butter, melted

The more usual meat-based filling of a Shepherd's Pie is substituted with a tasty mix of mushrooms and beans to produce a delicious vegetarian dish. Use brown lentils instead of aduki beans, if preferred.

SHEPHERDLESS PIE

 SERVES 4   PREP 15 MINS   COOK 50 MINS

EQUIPMENT
ovenproof dish

INGREDIENTS

FOR THE TOPPING
1½lb (675g) Russet Burbank potatoes, peeled and quartered
2 pats of butter

FOR THE FILLING
1 tbsp olive oil
1 onion, finely chopped
1 bay leaf
salt and freshly ground black pepper
3 celery stalks, finely chopped
3 carrots, finely chopped
7oz (200g) cremini mushrooms, coarsely chopped
handful of thyme sprigs, leaves picked
splash of dark soy sauce
14oz can aduki beans, drained and rinsed
⅔ cup hot vegetable stock

1 Preheat the oven to 400°F (200°C). To make the topping, cook the potatoes in a large saucepan of salted boiling water for 15–20 minutes, until soft. Drain, then return the potatoes to the pan and mash. Add a pat of butter and mash again, then set aside.

2 Heat the olive oil in a large frying pan over low heat. Add the onion, bay leaf, and a pinch of salt, and sweat for about 5 minutes, until the onion is soft. Next, add the celery and carrots and continue to sweat gently for another 5 minutes.

3 Pulse the mushrooms in a food processor until broken down; you want them shredded but not mushy. Add these to the pan, along with the thyme leaves and soy sauce, and cook for another 5–10 minutes, until the mushrooms begin to release their juices. Add the aduki beans, and season well with salt and pepper. Pour in the stock, bring to a boil, reduce the heat slightly, and simmer gently for 5 minutes.

4 Pour the filling into the dish, and top with the set-aside mashed potatoes. Dot with the remaining butter and bake until the top starts to become crisp and golden. Serve hot.

These exotic little hand pies can be served hot or cold. Try swapping the potatoes in the filling for sweet potatoes and playing with the spicing until you get the balance of flavors you prefer.

VEGETABLE SAMOSAS

 MAKES 16   PREP 45 MINS PLUS CHILLING   COOK 35–40 MINS   FREEZE UNCOOKED, UP TO 1 MONTH

1 To make the dough, sift the flour into a bowl with the salt. Stir in the vegetable oil and gradually add ½ cup warm water, mixing to form a dough. On a floured surface, knead the dough until smooth, then wrap in plastic wrap and chill for at least 30 minutes.

2 For the filling, cook the potatoes in a large saucepan of boiling water for 15–20 minutes, or until tender. Drain and, when the potatoes are cool enough to handle, peel and chop into small pieces.

3 Blanch the cauliflower florets and fresh peas, if using, in another pan of boiling water for 2–3 minutes, or until just tender, then drain.

4 Heat the oil in a large frying pan and fry the shallots for 3–4 minutes, stirring frequently, until soft. Add the potatoes, cauliflower, peas, curry powder, cilantro, and lemon juice and cook over low heat for 2–3 minutes, stirring occasionally. Set aside to cool.

5 Divide the dough into 8 equal pieces and roll them out on a floured surface so each forms a 7in (18cm) circle. Cut each circle in half and shape into a cone, dampening the edges to seal. Spoon a little of the filling into each cone, dampen the top edge of the dough, and press down over the filling to enclose it. Repeat with the rest of the dough and filling.

6 Half-fill the deep-fat fryer or saucepan with oil and heat to 350°F (180°C). Fry the samosas in batches for 3–4 minutes, or until golden brown on both sides. Drain on paper towels and serve hot or cold. If serving these as an appetizer, arrange 2 on a plate with ribbons of cucumber and some raita or chutney. The samosas can be prepared 1 day ahead, chilled, and fried just before serving.

EQUIPMENT
deep-fat fryer or large saucepan

INGREDIENTS

FOR THE DOUGH
2 cups all-purpose flour, plus extra for dusting
½ tsp salt
6 tbsp vegetable oil or ghee (clarified butter), plus extra for frying

FOR THE FILLING
1lb (450g) potatoes, unpeeled
8oz (225g) cauliflower, chopped into small pieces
6oz (175g) peas, thawed if frozen
3 tbsp vegetable oil or ghee (clarified butter)
2 shallots, sliced
2 tbsp curry powder or paste
2 tbsp chopped cilantro leaves
1 tbsp lemon juice

Late summer is a perfect time to make this delicious Mediterranean-inspired tart. The sweet, rich flavors of the vegetables are offset nicely with the sharp tang of the goat cheese.

ROASTED VEGETABLE AND GOAT CHEESE TART

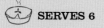 SERVES 6   PREP 30 MINS PLUS CHILLING   COOK 1¼–1½ HRS   FREEZE CRUST, UP TO 1 MONTH

EQUIPMENT
8in (20cm) round tart pan, baking beans

INGREDIENTS

FOR THE DOUGH
(For visual step-by-step instructions, see pie dough p.104)
1 cup all-purpose flour, plus extra for dusting
5 tbsp butter, chilled and cubed
1oz (30g) aged Cheddar cheese, finely grated
1 large egg yolk

FOR THE FILLING
½ red bell pepper, finely chopped
½ red onion, finely chopped
2 garlic cloves, finely chopped
2 baby zucchini, finely sliced
2 baby eggplants, finely sliced
4 baby plum tomatoes, halved
1 tbsp olive oil
½ tsp dried basil
salt and freshly ground black pepper
½ cup half-and-half
2 large eggs
3½oz (100g) log goat cheese, thinly sliced

1 To make the dough, rub the flour and butter together with your fingertips until the mixture resembles fine bread crumbs. Stir the cheese and egg yolk into the flour mixture. Add 1–2 teaspoons of cold water, and bring the ingredients together to form a smooth dough. Wrap and chill for 30 minutes.

2 Preheat the oven to 400°F (200°C). Place the bell pepper, onion, garlic, zucchini, eggplants, and tomatoes in a roasting pan. Add the olive oil and basil, season, and toss well to coat the vegetables. Roast for 20 minutes, or until the vegetables are tender. Reduce the oven temperature to 350°F (180°C).

3 Roll out the dough on a floured surface to a circle large enough to line the tart pan. Place the dough in the pan, pressing down firmly into the bottom and around the edges. Trim off any excess dough, prick the bottom of the tart with a fork, and line with parchment paper. Place the pan on a baking sheet and fill with baking beans. Bake for 15 minutes, then remove the beans and paper, and bake for another 10 minutes.

4 Place the half-and-half and eggs in a measuring cup, season well, and whisk to combine. Arrange the roasted vegetables over the tart crust, and place the sliced goat cheese on top. Carefully pour the egg mixture over the vegetables and cheese, then bake for 30–35 minutes, until golden.

A cross between an Indian samosa and a Cornish Pasty, here a gently spiced vegetable filling is encased in pie dough and baked. You can vary the vegetables used according to the season.

CURRIED VEGETABLE PIES

MAKES 4   PREP 15 MINS   COOK 45 MINS   FREEZE UP TO 1 MONTH

1 Preheat the oven to 400°F (200°C). Cook the carrots and potatoes in a large saucepan of boiling, salted water for 15 minutes, until soft, then drain well.

2 Roll out the dough on a floured surface and cut out 4 rounds using the pastry cutter. Place the dough rounds on a baking sheet and brush the edges with a little of the beaten egg.

3 Place the carrots and potatoes in a bowl, and gently mix with the curry paste and yogurt. Add the garlic, ginger, scallions, cilantro, and lemon juice, and season well with salt and pepper. Stir in gently until well mixed.

4 Divide the vegetable mixture evenly among the dough circles, spooning it into the center of each one. Fold over the dough to make a half-moon shape and pinch the edges together to seal. Using a sharp knife, cut 2 slashes in the top of each pie, then brush all over with the remaining beaten egg. Bake for 20–30 minutes, until golden. Serve hot or cold.

EQUIPMENT
6in (15cm) round pastry cutter, baking sheet

INGREDIENTS

FOR THE FILLING
2 carrots, cubed
2 potatoes, peeled and finely cubed
salt and freshly ground black pepper
1 tbsp curry paste
2 tbsp Greek-style yogurt
1 garlic clove, grated or finely chopped
1in (2cm) piece fresh ginger,
  peeled and finely chopped
2 scallions, finely sliced
handful of cilantro, finely chopped
juice of ½ lemon

FOR THE DOUGH
1lb (450g) store-bought pie dough
  (or to make your own, see p.104)
all-purpose flour, for dusting
1 large egg, lightly beaten, to glaze

Some people have been put off beets because they have only tried the pickled kind. Try roasting fresh beets and you will soon be won over by their sweet, earthy flavor. Tangy goat cheese is a perfect pairing here.

BEET TARTE TATIN

SERVES 6   PREP 20 MINS   COOK 35–45 MINS

EQUIPMENT
9in (23cm) cast-iron frying pan, or a similar pan with an ovenproof handle

INGREDIENTS

FOR THE FILLING
2 tbsp butter
2 tbsp balsamic vinegar
1 tbsp granulated sugar
1 tbsp sage, finely chopped
salt and freshly ground black pepper
1lb (450g) cooked beets, not preserved in vinegar, drained and chopped
3½oz (100g) firm or semifirm goat cheese, finely sliced

FOR THE PASTRY
7oz (200g) sheet store-bought puff pastry (or to make your own, see pp.110–113)
all-purpose flour, for dusting

1 Preheat the oven to 400°F (200°C). Melt the butter in the frying pan. Add the balsamic vinegar and granulated sugar and cook briefly, until the sugar dissolves and the mixture turns syrupy. Scatter the chopped sage over the bottom of the frying pan and season well with salt and pepper.

2 Fry the beets in the balsamic glaze for 5–10 minutes over medium heat, or until they start to darken and the juices reduce, until they just cover the bottom of the pan. Spread the beets out evenly in the frying pan, packing them in tightly, then use the sliced goat cheese to cover the beets.

3 Roll out the pastry on a lightly floured surface to a circle a little larger than the pan and about ¼–⅜in (5–7mm) thick, and drape it over the frying pan. Trim the excess pastry around the edges with a small, sharp knife. Now take any excess pastry and tuck it under the edges of the beets, to make an edge to the tart when you turn it over and to contain the juices.

4 Bake for 25–30 minutes until the pastry is puffed up and golden brown. Remove from the oven and place a large, flat serving plate over the top. Holding the bottom of the frying pan with a dish towel, flip the tart over onto the plate in a quick movement. Leave the tart with the frying pan on top for 1–2 minutes, to allow all the beets to dislodge before taking it off.

5 Serve the tart warm, or at room temperature, as it is, or with extra goat cheese crumbled over to make a more substantial dish. Best eaten the same day.

Use either homemade or store-bought pie dough to make this double-crusted pie. Suitable for vegetarians, its rich, cheesy filling is offset by the sharpness of the onions.

CHEESE AND ONION PIE

 SERVES 4 PREP 15 MINS PLUS COOLING COOK 40 MINS FREEZE UP TO 6 MONTHS

EQUIPMENT
7in (18cm) round pie pan

INGREDIENTS

FOR THE FILLING
1 tbsp olive oil
1 large onion, finely chopped
salt and freshly ground black pepper
2 large eggs
7oz (200g) aged Cheddar cheese, grated

FOR THE DOUGH
12oz (350g) ready-made pie dough
(or to make your own, see p.104)
all-purpose flour, for dusting

1 Preheat the oven to 400°F (200°C). Heat the olive oil in a small pan over low heat. Add the onion and a pinch of salt, and sweat for 2 minutes until transparent and just starting to soften. Transfer to a bowl and set aside to cool completely.

2 Lightly beat 1 of the eggs in a small bowl and stir into the cooled onion with the cheese. Season with salt and pepper.

3 Halve the pie dough, then roll out each piece on a floured surface. Use one of the dough circles to line the pie pan, allowing the dough to hang over the edge, and fill with the cheese and onion mixture. Dampen the edge of the dough with water, then top with the other circle of dough. Trim away the excess dough. Using your thumb and finger, pinch the edges of the dough together to seal. Cut 2 slits in the top to allow the steam to escape.

4 Lightly beat the remaining egg and brush all over the top of the pie. Bake for 25–35 minutes, until cooked and golden. Serve with a tossed salad and boiled or steamed new potatoes.

A well-cooked onion tart is one of the most delightful dishes imaginable. Take care to cook the onions slowly, so that they become soft and sweet, and use a rich, buttery crust for the best result.

ONION TART

SERVES 8   **PREP 25 MINS PLUS CHILLING**   **COOK 1 HR – 1 HR 10 MINS**   **FREEZE UP TO 2 MONTHS**

1 Heat the olive oil and butter in a saucepan. Add the onions and season well with salt and pepper. When sizzling, reduce the heat to low, cover, and cook for 20 minutes, stirring occasionally, until the onions are soft but not brown. Uncover the pan, increase the heat, and cook the onions for another 5–10 minutes to allow any water to evaporate.

2 Put the onions in the tart crust and spread them out. Beat together the cream, egg, egg yolk, and salt and pepper. Place the tart on a baking sheet and pour the cream mixture over the onions. Use a fork to help distribute the cream evenly, by pushing the onions from side to side a little.

3 Bake for 30 minutes, until just set, lightly golden, and puffy on top. Remove from the oven, trim the edges of the crust, and set aside to cool for 10 minutes before eating warm or cold. This tart is best eaten the day it is made, but it can be chilled overnight and gently reheated in a medium oven. The pie crust can be prepared up to 2 days in advance, wrapped in plastic wrap, and chilled in the refrigerator until needed.

EQUIPMENT
9in (22cm) tart pan with removable bottom

INGREDIENTS

FOR THE FILLING
2 tbsp olive oil
2 tbsp butter
1¼lb (500g) finely sliced onions
sea salt and freshly ground black pepper
¾ cup heavy cream
1 large egg, plus 1 egg yolk

FOR THE DOUGH
store-bought prebaked pie crust
  (or to make your own, see p.104
  and pp.122–123)

Tarte Tatin is usually a sweet tart, but try making a savory version for an interesting twist on a classic, using shallots or beets. Contrast the sweet and sour flavors with a simple green salad.

CARAMELIZED SHALLOT TARTE TATIN

SERVES 4–6　　　**PREP 20 MINS PLUS CHILLING**　　　**COOK 45 MINS**

EQUIPMENT
large ovenproof frying pan

INGREDIENTS

FOR THE DOUGH
(For visual step-by-step instructions,
see pie dough p.104)
1 cup all-purpose flour,
plus extra for dusting
a pinch of sea salt
5 tbsp butter
or 9oz (250g) store-bought
pie dough

FOR THE FILLING
2 tbsp butter
2 tbsp extra virgin olive oil
14oz (400g) shallots, peeled and
split in half lengthwise
2 tbsp balsamic vinegar
a few sprigs of thyme

1 To make the dough, combine the flour, salt, and butter in a food processor, and mix to form fine bread crumbs, or to make by hand, rub with your fingertips. With the motor running, add enough cold water, a tablespoon at a time, until the dough starts to stick together. If making by hand, add the water in the same way, but bring the dough together between each addition. Form the dough into a ball, wrap in plastic wrap, and chill in the refrigerator for 30 minutes.

2 Preheat the oven to 400°F (200°C). Melt the butter with the olive oil in the frying pan. Put the shallots in, cut-side down, and cook very gently for 10 minutes until browned. Turn them over and cook for another 5 minutes. Add the vinegar and 2 tablespoons water, then remove from the heat. Tuck the thyme sprigs between the shallots.

3 Roll out the dough on a lightly floured surface to a circle a little larger than the frying pan. Lay the dough over the shallots, trim, and tuck it in. Transfer the pan to the oven and cook for 30 minutes, or until the dough is golden brown.

4 Remove the pan from the oven and bang gently to loosen the shallots. Run a knife around the edges of the dough, then put a large plate over the pan and quickly turn it over. Serve warm with a tossed salad.

The slow-cooked onions melt down to a soft sweetness, and combined with the tangy saltiness of the blue cheese make this a wonderful vegetarian quiche, which is perfect to serve on any occasion.

ONION AND ROQUEFORT QUICHE

 SERVES 6–8   PREP 30 MINS   COOK 1½ HRS   FREEZE UP TO
                         PLUS CHILLING   1 MONTH

1 To make the dough, sift the flour onto a surface and make a well in the center. Add the egg yolk, salt, 3 tablespoons water, and butter to the well. Mix the ingredients with your fingertips, then work the flour into the ingredients until bread crumbs form. Press the dough into a ball.

2 On a lightly floured surface, knead the dough by pushing it away from you with the heel of your hand for 1–2 minutes, until it is smooth and peels away from the surface in one piece. Form into a ball, wrap in plastic wrap, and chill for 30 minutes until firm.

3 Grease the pan. Roll out the dough on a floured surface to a 12in (30cm) circle and use to line the pan, allowing the sides to overhang. Trim off the excess dough. Press the dough evenly up the side, then prick the bottom with a fork. Chill for 15 minutes, until firm.

4 Preheat the oven to 425°F (220°C). Line the crust with wax paper. Fill with baking beans and bake for 15 minutes. Remove the paper and beans and reduce the oven temperature to 375°F (190°C). Bake for 5–8 minutes, until browned. Set aside.

5 Melt the butter. Add the onions, thyme, and seasoning. Put greased foil on top and cover with the lid. Cook, stirring occasionally, for 20–30 minutes, until soft but not brown. Whisk the egg, yolk, milk, salt and pepper, nutmeg, and cream. Crumble the cheese into the onions; stir until melted. Cool slightly. Spread it evenly into the crust. Put the pan on a baking sheet. Pour the custard over the onions, and mix in with a fork. Bake for 30–35 minutes, until a skewer inserted into the center comes out clean and the custard wobbles slightly. Serve warm or at room temperature.

EQUIPMENT
10in (25cm) tart pan, baking beans

INGREDIENTS

FOR THE DOUGH
(For visual step-by-step instructions,
  see pie dough p.104)
1½ cups all-purpose flour,
  plus extra for dusting
1 large egg yolk
½ tsp salt
7 tbsp unsalted butter, softened,
  plus extra for greasing

FOR THE FILLING
2 tbsp unsalted butter
1¼lb (500g) onions, sliced
2–3 thyme sprigs, leaves picked
salt and freshly ground black pepper
1 large egg, plus 1 large egg yolk
½ cup milk
a pinch of ground nutmeg
¼ cup heavy cream
6oz (175g) vegetarian Roquefort-style
  blue cheese, or regular Roquefort

A mixture of Gruyère and feta cheese is used to flavor this classic spinach tart. Picking up a bag of baby spinach and some store-bought pie dough from the supermarket makes this a great last-minute dish.

SPINACH, CHEESE, AND THYME TART

 SERVES 6   PREP 15 MINS   COOK 1¼ HRS   ❄ FREEZE UP TO 1 MONTH

EQUIPMENT
9in (23cm) tart pan with removable bottom, baking beans

INGREDIENTS

FOR THE DOUGH
10oz (300g) store-bought pie dough (or to make your own, see p.104)

FOR THE FILLING
1 tbsp olive oil
1 onion, finely chopped
salt and freshly ground black pepper
2 garlic cloves, grated or finely chopped
leaves from 1 bunch fresh thyme
9oz (250g) baby spinach
4½oz (125g) each Gruyère and feta cheese
¾ cup heavy cream
2 large eggs

1 Preheat the oven to 400°F (200°C). Roll out the dough on a floured surface and use to line the tart pan. Trim off the excess dough, line the tart crust with wax paper, and fill with baking beans. Bake for 15–20 minutes. Remove the beans and paper. Bake for another 1–2 minutes to crisp. Set aside. Reduce the heat to 350°F (180°C).

2 Heat the olive oil in a frying pan over low heat. Add the onion and a pinch of salt, and sweat gently for 5 minutes, until soft. Add the garlic and thyme, and cook for a few seconds, then add the spinach and stir for 5 minutes, until the spinach wilts.

3 Assemble the tart (see below). Bake for 30–40 minutes, until set and golden. Set aside to cool for 10 minutes. Serve warm or at room temperature.

For the tart filling

1 Spoon the onion and spinach mixture into the tart crust and make sure it covers the bottom.

2 Sprinkle over grated Gruyère, and scatter evenly with feta cubes. Season with salt and pepper.

3 Mix the cream and 2 eggs in a measuring cup, until combined, and carefully pour over the tart filling.

A traditional Greek recipe, this crispy filo pie will become a firm family favorite. For variety, add a pinch of grated nutmeg to the filling. This pie is best served either warm or at room temperature.

FILO PIE WITH SPINACH, RICOTTA, PINE NUTS, AND RAISINS

 SERVES 4   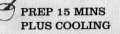 PREP 15 MINS PLUS COOLING   COOK 35 MINS

1 Preheat the oven to 350°F (180°C). Heat the olive oil in a frying pan over low heat. Add the onion and a pinch of salt, and sweat gently for about 5 minutes, until soft. Add the garlic, and cook for a few more seconds, until the garlic turns white.

2 Add the spinach, and cook, stirring, for about 3 minutes, until it wilts. Season well with salt and pepper. Remove from the heat, stir in the raisins and pine nuts, and set aside to cool. Add the ricotta and beaten egg, and stir well.

3 Lay 2 sheets of filo dough one on top of the other in the cake pan, letting them hang over the edge on 2 sides. Next, lay 2 more sheets of filo dough at right angles to the first layer. Continue in this way until you have used 8 sheets for the bottom of the pie.

4 Spoon the spinach and ricotta mixture into the pie. Fold in the edges of the dough, and top the pie with the remaining 4 sheets of filo dough, tucking them in neatly. Brush all over with the melted butter, and bake for 20–30 minutes until golden and crisp.

EQUIPMENT
8in (20cm) round or square cake pan with removable bottom

INGREDIENTS

FOR THE FILLING
1 tbsp olive oil
1 onion, finely chopped
salt and freshly ground black pepper
2 garlic cloves, grated or finely chopped
1¼lb (550g) fresh
    spinach leaves
handful of raisins
½ cups pine nuts, roasted
7oz (200g) ricotta cheese
1 large egg, lightly beaten

FOR THE DOUGH
12 sheets store-bought
    filo dough
2 tbsp
    butter, melted

I love the vibrant color of this tart, which will become a perennial favorite with both friends and family. Be sure to wash the spinach and watercress to remove any dirt and drain well before using.

CREAMY SPINACH TART

SERVES 4–6   PREP 15 MINS   COOK 1 HR

EQUIPMENT
8in (20cm) fluted tart pan with removable bottom, baking beans

INGREDIENTS

FOR THE DOUGH
10oz (300g) store-bought pie dough (or to make your own, see p.104)
all-purpose flour, for dusting
1 large egg, lightly beaten, to glaze

FOR THE FILLING
1 tbsp olive oil
1 onion, finely chopped
salt and freshly ground black pepper
2 garlic cloves, grated or finely chopped
1lb (450g) fresh spinach
7oz (200g) watercress
¾ cup heavy cream
2 large eggs
a pinch of freshly grated nutmeg

1 Preheat the oven to 400°F (200°C). Roll out the dough on a lightly floured surface and use to line the tart pan. Trim off the excess, then line the crust with wax paper, and fill with baking beans. Bake for 15–20 minutes, until the edges are golden. Remove the beans and paper, brush the bottom of the crust with a little of the beaten egg, and bake for another 2–3 minutes to crisp. Set aside. Reduce the oven temperature to 350°F (180°C).

2 For the filling, heat the olive oil in a large frying pan over low heat. Add the onion and a pinch of salt and sweat gently for about 5 minutes, until soft. Add the garlic and cook for a few more seconds, until the garlic turns white, then spoon into the crust.

3 Put the spinach and watercress in a food processor, and pulse a couple of times until broken up but not mushy. Pour in the cream and the 2 eggs, and pulse again until everything is combined. Season well with salt and pepper and pulse once more. Carefully pour into the tart crust and sprinkle the nutmeg over the top. Bake for 20–30 minutes, until set. Set aside to cool for 10 minutes before releasing from the pan. Serve with boiled or steamed new potatoes and a fresh tomato salad.

Spinach and goat cheese are the classic combination for a tasty quiche. Serve warm or cold for a summer lunch or picnic with salad. It is best eaten on the day it is made, but can be chilled overnight.

SPINACH AND GOAT CHEESE QUICHE

SERVES 4–6   PREP 20 MINS PLUS CHILLING   COOK 55 MINS – 1 HR   FREEZE CRUST, UP TO 2 MONTHS

1 To make the dough, rub the flour, butter, and salt together with your fingertips until the mixture resembles fine bread crumbs. Add 3–4 tablespoons cold water a little at a time and bring the mixture together to form a soft dough. Add a little more water if it is too dry. Wrap in plastic wrap and chill for 30 minutes. Preheat the oven to 350°F (180°C).

2 Roll out the dough on a floured surface to a large circle about ⅛in (3mm) thick, and use to line the tart pan, making sure it overlaps the sides. Trim all but ½in (1cm) of the overhanging dough. Prick the bottom with a fork, line with wax paper, and fill with baking beans. Place on a baking sheet and bake for 20–25 minutes, until the dough is lightly cooked. Remove the beans and paper and bake for another 5 minutes to crisp. Trim any ragged edges from the dough crust while it is still warm.

3 For the filling, cook the spinach in a large frying pan with the olive oil and garlic for 2–3 minutes, until it softens. Place the spinach in a sieve and press out any excess water. Set aside to cool.

4 Once the spinach is cool, purée it in a blender with the goat cheese, half-and-half, and eggs until the mixture is smooth. Season well with salt and pepper.

5 Place the tart on a baking sheet and carefully pour in the spinach and goat cheese mixture. Bake for 30 minutes until the mixture has just set. Set aside to cool for at least 15 minutes before serving.

EQUIPMENT
9in (22cm) tart pan with removable bottom, baking beans

INGREDIENTS

FOR THE DOUGH
(For visual step-by-step instructions, see pie dough p.104)
1 cup all-purpose flour, plus extra for dusting
5 tbsp unsalted butter, at room temperature, cut into small pieces
½ tsp salt

FOR THE FILLING
7oz (200g) baby spinach
1 tbsp olive oil
1 garlic clove, crushed
7oz (200g) soft goat cheese
½ cup half-and-half
2 large eggs
salt and freshly ground black pepper

Make sure you chill these pasties in the refrigerator before baking; this helps firm up the dough and hold them together during cooking. These much-loved, wholesome pies are delicious hot or cold.

WHOLE WHEAT SPINACH AND POTATO PASTIES

 MAKES 4   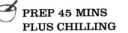 PREP 45 MINS
PLUS CHILLING   🕐 COOK 30–35 MINS   ❄ FREEZE UP TO
1 MONTH

1 To make the dough, rub the two kinds of flour and butter together with your fingertips until the mixture resembles bread crumbs. Add the salt and about ¼ cup cold water, to bring the mixture together to form a soft dough. Wrap and chill for 30 minutes.

2 For the filling, cook the potato chunks in a small saucepan of boiling water for 10 minutes. Drain and set aside to cool. Place the spinach in a colander and pour boiling water over it from a kettle to wilt it. Squeeze out all the liquid and chop finely. Place the spinach in a large bowl with the garlic, cheeses, nutmeg, salt and pepper, and stir well. Set aside.

3 Preheat the oven to 375°F (190°C). Line the baking sheets with parchment paper. Stir the cooled potato into the spinach and cheese mixture.

4 On a well-floured surface, cut the dough into 4 equal pieces. Roll each piece into a circle about 8in (20cm) across and a thickness of ¼in (5mm). Using a small plate (about 8in [20cm] in diameter) cut out a circle from each rolled circle of dough. Arrange one-quarter of the filling on half of each circle, leaving a ½in (1cm) border around the edge. Brush the edges with the beaten egg, bring them together to seal, and crimp for a decorative finish. Chill the pies for 10 minutes.

5 Place the pies on the prepared baking sheets and brush with the remaining beaten egg. Cut a slit in the top of each pasty and bake for 20–25 minutes. Serve the pasties either hot or cold.

EQUIPMENT
2 baking sheets

INGREDIENTS

FOR THE DOUGH
(For visual step-by-step instructions,
** see pie dough p.104)**
1 cup whole wheat flour
1 cup all-purpose flour,
** plus extra for dusting**
11 tbsp butter, chilled and cubed
½ tsp salt
1 large egg, beaten, to glaze

FOR THE FILLING
10oz (300g) unpeeled waxy potatoes, such
** as Yukon Golds, cut into small chunks**
8oz (225g) spinach
1 garlic clove, finely chopped
9oz (250g) ricotta cheese
2½oz (75g) vegetarian-style Grana Padano,
** or regular Grana Padano cheese, grated**
freshly grated nutmeg
salt and freshly ground black pepper

Long, slow cooking of the fennel ensures a soft, sweet filling for this tart. It is best served on the day it is made, but if making it in advance it can be stored in the refrigerator overnight.

ROASTED FENNEL AND PARMESAN TART

SERVES 6–8   **PREP 20 MINS PLUS CHILLING**   **COOK 1¼ HRS**   **FREEZE CRUST, UP TO 2 MONTHS**

EQUIPMENT
9in (22cm) fluted tart pan with removable bottom, baking beans

INGREDIENTS

FOR THE DOUGH
(For visual step-by-step instructions, see pie dough p.104)
1 cup all-purpose flour, plus extra for dusting
5 tbsp unsalted butter, softened
½ tsp salt

FOR THE FILLING
2 large fennel bulbs, 10oz (300g) trimmed weight, finely sliced (green fronds reserved)
1 onion, finely sliced
2 tbsp olive oil
1 tbsp butter, softened
juice and zest of 2 lemons
1¼ cups heavy cream
2 large eggs
2oz (50g) vegetarian Parmesan-style cheese, or regular Parmesan, grated
salt and freshly ground black pepper

1 To make the dough, rub the flour, butter, and salt together with your fingertips until the mixture resembles fine bread crumbs. Add 3–4 tablespoons of water, a little at a time, and bring together to form a soft dough. Wrap in plastic wrap and chill for 30 minutes.

2 Preheat the oven to 350°F (180°C). Roll out the dough on a floured surface to a large circle about ⅛in (3mm) thick and use to line the tart pan, making sure it overlaps the sides. Trim all but ½in (1cm) of the overhanging dough. Prick the bottom of the dough with a fork, line with wax paper, fill with baking beans, and put on a baking sheet. Bake for 20–25 minutes, until the dough is lightly cooked. Remove the beans and paper and bake for another 5 minutes to crisp. Trim off any ragged edges from the crust.

3 Meanwhile, cook the fennel and onion in the olive oil, butter, and lemon juice for 20 minutes, until soft. Stir occasionally to prevent it from sticking. If it looks like it's starting to burn, cover the pan with a lid, but remove it for the last 5 minutes of cooking time, to evaporate any excess water. Set aside to cool.

4 Whisk the cream, eggs, Parmesan, and lemon zest together and season well. Add a tablespoon or two of the reserved fennel fronds, finely chopped.

5 Pile the cooked fennel mixture into the crust and spread it around evenly without packing it too tightly. Carefully pour the cream mixture over the fennel and bake for 30 minutes until just set. Set aside to cool for 30 minutes before eating warm or cold.

These delicious strudels make a fantastic vegetarian alternative at any party. Preparing them a few hours in advance means that there is no last-minute panic when serving lots of dishes at the same time.

BUTTERNUT SQUASH AND GOAT CHEESE STRUDELS

 MAKES 4   PREP 15 MINS   COOK 30–35 MINS   FREEZE UP TO 1 MONTH

1 Preheat the oven to 400°F (200°C). Heat the olive oil in a frying pan over medium heat. Add the onions and cook for about 5 minutes, until soft. Add the vinegar, sugar, season well with salt and black pepper, and cook over low heat for 5 minutes.

2 If using filo, lay out 4 sheets of filo dough, one for each strudel, on a well-floured surface. Brush the sheets with melted butter, cover with a second layer, and brush again. Repeat with the remaining filo sheets. Brush the top layer with butter, being careful to brush around the edges first (this will help to seal the strudels later).

3 Now scatter the grated butternut squash evenly over the strudel bases, leaving a clean border of at least ¾in (2cm) around all the edges except those nearest to you. Scatter the cooked onions on top, then the chopped sage. Finally, add the goat cheese, and season with pepper and a little salt.

4 Fold in the 2 sides of each strudel that are free of filling, then carefully roll up, starting with the side nearest you. Take care to tuck the sides in as you roll, and finish with the seams tucked underneath. Transfer the strudels to the baking sheet and brush the tops with any remaining melted butter.

5 Bake at the top of the oven for 20–25 minutes, until golden brown and crisp. If serving hot, set the strudels aside to cool for at least 10 minutes; they are also good cold. The uncooked strudels can be stored in the refrigerator, covered, a few hours before baking. The cooked strudels can be warmed 1 day later.

EQUIPMENT
baking sheet

INGREDIENTS

FOR THE FILLING
2 tbsp olive oil
3 red onions, finely sliced
2 tbsp balsamic vinegar
a pinch of sugar
salt and freshly ground black pepper
1lb 2oz (500g) butternut squash, peeled, seeded, and coarsely grated
2 tbsp finely chopped sage leaves
9oz (250g) soft goat cheese, cubed

FOR THE PASTRY
1 quantity strudel pastry (see pp.114–115), or 1 pack (12 sheets) filo dough, about 10in x 10in (25cm x 25cm)
all-purpose flour, for dusting
4 tbsp unsalted butter, melted

Squash·is a wonderfully versatile vegetable. Roasting it gives it a depth of flavor, and contrasting it with a salty cheese, such as Dolcelatte, complements its sweet, earthy tones.

THYME-ROASTED BUTTERNUT SQUASH AND DOLCELATTE TART

 SERVES 6   **PREP 25 MINS PLUS CHILLING**   **COOK 1½ HRS**   **FREEZE UP TO 1 MONTH**

EQUIPMENT
8in (20cm) tart pan with
removable bottom, baking beans

INGREDIENTS

FOR THE DOUGH
(For visual step-by-step instructions,
see pie dough p.104)
1¼ cups all-purpose flour
8 tbsp butter, chilled

FOR THE FILLING
1lb (450g) butternut squash, peeled
and seeded
1–2 tbsp olive oil
leaves from 1 bunch fresh thyme
or 1 tsp dried thyme
14oz (400g) arugula
2 large eggs, plus 1 large egg yolk
1¼ cups heavy cream
2oz (50g) vegetarian Parmesan-style cheese
or regular Parmesan, grated
grated nutmeg
salt and freshly ground black pepper
4oz (115g) Dolcelatte cheese

1 To make the dough, put the flour and butter into a food processor and pulse until it resembles bread crumbs. Add just enough water to bring it together into a dough. Roll it out on a floured surface, and use to line the tart pan. Chill for 30 minutes.

2 Preheat the oven to 350°F (180°C). Prick the bottom of the crust, line it with wax paper, and fill with baking beans. Bake for 10 minutes, then remove the paper and beans, and bake for another 10 minutes to crisp up.

3 Slice the squash into thick slices, put on a baking sheet, brush lightly with olive oil, and sprinkle the thyme over the top. Bake for 30 minutes, or until tender. Meanwhile, place the arugula and a little olive oil in a saucepan and wilt over medium heat for 1–2 minutes. Drain and set aside to cool. Whisk the eggs, egg yolk, cream, Parmesan, and nutmeg together and season to taste with salt and pepper.

4 Squeeze the arugula dry and spread it across the bottom of the crust, then add slices of squash and crumble over the Dolcelatte. Pour in the egg mixture and bake for 30–40 minutes, or until the filling is set. Remove from the oven and set it aside for 10 minutes before serving.

These crisp little filo parcels are a version of a popular Middle Eastern snack. Variations of these savory snacks are available all over the Middle East and North Africa.

SPICY BUTTERNUT SQUASH AND FETA PARCELS

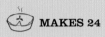 MAKES 24   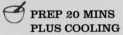 PREP 20 MINS
PLUS COOLING   ⏰ COOK 30 MINS   ❄ FREEZE UP TO
1 MONTH

1 Place the squash in a small saucepan and pour in enough water just to cover it. Bring to a boil, cover, then reduce the heat, and simmer gently for 5 minutes, or until tender. Drain and set aside to cool.

2 Preheat the oven to 350°F (180°C) and grease the baking sheet. Mix the squash with the pine nuts and feta. Season with black pepper and add the spices and chile flakes. Set aside.

3 Lay the filo sheets on top of each other and cut into 4 long strips, about 3in (7.5cm) wide. Stack the strips on top of each other and cover with dampened paper towels.

4 Taking one strip of dough at a time, brush with melted butter and fill one end with a heaping teaspoon of the squash mixture to 1in (2.5cm). Fold over the end of the strip of dough to cover the filling.

5 Fold a corner of the dough over diagonally to form a triangular pocket of filled dough. Working upward, keep folding diagonally, from one side to the other, to retain the triangular shape, until all the dough is folded. Make sure any gaps in the dough are pressed closed. Keep the triangles in a pile on a lightly floured surface, covered with a damp cloth to stop them from drying out, while preparing the other pastries. Transfer the triangles to the baking sheet.

6 Brush with the remaining butter and bake for 20–25 minutes, until crisp and golden. Serve while still warm. The pastries can be prepared up to 24 hours before baking and chilled.

EQUIPMENT
baking sheet

INGREDIENTS

FOR THE FILLING
4oz (100g) butternut squash, peeled, seeded, and finely cubed
1oz (25g) roasted pine nuts
3oz (100g) feta cheese, finely crumbled
freshly ground black pepper
½ tsp ground coriander
½ tsp ground cumin
½ tsp dried chile flakes

FOR THE DOUGH
6 sheets filo dough, 16in x 12in (40cm x 30cm)
4 tbsp butter, melted, plus extra for greasing
all-purpose flour, for dusting

If you don't have much time, use store-bought puff pastry rather than making your own. Buy a butter-based one, and it will be all but indistinguishable from the homemade variety.

SWEET POTATO, RED ONION, AND THYME GALETTES WITH CHILE

 MAKES 4   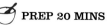 **PREP 20 MINS**    **COOK 50 MINS**

EQUIPMENT
1 or 2 baking sheets

INGREDIENTS

FOR THE FILLING
2 medium-sized sweet potatoes,
10oz (300g) peeled weight
2 red onions, cut into ½in (1cm) cubes
1 tbsp olive oil
salt and freshly ground black pepper
½ red chile, seeded and finely chopped
1 tsp finely thyme, chopped

FOR THE PASTRY
12oz (375g) store-bought puff pastry
(or to make your own, see pp.110–113)
all-purpose flour, for dusting
1 large egg yolk, beaten

1 Preheat the oven to 400°F (200°C). Cut the sweet potatoes into ½in (1cm) cubes. Toss the sweet potato and red onions in the olive oil in a large bowl and season well with salt and pepper. Turn the vegetables onto a baking sheet and bake for 30 minutes, until softened and golden at the edges.

2 Roll out the puff pastry on a lightly floured surface into a square about 12in x 16in (30cm x 40cm) and cut it into quarters. Lay the pastry rectangles on one or two baking sheets. Brush them with beaten egg yolk.

3 Toss the cooked vegetables with the chopped chile and thyme, and divide the mixture equally between the 4 pastry rectangles. Spread the vegetables out, leaving a ½in (1cm) clear edge to the pastry.

4 Bake the galettes for 20 minutes, or until the pastry is puffed up and golden brown at the edges, and the bottom is firm to the touch and golden. Best eaten hot, but set aside to cool for 5 minutes before serving with a leafy green salad. The cooked galettes can be stored in the refrigerator for up to 2 days and warmed again before serving.

Any combination of mushrooms can be used in this rich, nutty tart. For an added depth of flavor, reconstitute a handful of dried porcini in stock or boiling water, then chop and add them to the filling.

MIXED MUSHROOM AND WALNUT TART

 SERVES 6   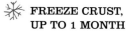 **PREP 15 MINS**   **COOK 1 HR**   ❄ **FREEZE CRUST, UP TO 1 MONTH**

EQUIPMENT
5in x 14in (12cm x 35cm) rectangular, fluted tart pan with removable bottom, baking beans

INGREDIENTS

FOR THE DOUGH
9oz (250g) store-bought pie dough (or to make your own, see p.104)
all-purpose flour, for dusting
1 large egg, lightly beaten, to glaze

FOR THE FILLING
3–4 tbsp olive oil
5oz (140g) exotic mushrooms (such as porcini or shiitake), coarsely chopped
7oz (200g) cremini mushrooms, coarsely chopped
3 garlic cloves, grated or finely chopped
2oz (50g) walnut halves, coarsely chopped
salt and freshly ground black pepper
2 handfuls of fresh spinach leaves, coarsely chopped
¾ cup heavy cream
2 large eggs

1 Preheat the oven to 400°F (200°C). Roll out the dough on a floured surface and use to line the tart pan. Trim away the excess dough. Line the crust with wax paper and fill with baking beans. Bake for 15–20 minutes, until the edges are golden, then remove the beans and paper, brush the bottom of the crust with a little of the beaten egg, and bake for another 2–3 minutes to crisp. Remove from the oven and set aside. Reduce the heat to 350°F (180°C).

2 Heat the olive oil in a large, deep-sided frying pan over low heat. Add the mushrooms, garlic, and walnuts, and season well with salt and pepper. Cook, stirring occasionally, for about 10 minutes, until the mushrooms release their juices. Add in the spinach, and cook, stirring, for another 5 minutes, until just wilted. Spoon the mixture into the crust.

3 Mix together the cream and the eggs. Season well with salt and pepper and pour the cream mixture over the mushroom filling. Sprinkle with a pinch of black pepper and bake for 15–20 minutes, until set. Set aside to cool for 10 minutes before releasing from the pan. Serve hot or cold.

These tempting little tarts make a great appetizer, being both meat-free and easy to finish at the last minute. For an even faster version, use a jar of good-quality hollandaise sauce.

CREAMY MUSHROOM HOLLANDAISE TARTLETS

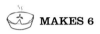 MAKES 6   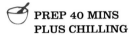 PREP 40 MINS PLUS CHILLING   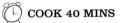 COOK 40 MINS

1 To make the dough, pulse the flours and butter in a food processor until the mixture resembles bread crumbs. Add the egg and process until the dough comes together into a ball, adding 1–2 drops of water if necessary. Put the dough on a floured surface, divide into 6 pieces, roll out, and use to line the pans. Prick the bottom of the dough, then chill for 30 minutes.

2 Preheat the oven to 400°F (200°C). Line the crusts with wax paper and fill with baking beans. Bake for 10 minutes, then remove the paper and beans and bake for another 5 minutes, or until crisp. Set aside. Don't turn off the oven.

3 Pour boiling water over the dried mushrooms and let soften for 10 minutes. Melt the butter in a frying pan and cook the onion and mushrooms over medium heat. Drain the dried mixed mushrooms, chop, and add to the onion mix. Once all the mushrooms have wilted, increase the heat and boil until the liquid has evaporated. Add the lemon juice and seasoning. Cool.

4 Purée the mushroom mixture with the cream cheese in a food processor until fairly smooth. Season. For the hollandaise, melt the butter in a small saucepan. Blend the yolks, black pepper, and vinegar in a food processor for 1 minute, then gradually add the melted butter while the processor is running, until the sauce is thickened. Adjust the seasoning and set aside.

5 Turn the oven to 375°F (190°C). Spoon the filling into the tartlets, pour the sauce over the top, and bake for 10 minutes. Serve hot, topped with chopped chives.

EQUIPMENT
6 tartlet pans with
removable bottoms, baking beans

INGREDIENTS

FOR THE DOUGH
(For visual step-by-step instructions, see pie dough p.104)
½ cup all-purpose flour,
   plus extra for dusting
½ cup whole wheat all-purpose flour
6 tbsp butter, chilled and cubed
1 small egg

FOR THE FILLING
½oz (15g) dried wild mushrooms
2 tbsp unsalted butter
1 red onion, chopped
14oz (400g) mixed mushrooms,
   such as portabello, oyster,
   shiitake, cremini, or button, sliced
juice of ½ lemon
6oz (175g) cream cheese
salt and freshly ground black pepper

FOR THE HOLLANDAISE SAUCE
16 tbsp unsalted butter
4 large egg yolks
freshly ground black pepper
1 tbsp white wine vinegar
small bunch of chives, chopped

The addition of rolled oats to a classic pie dough gives this tart a nutty flavor. Unusually, yogurt is used in the filling instead of cream, which lends a tanginess to the finished dish.

GOAT CHEESE TARTLETS

 MAKES 4   PREP 25 MINS PLUS CHILLING   COOK 35–40 MINS   FREEZE CRUST, UP TO 1 MONTH

EQUIPMENT
4 x tartlet pans with removable bottoms, 5in (12.5cm) in diameter and 1in (2.5cm) deep, baking beans

INGREDIENTS

FOR THE DOUGH
(For visual step-by-step instructions, see pie dough p.104)
½ cup all-purpose flour, plus extra for dusting
a pinch of salt
¼ cup rolled oats
4 tbsp butter, chilled and cubed

FOR THE FILLING
2 large eggs
⅓ cup Greek yogurt
⅔ cup milk
2 tbsp chives, chopped
salt and freshly ground black pepper
3oz (85g) goat cheese, crumbled

1 To make the dough, sift the flour and salt into a large bowl and stir in the oats. Rub in the butter with your fingertips until the mixture resembles bread crumbs. Sprinkle over 2 tablespoons of chilled water and mix in with a butter knife. Gather the dough together and, on a floured surface, knead lightly for a few seconds, or until smooth. Wrap the dough in plastic wrap and chill for 30 minutes.

2 Preheat the oven to 400°F (200°C) and place a baking sheet inside to heat. Divide the dough into 4 pieces. Roll out each one thinly on a lightly floured surface and use to line the tartlet pans. Prick the bottom of the dough several times with a fork, then line each pan with foil and fill with baking beans. Bake for 10 minutes, then remove the foil and beans and return to the oven for 5 minutes. Remove from the oven and set aside. Reduce the heat to 350°F (180°C).

3 Whisk the eggs, yogurt, milk, chives, and salt and pepper in a bowl. Divide the cheese between the crusts, then carefully pour over the egg mixture. Bake for 20–25 minutes until the filling is lightly set and beginning to brown.

4 Set aside to cool slightly, then remove from the pans and serve warm, or at room temperature. Make the dough and line the tartlet pans up to 1 day in advance. If serving cold, the tartlets can be refrigerated, and covered with plastic wrap, for up to 48 hours.

A classic Swedish recipe, all the flavor comes from the buttery crisp dough and the strong cheese. Serve with a tossed salad and a sharp dressing to complement the richness of the tart.

SWEDISH CHEESE TART

 SERVES 6–8   PREP 20 MINS PLUS CHILLING   COOK 55 MINS – 1 HR   FREEZE CRUST, UP TO 2 MONTHS

1 To make the dough, rub the flour, butter, and salt together with your fingertips until the mixture resembles fine bread crumbs. Add 3–4 tablespoons cold water a little at a time and bring the mixture together to form a soft dough. Wrap in plastic wrap and chill for 30 minutes. Preheat the oven to 350°F (180°C).

2 Roll out the dough on a well-floured surface to a large circle about ⅛in (3mm) thick and use to line the tart pan, making sure it overlaps the sides. Trim all but ½in (1cm) of the overhanging dough, then use your fingers to push the dough down into the corners of the pan, making sure it clings to the sides well. Prick the bottom of the dough with a fork, line with wax paper, and fill with baking beans. Place the tart crust on a baking sheet and bake for 20–25 minutes, until the dough is lightly cooked. Remove the beans and paper and bake for another 5 minutes to crisp. Trim off any ragged edges from the crust while warm.

3 Whisk together the half-and-half, milk, and eggs and season well with black pepper, and a little salt—not too much, since the cheese is salty.

4 Scatter the cheese over the bottom of the cooked tart crust, spreading it out evenly. Put the tart crust on a baking sheet and carefully pour the cream mixture over the cheese. Bake for 30 minutes, until just set, slightly puffy, and golden brown.

5 Set the tart aside to rest for at least 15 minutes before serving warm or at room temperature. Best eaten on the day it is made, but can be stored in the refrigerator overnight.

EQUIPMENT
9in (22cm) fluted tart pan wtih removable bottom, baking beans

INGREDIENTS

FOR THE DOUGH
(For visual step-by-step instructions,
   see pie dough p.104)
1 cup all-purpose flour,
   plus extra for dusting
5 tbsp unsalted butter, softened
½ tsp salt

FOR THE FILLING
¾ cup half-and-half
⅓ cup whole milk
2 large eggs
salt and freshly ground black pepper
9oz (250g) Västerbotten cheese,
   or other sharp cheese such as
   aged Cheddar, grated

Spinach seems to work well with strong, sharp cheeses, such as Stilton, goat cheese, or feta. Here, the classic filling is given a makeover, encased in a filo pie with herbs, and baked until crisp.

HERBY FETA FILO PIE

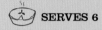 SERVES 6   PREP 30 MINS PLUS COOLING   COOK 1 HR

EQUIPMENT
8in (20cm) round springform pan

INGREDIENTS

FOR THE FILLING
2lb (900g) spinach, rinsed
7 tbsp butter,
plus extra for greasing
2 onions and garlic cloves, finely chopped
4oz (120g) roasted peppers in oil,
drained and chopped
a handful of basil leaves
3 tbsp mint leaves, chopped
3 tbsp parsley, chopped
salt and freshly ground black pepper
10oz (300g) feta cheese, crumbled

FOR THE DOUGH
6 sheets store-bought filo dough,
16in x 12in (40cm x 30cm)

1 Pack the spinach leaves into a large saucepan, cover, and cook for 8–10 minutes, until just wilted. Drain well. Set aside, still draining, to cool.

2 Melt 2 tbsp butter until bubbling and gently fry the onions, stirring occasionally, for 3 minutes. Add the garlic and fry for another 2 minutes. Stir in the peppers and herbs, and set aside. Preheat the oven to 400°F (200°C). Grease and line the pan.

3 Blot the spinach with paper towels, then chop finely. Stir into the onion mixture, and season to taste. Melt the remaining butter. Brush the pan with a little melted butter and assemble the pie (see below).

4 Brush the top of the dough with any remaining butter and place the pan on a baking sheet. Bake for 35–40 minutes, until crisp and golden. Be sure to let the pie to stand for 10 minutes before carefully releasing from the pan. Serve hot or warm, cut into wedges. Good with a crisp salad or seasonal vegetables.

Layering filo sheets

1 Cover the bottom with a sheet of dough, leaving the edges to overhang, and brush with butter.

2 Continue with 5 more sheets, brushing each with butter. Leave the edges overhanging.

3 Add half the filling, then feta, then filling. Put the overhanging dough over the top, brushing with butter.

A simple yet sophisticated tart, the flavors of this dish belie the simple list of ingredients. Try to use really fresh ricotta and the young tips of the rosemary. Best eaten on the day it is made.

RICOTTA, ROSEMARY, AND PINE NUT TART

SERVES 6   PREP 30 MINS PLUS CHILLING   COOK 1–1¼ HRS   FREEZE CRUST, UP TO 1 MONTH

EQUIPMENT
8in (20cm) round tart pan

INGREDIENTS

FOR THE DOUGH
(For visual step-by-step instructions, see pie dough p.104)
1 cup all-purpose flour, plus extra for dusting
5 tbsp butter, chilled and cubed
1 tsp dried rosemary
1 large egg yolk

FOR THE FILLING
1 tbsp olive oil
2 red onions, finely sliced
2 garlic cloves, finely chopped
salt and freshly ground black pepper
9oz (250g) ricotta cheese
2 large eggs
3oz (85g) roasted pine nuts
1 tbsp fresh rosemary leaves, finely chopped

1 To make the dough, rub the flour and butter together with your fingertips until the mixture resembles fine bread crumbs. Add the rosemary and egg yolk to the flour mixture, then add 1–2 teaspoons cold water and bring together to form a smooth dough. Wrap in plastic wrap and chill for 30 minutes.

2 Meanwhile, heat the olive oil in a nonstick frying pan over medium heat. Add the onions and cook for 10 minutes. Add the garlic and cook for another 2 minutes. Season well and transfer to a large bowl. Add the ricotta and stir well. Add the eggs and beat the mixture until it is well combined. Stir in the pine nuts and fresh rosemary. Set aside.

3 Preheat the oven to 350°F (180°C). Roll out the dough on a floured surface to a circle large enough to line the tart pan. Place the dough in the pan, pressing down firmly into the bottom and around the edges. Trim off any excess dough, prick the bottom with a fork, and line with parchment paper. Place the pan on a baking sheet and fill with baking beans. Bake for 20 minutes. Remove the beans and paper and bake for another 5 minutes.

4 Pour the ricotta and onion mixture into the dough case and bake for 25–30 minutes, until golden.

The classic ingredients of a Waldorf salad can be turned into a delicious tangy tart. Adding chopped walnuts to the dough gives the crust added texture and taste. Serve with salad for a summer lunch.

STILTON, APPLE, AND CELERY TART

 SERVES 6–8    PREP 30 MINUTES PLUS CHILLING   COOK 1 HR – 1 HR 5 MINS   FREEZE CRUST, UP TO 1 MONTH

1 To make the dough, rub the flour and butter together with your fingertips until the mixture forms fine bread crumbs. Add the egg yolk and chopped walnuts to the flour mixture, then add 2–3 tablespoons cold water and bring together to form a smooth dough. Wrap in plastic wrap and chill for 30 minutes.

2 For the filling, melt the butter in a medium nonstick frying pan and gently fry the celery for 5 minutes. Remove from the pan with a slotted spoon. Add the apple slices to the pan and gently fry for another 5 minutes, or until just browning.

3 Purée the Stilton, milk, eggs, and plenty of black pepper in a food processor until well combined.

4 Preheat the oven to 350°F (180°C). Roll out the dough on a floured surface to a circle large enough to line the tart pan. Place the dough in the pan, pressing down firmly into the bottom and around the edges. Trim off any excess dough, prick the bottom with a fork, and line with parchment paper. Place the pan on a baking sheet and fill with baking beans. Bake for 20 minutes. Remove the beans and paper and bake for another 5 minutes to crisp up the bottom.

5 Sprinkle the celery and walnuts over the pie crust and arrange the apples in 3 rows, over the top. Carefully pour the Stilton mixture over the apple slices and bake for 25–30 minutes, until golden.

EQUIPMENT
8in (20cm) loose-bottomed square tart pan

INGREDIENTS

FOR THE DOUGH
(For visual step-by-step instructions, see pie dough p.104)
1¼ cups all-purpose flour, plus extra for dusting
8 tbsp butter, chilled and cubed
1 large egg yolk
2 tbsp walnuts, very finely chopped

FOR THE FILLING
2 tbsp butter
4 stalks celery (4oz [115g]), finely chopped
2 red apples, e.g., Gala, quartered, cored, and each sliced into 16 pieces
5oz (140g) Stilton cheese, coarsely crumbled
⅔ cup whole milk
2 large eggs
freshly ground black pepper
¼ cup coarsely chopped walnuts

These little cigar-shaped filo pastries are stuffed with flavored feta and quickly baked to a crisp, golden finish. A handful of toasted pine nuts or some chopped dill make a good addition to this basic recipe.

BOREKS

 MAKES 20   PREP 25 MINS   COOK 10–12 MINS   ❄ FREEZE UP TO
                                                                                        1 MONTH

EQUIPMENT
baking sheet

INGREDIENTS

FOR THE FILLING
6oz (175g) feta cheese, finely crumbled
a pinch of ground nutmeg
1 tsp dried mint
freshly ground black pepper

FOR THE DOUGH
8 sheets of store-bought filo dough,
16in x 12in (40cm x 30cm)
4 tbsp butter, melted,
plus extra for greasing
all-purpose flour, for dusting

1 Preheat the oven to 350°F (180°C). Place the feta cheese in a bowl, add the nutmeg and mint, then season to taste with black pepper.

2 Lay the filo sheets on top of each other and cut into 3 long strips, 4in (10cm) wide.

3 Taking one strip of filo dough at a time, brush with melted butter and place 1 heaping teaspoon of the cheese mixture at one end. Roll up the filo, like a cigar, folding the ends in about one-third of the way down to encase the filling completely, then continue to roll. Make sure the ends are tightly sealed.

4 On a lightly floured surface, keep the rolled pastries in a pile, covered with a damp dish cloth, while preparing the remainder.

5 Place the pastries in a single layer on a large greased baking sheet. Brush with the remaining butter and bake for 10–12 minutes, or until crisp and golden. Best served hot or slightly warm. The pastries can be prepared 24 hours ahead of baking.

This quiche is an all-time spring favorite. A hidden layer of cream cheese and Cheddar under the asparagus adds flavor to the finished dish. Serve warm or cold with a crisp tossed salad.

ASPARAGUS CREAM CHEESE QUICHE

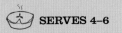 **SERVES 4–6**   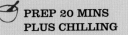 **PREP 20 MINS PLUS CHILLING**   ⏰ **COOK 35 MINS**

1 Sift the flour and salt into a bowl. Add the fat and rub in with your fingertips until the mixture resembles fine bread crumbs. Mix with 2 tablespoons of cold water to form a firm dough. Knead gently on a lightly floured surface. Roll out and use to line the tart pan set on a baking sheet. Chill for 30 minutes.

2 Preheat the oven to to 350°F (180°C). Toss the asparagus in a little olive oil and cook on a hot grill pan for 2 minutes each side, until bright green and just tender.

3 Spread the cream cheese over the bottom of the prepared pie crust. Sprinkle with the thyme, some black pepper, and the Cheddar. Trim the asparagus spears to fit the crust, as necessary. Scatter the asparagus trimmings over the cheese and lay the whole spears attractively on top.

4 Beat the eggs and half-and-half together with a little salt and black pepper, and pour into the pie crust. Bake for 30 minutes, or until golden and set. Serve warm or cold.

EQUIPMENT
8in (20cm) tart pan,
baking beans

INGREDIENTS

FOR THE DOUGH
(For visual step-by-step instructions,
  see pie dough p.104)
1 cup all-purpose flour
a pinch of salt
3 tbsp lard, chilled and cubed
3 tbsp butter, chilled and cubed

FOR THE FILLING
6oz (175g) green asparagus spears
a little olive oil
4oz (115g) cream cheese
2 tsp chopped thyme
salt and freshly ground black pepper
3oz (85g) aged Cheddar cheese, grated
2 large eggs
⅔ cup half-and-half

A perfect dish to cook in spring, this tart looks as good as it tastes. Puréeing the peas gives them a wonderfully vibrant green color and adds a sweet, fresh flavor to the creamy filling.

ASPARAGUS, PEA, AND MINT TART

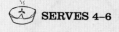 **SERVES 4–6**   **PREP 25 MINS PLUS CHILLING**   **COOK 1 HR – 1 HR 5 MINS**   **FREEZE CRUST, UP TO 1 MONTH**

EQUIPMENT
8in (20cm) tart pan, baking beans

INGREDIENTS

FOR THE DOUGH
(For visual step-by-step instructions, see pie dough p.104)
1 cup all-purpose flour, plus extra for dusting
5 tbsp butter, chilled and cubed
¼ cup finely grated vegetarian-style Parmesan, or regular Parmesan cheese
1 large egg yolk

FOR THE FILLING
1 cup frozen peas
4½oz (125g) fine asparagus stems, cut into 2⅓in (6cm) lengths
½ cup whole milk
2 large eggs
2 garlic cloves, roughly chopped
salt and freshly ground black pepper
3 tbsp mint leaves, chopped
2oz (50g) Cheddar cheese, grated

1 To make the dough, rub the flour and butter together with your fingertips until the mixture resembles fine bread crumbs. Stir the Parmesan cheese and egg yolk into the flour mixture. Add 1–2 tablespoons cold water and bring together to form a smooth dough. Wrap and chill for 30 minutes.

2 For the filling, cook the peas in a small saucepan of boiling water for 2 minutes, or until tender. Drain. Steam the asparagus for 5 minutes, or until just tender. Drain and place on paper towels to absorb any excess moisture. Purée the peas, milk, eggs, garlic, and plenty of seasoning in a food processor until well combined.

3 Preheat the oven to 350°F (180°C). Roll out the dough on a floured surface to a circle large enough to line the tart pan. Place the dough in the pan, pressing down well into the bottom and around the edges. Trim off any excess dough, prick the bottom with a fork, and line with parchment paper. Place the pan on a baking sheet and fill with baking beans. Bake for 20 minutes, then remove the beans and paper and bake for another 5 minutes.

4 Sprinkle the chopped mint over the tart crust and arrange the asparagus spears, like the spokes of a wheel, on top. Carefully pour the creamy pea mixture over the asparagus and sprinkle the Cheddar cheese on top. Bake for 25–30 minutes, until golden.

For a meat-free feast, try cooking up the best your garden has to offer in this delicious potato-topped pie. The types of vegetables used can be varied according to the season. Serve hot.

KITCHEN GARDEN PIE

🍲 SERVES 4   🥄 PREP 20 MINS   ⏰ COOK 1¼–1½ HRS

1 Preheat the oven to 400°F (200°C). Place the leeks, parsnips, squash, carrots, onion, and garlic in a large roasting pan. Add the olive oil, chile flakes, and rosemary, season well, and toss to coat the vegetables. Roast for 35–45 minutes, or until the vegetables are tender.

2 To make the topping, cook the potatoes in a saucepan of boiling, salted water for 15 minutes, or until tender. Drain and mash, stir in the butter, whole milk, and Cheddar cheese. Mix well to combine, season to taste, and set aside.

3 Place the parsley, bread, and Parmesan in a food processor, and pulse to form fine crumbs. Season, and stir in the lemon zest.

4 Melt the butter in a medium pan. Stir in the flour and cook for 2–3 minutes over medium heat, stirring constantly with a wooden spoon, until a smooth paste is formed. Gradually add the milk, stirring constantly, to make a white sauce. Stir in the mustard powder, Cheddar cheese, and roasted vegetables, and season well.

5 Transfer to the ovenproof dish. Top with the mashed potatoes, spreading them in an even layer, and sprinkle the bread crumb mixture over the top. Place the dish on a baking sheet and bake for 20 minutes.

EQUIPMENT
3 quart ovenproof dish

INGREDIENTS

FOR THE FILLING
3½oz (100g) baby leeks, sliced
7oz (200g) parsnips, chopped
 into bite-sized pieces
10oz (300g) butternut squash,
 chopped into bite-sized pieces
7oz (200g) baby carrots,
 chopped into bite-sized pieces
1 red onion, finely chopped
2 garlic cloves, finely chopped
2 tbsp olive oil
½ tsp dried red chile flakes
2 tbsp fresh rosemary, chopped
 or 1 tsp dried rosemary
salt and freshly ground black pepper
small bunch of curly parsley,
 stems removed
2oz (50g) white bread
1oz (30g) Parmesan cheese, grated
zest of 1 lemon
4 tbsp butter
¼ cup all-purpose flour
2 cups whole milk
½ tsp English mustard powder, e.g., Coleman's
2oz (60g) aged Cheddar cheese, grated

FOR THE TOPPING
2¼lb (1kg) floury potatoes, such as
 Russet Burbanks, peeled and chopped
 into small chunks
4 tbsp butter
¼ cup whole milk
2oz (60g) aged Cheddar cheese, grated

Sometimes a few staple ingredients can be combined to produce a simple yet sumptuous dish. Baked in minutes, these are great served fresh from the oven with new potatoes and a tomato salad.

BROCCOLI, TOMATO, AND MOZZARELLA GALETTES

 MAKES 4   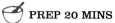 PREP 20 MINS   COOK 35 MINS

EQUIPMENT
baking sheet

INGREDIENTS

FOR THE FILLING
6oz (175g) broccoli, cut into tiny florets
salt and freshly ground black pepper
3½oz (100g) mozzarella, grated
6 sun-dried tomatoes in oil,
drained and finely chopped
6 tbsp crème fraîche, plus
extra for brushing

FOR THE PASTRY
13oz (375g) sheet store-bought puff pastry
(about 9in x 16in/23cm x 40cm),
(or to make your own, see pp.110–113)

1 Cook the broccoli in a saucepan of boiling, lightly salted water for 2 minutes, until almost tender. Drain, rinse with cold water, and drain again. Preheat the oven to 425°F (220°C). Sprinkle a little water over the baking sheet to dampen.

2 Place the broccoli florets in a large bowl, add the mozzarella, tomatoes, and crème fraîche. Season with salt and pepper and stir well to combine.

3 Cut the pastry into quarters. Pile one-quarter of the filling at one end of each oblong, leaving a border, then brush the pastry edges with water. Fold over the uncovered halves of pastry, press the edges together to seal, and transfer to the dampened baking sheet. Make a few slashes in the tops and brush some crème fraîche over the top to glaze. Bake for 30 minutes, until puffy, crisp, and golden.

If you don't have a food processor, try making a traditional pie dough the old-fashioned way. It only takes minutes to prepare and is surprisingly satisfying when you have the time. ❄

BROCCOLI AND MUSHROOM QUICHE

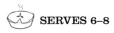 SERVES 6–8

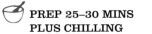 PREP 25–30 MINS
PLUS CHILLING

🕐 COOK 50 MINS –
1 HR

❄ FREEZE UP TO
1 MONTH

1 To make the dough, sift the flour on to a work surface and make a well in the center. Put the egg yolk, salt, butter, and 3 tablespoons water in the well. Work the flour into the other ingredients with your fingertips until coarse bread crumbs form. Press the dough lightly into a ball. If it is too dry, sprinkle with more water. On a lightly floured surface, knead the dough for 1–2 minutes, until it is very smooth. Shape into a ball, wrap in plastic wrap, and chill for 30 minutes.

2 Preheat the oven to 425°F (220°C). Grease the tart pan. Roll out the dough on a floured surface to a 12in (30cm) circle, and use to line the pan. With your thumb and forefingers, press the dough evenly up the side, from the bottom, to increase the height of the dough rim. Prick the bottom with a fork and chill for at least 15 minutes, until firm.

3 Line the dough with foil, fill with baking beans, and bake for 12–15 minutes until starting to turn golden. Remove the foil and beans, reduce the heat to 375°F (190°C) and bake for another 5 minutes.

4 Cook the broccoli in a saucepan of salted boiling water for 3–5 minutes, then drain. Melt the butter in a frying pan, add the mushrooms and garlic and sauté until all the liquid has evaporated. Whisk together the eggs, yolks, milk, cream, seasoning, and nutmeg. Spread the mushrooms in the crust. Lay the broccoli on top and sprinkle the cheese over the top. Ladle the egg mix over to fill almost to the rim. Bake for 30–35 minutes, until browned and the filling wobbles slightly in the center. Serve at room temperature.

EQUIPMENT
10in (25cm) fluted tart pan, baking beans

INGREDIENTS

FOR THE DOUGH
(For visual step-by-step instructions, see pie dough p.104)
1 cup all-purpose flour,
plus extra for dusting
1 large egg yolk
½ tsp salt
7 tbsp unsalted butter,
softened, plus extra for greasing

FOR THE FILLING
1–2 heads of broccoli, total weight
about 1lb 2oz (500g), cut into florets
salt and freshly ground black pepper
2 tbsp butter
3oz (85g) cremini mushrooms, sliced
3oz (85g) button mushrooms, halved
2 garlic cloves, finely chopped
3 large eggs, plus 2 large egg yolks
1½ cups milk
1 cup heavy cream
a pinch of ground nutmeg
4 oz (115g) aged Cheddar cheese, grated

This classic leek pie originates from the Picardy region of northern France. Although not traditional, the inclusion of blue cheese adds piquancy to the gentle sweetness of the leeks. Serve warm or cold.

FLAMICHE

SERVES 4–6   **PREP 20 MINS**   **COOK 40–45 MINS**

EQUIPMENT
7in (18cm) cake pan with removable bottom

INGREDIENTS

FOR THE FILLING
4 tbsp unsalted butter
2 tbsp olive oil
1lb 2oz (500g) leeks, washed, trimmed, and finely shredded
sea salt and freshly ground black pepper
grated nutmeg
2 tbsp all-purpose flour
1 cup milk
3½oz (100g) vegetarian blue cheese, or regular blue cheese, such as Stilton (optional)

FOR THE PASTRY
1lb 2oz (500g) store-bought puff pastry (or to make your own, see pp.110–113)
flour, for dusting
oil, for greasing
1 large egg, beaten, to glaze

1 Preheat the oven to 400°F (200°C). Melt the butter and olive oil in a large saucepan. Add the leeks and cook over low heat for 10 minutes, stirring occasionally, until well softened but not browned. Season well with salt, black pepper, and a little nutmeg. Scatter the flour over the surface of the leeks and stir it in well.

2 Pour the milk onto the leeks, a little at a time, stirring constantly. The mixture will thicken to begin with, then gradually loosen as all the milk is added. Bring to a boil, reduce the heat, and cook for 3–5 minutes, until well thickened. Remove from the heat and stir in the cheese (if using).

3 Roll out the pastry on a well-floured surface into an 8in x 16in (20cm x 40cm) rectangle, about ⅛–¼in (3–5mm) thick. Place the pan onto one short edge of the pastry and cut a circle around it to make the lid; the remaining pastry should be large enough to line the bottom of the pan. Oil the pan, trim the remaining pastry and use it to line the pan, allowing the sides to overhang slightly. Brush the inside with a little beaten egg and set aside for 5 minutes.

4 Fill the pastry crust with the leek mixture and brush a little beaten egg around the edges of the pastry. Top with the disk of pastry and press around the edges to seal. Brush the top with beaten egg, then cut 2 small slits in the top to allow steam to escape.

5 Bake for 25–30 minutes, until puffed up and golden brown. Remove from the oven, trim the excess pastry, and set aside to cool for at least 10 minutes before serving. Chill the flamiche overnight. Gently reheat, or bring back to room temperature to serve.

The humble leek is a vastly underrated vegetable. Commonly used to complement other vegetables, leeks and onions both flourish alone when cooked slowly to bring out their natural sweetness.

LEEK QUICHE

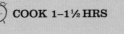 SERVES 6–8   PREP 30 MINS PLUS CHILLING   COOK 1–1½ HRS   FREEZE PIE CRUST, UP TO 2 MONTH

1 To make the dough, rub the flour, butter, and salt together with your fingertips until the mixture resembles fine bread crumbs. Add 4–6 tablespoons cold water a little at a time and bring the mixture together to form a soft dough. Add a little extra water if it is too dry. Wrap in plastic wrap and chill for 30 minutes. Preheat the oven to 350°F (180°C).

2 Roll out the dough on a floured surface to a large circle about ¼in (5mm) thick, and use to line the pan, making sure the dough overlaps the sides. Trim all but ½in (1cm) of the overhanging dough. Prick the bottom of the dough with a fork, line with wax paper, and fill with baking beans. Place the crust on a baking sheet and bake for 20–25 minutes, until the dough is lightly cooked. Remove the beans and paper and bake for another 5 minutes to crisp. Trim off any ragged edges from the pie crust while still warm.

3 To make the the filling, melt the butter in a large saucepan, add the leeks and cook over medium heat for 15 minutes, stirring occasionally until soft, but not brown. Place the leeks in the crust and spread them out evenly to cover the bottom.

4 Whisk the half-and-half, crème fraîche, eggs, thyme, and seasoning together in a bowl. Place the pie crust on a baking sheet and carefully pour the cream mixture over the leeks. Bake for 45 minutes, until the mixture has just set and is lightly golden.

5 Remove the tart from the oven and set aside to cool for at least 15 minutes before eating warm or cold. This is best eaten the day it is made, but it can be stored in the refrigerator overnight.

EQUIPMENT
9in (22cm) fluted tart pan with removable bottom and deep sides (1¼in/3cm)

INGREDIENTS

FOR THE DOUGH
(For visual step-by-step instructions, see pie dough p.104)
1 cup all-purpose flour, plus extra for dusting
7 tbsp unsalted butter, at room temperature, cut into small pieces
½ tsp salt

FOR THE FILLING
4 tbsp butter
1lb 2oz (500g) leeks, prepared weight, sliced into ½in (1cm) disks
¾ cup half-and-half
⅓ cup crème fraîche
2 large eggs
½ tbsp thyme, finely chopped
salt and freshly ground black pepper

This pie is full of woody forest flavors and would make an ideal supper dish served with creamy mashed potatoes and a green vegetable. It is also perfect as a vegetarian Christmas alternative.

CHESTNUT AND MUSHROOM PIE

 SERVES 4–6   PREP 15 MINS   COOK 35–40 MINS

EQUIPMENT
9in (23cm) pie dish

INGREDIENTS

FOR THE FILLING
1 tbsp olive oil
1 red onion, finely chopped
2 garlic cloves, finely chopped
1lb 2oz (500g) mixed mushrooms, such as portabello, oyster, shiitake, cremini, button, sliced if large or left whole
¾ cup red wine
leaves from 4 sprigs of fresh thyme or 1 tsp dried thyme
salt and freshly ground black pepper
5½oz (150g) cooked and peeled chestnuts, halved

FOR THE PASTRY
7½oz (215g) sheet store-bought puff pastry (or to make your own, see pp.110–113)
1 large egg, beaten, to glaze

1 Heat the olive oil in a large, heavy-bottomed, nonstick frying pan and gently fry the onion for 3 minutes. Add the garlic and cook for another 1–2 minutes.

2 Add the mushrooms, red wine, and thyme. Season well, bring to simmer, and cook over medium heat for 5 minutes. Stir the chestnuts into the mushroom mixture and cook for another 5 minutes, stirring occasionally. Spoon the mushroom mixture into the pie dish. Preheat the oven to 400°F (200°C).

3 Cut enough ¾in (2cm) wide strips from the edge of the pastry to fit around the rim of the pie dish. Brush the edge of the dish with water and place the strips on the rim. Cover the pie with the remaining pastry, trim, and press firmly to seal. Brush with the beaten egg and cut a hole in the center of the lid to allow steam to escape. Place on a baking sheet and bake for 15–20 minutes, or until browned.

Salting the grated zucchini is an important stage of this recipe.
It helps to draw out as much moisture as possible from them, which
stops the delicate filo dough from becoming soggy after cooking.

ZUCCHINI AND FETA PIE

 **SERVES 4–6** **PREP 1 HR** **COOK 50–55 MINS**

1 Toss the grated zucchini in the salt and drain in
a colander over a bowl for 30 minutes. To help the
liquid drain, cover them with a clean saucer and put
a heavy weight on top. After 30 minutes, push the
zucchini down firmly with your hand to make sure
that as much liquid as possible is extracted.

2 Heat the olive oil in a frying pan, add the onion
and garlic and fry for 5 minutes, until soft. Add
the zucchini and cook for 10–15 minutes over low heat,
stirring occasionally, so that all the liquid evaporates.
Set the zucchini mixture aside to cool.

3 Preheat the oven to 350°F (180°C). Mix the the
eggs, yogurt, and mint into the zucchini mix,
and season well with black pepper. Mix in the feta.

4 Brush the bottom of the pan with a little olive oil.
Layer the first sheet of filo into the pan lengthwise,
and brush with a little olive oil. Lay the next one at
right angles to the first, making sure it touches one
of the short edges of the pan, and brush with more oil.
Place a third in the same direction touching the other
edge and again brush with oil. Repeat until you have
used 6 pieces of filo. Spread the filling evenly over the
bottom of the pie. Lay 1 piece of filo lengthwise over
the filling. Fold half the overhanging edges over the
top piece of filo. Brush with oil and add another piece
lengthwise, folding the remaining edges over and
brushing with oil. Put a third sheet of filo on top and
place the last piece over the pie, tucking any edges in.

5 Brush the top with a little olive oil and bake
for 35–40 minutes. Set aside to cool for at least
10 minutes before serving hot or warm. This pie can
be refrigerated, covered, for up to 2 days. It can be
eaten cold, or reheated before use.

EQUIPMENT
8in x 13in (23cm x 34cm) baking pan

INGREDIENTS

FOR THE FILLING
1lb 5oz (600g) zucchini,
   trimmed and coarsely grated
1 tsp fine salt
6 tbsp olive oil
1 red onion, finely chopped
1 garlic clove, crushed
2 large eggs, beaten
1 tbsp Greek yogurt
3–4 tbsp chopped mint
freshly ground black pepper
7oz (200g) feta cheese, crumbled

FOR THE DOUGH
10 sheets store-bought filo dough
olive oil, for brushing

These light, delicate mini quiches are filled with the produce of an early summer harvest. Using cheese in the crust adds a sharpness, which contrasts nicely with the sweetness of the vegetables.

ZUCCHINI, FAVA BEAN, AND PEA MINI QUICHES

 MAKES 6   PREP 15 MINS PLUS CHILLING AND COOLING   COOK 35–40 MINS   FREEZE UP TO 1 MONTH

1 Preheat the oven to 350°F (180°C). In a food processor, spin the flour for a minute, then drop the butter down the chute in small pats. To make by hand, rub the butter into the flour until it resembles bread crumbs. Once incorporated, add the egg yolk, Parmesan, and some salt and pepper. Turn onto a work surface and bring the dough together with a little milk. Wrap in plastic wrap and chill for 30 minutes.

2 Bring a saucepan of salted water to a boil and drop in the fava beans. Blanch them for 3 minutes, then drain under cold running water, and shell them.

3 Grease the tart pans with butter, then dust with flour. Roll the dough out on a lightly floured surface and use to line the tart pans. Chill in the refrigerator for 10 minutes, then line the crusts with wax paper and baking beans and bake for 8 minutes. Remove paper and beans, set aside to cool, then fill with the vegetables.

4 Mix together the egg yolks and cream, add the chopped mint, season with some salt and pepper, and pour over the tarts, right up to the top. Bake for 25 minutes until the custard has just set. Let them stand for 5 minutes before serving with a few dressed mixed leaves.

EQUIPMENT
6 x 4in x 2in (10cm x 4cm) fluted tart pans, baking beans

INGREDIENTS

FOR THE DOUGH
(For visual step-by-step instructions, see pie dough p.104)
1½ cups all-purpose flour, plus extra for dusting
7 tbsp unsalted butter, plus extra for greasing
1 egg yolk
2oz (40g) vegetarian Parmesan-style cheese or regular Parmesan, grated
salt and freshly ground black pepper
a little milk

FOR THE FILLING
1½lb (650g) fava beans in the pod (or 8oz/220g frozen)
7oz (200g) zucchini, cut into ½in (1cm) cubes
14oz (400g) fresh peas (4–4½oz/120g podded weight)
6 large egg yolks
⅔ cup heavy cream
1 tbsp chopped mint

These savory tartlets are good served either as an individual portion or as small as you like for a quick and easy canapé. If you are making bite-sized ones, reduce the cooking time accordingly.

APPLE AND CAMEMBERT TARTLETS

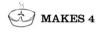 MAKES 4　　　　PREP 10 MINS　　　　COOK 25–30 MINS

EQUIPMENT
baking sheet

INGREDIENTS

FOR THE PASTRY
7oz (200g) ready-made puff pastry
(or to make your own, see pp.110–113)
all-purpose flour, for dusting
1 large egg yolk, beaten with a little water
1 tsp Dijon mustard

FOR THE FILLING
9oz (250g) Camembert cheese (underripe,
if possible), sliced very thinly
4 small sweet apples, such as
Fuji or Gala, sliced very thinly
salt and freshly ground black pepper

1 Preheat the oven to 400°F (200°C). Roll out the pastry on a lightly floured surface to about ¼in (5mm) thick. Cut out 4 x 6in (15cm) rounds with a saucer or a small plate. Brush the rounds with the egg yolk, and then with the mustard.

2 Lay 2 slivers of the sliced cheese over the pastry bases. If the cheese is too ripe to slice, pinch pieces off between your fingers and dot them over the surface of the pastry, leaving a ¾in (2cm) edge free. Lay the apple slices on top of the cheese in a circular pattern, overlapping them slightly. Season the apple with salt and pepper and finish the tarts by dotting the remaining cheese over the surface of the apple.

3 Bake for 25–30 minutes, until golden brown and puffed up. Cool for 5 minutes before serving.

These rustic pies are practically a national dish in Finland. They are made with rye flour and shaped into rough, hand-finished oval shapes, before being baked and topped with a traditional egg butter.

KARELIAN PIES

 MAKES 8   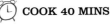 PREP 40 MINS   COOK 40 MINS
                                        PLUS CHILLING

1 Place the flours and salt in a large bowl and add 5–6 tablespoons cold water and mix well, to form a soft dough. Wrap in plastic wrap and chill in the refrigerator for 30 minutes.

2 Cook the potatoes in a saucepan of salted, boiling water for 15 minutes, or until tender. Drain, transfer to a food processor, and blend until smooth.

3 Heat the milk in a small pan until warm and add it to the food processor with the egg yolk, season, and process until well combined.

4 Place the eggs in a small pan of cold water, bring to a boil and simmer gently for 8 minutes. Remove from the pan, rinse under cold water, and set aside. Preheat the oven to 450°F (230°C) and line the baking sheets with parchment paper.

5 On a well-floured surface, divide the dough into 8 equal pieces. Form each piece of dough into a ball and roll it thinly into an oval shape about 4in x 6in (10cm x 15cm). Sprinkle each oval with rye flour and cover with a dish towel, to prevent it from drying out. Place a mound of the potato purée down the center of each oval (about 2 tablespoons), leaving a ¾in (2cm) border all around the edge. Fold the edges of the dough over and pinch them tightly to form an open oval pie.

6 Place the pies on baking sheets and brush the dough and potato with the melted butter. Bake for 10–15 minutes, until just starting to turn golden brown. Meanwhile, shell and finely chop the hard-boiled eggs. In a small bowl, cream the butter and stir in the chopped egg. Remove the pies from the oven and cover with a dish towel, so the crust does not harden. Serve the pies warm, topped with the egg butter.

EQUIPMENT
2 baking sheets

INGREDIENTS

FOR THE DOUGH
¾ cup rye flour,
  plus extra for dusting
¼ cup all-purpose flour,
  plus extra for dusting
½ tsp salt

FOR THE FILLING
1lb 2oz (500g) floury potatoes,
  such as Russet Burbanks, peeled
  and chopped into small chunks
salt
⅓ cup whole milk
1 large egg yolk
3 tbsp butter, melted

FOR THE EGG BUTTER
2 large eggs
8 tbsp butter, softened
salt and freshly ground black pepper

FRUIT PIES AND TARTS

A classic comfort food, apple pie is for many people the taste of home. Lard or vegetable shortening is used here to make the pie dough, but butter can easily be substituted if desired.

APPLE PIE

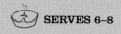 **SERVES 6–8**　　　　**PREP 30–35 MINS PLUS CHILLING**　　　　**COOK 50–55 MINS**　　　　**FREEZE UP TO 1 MONTH**

EQUIPMENT
9in (23cm) shallow pie dish

INGREDIENTS

FOR THE DOUGH
(For visual step-by-step instructions, see sweet pie dough p.105)
2 cups all-purpose flour, plus extra for dusting
½ tsp salt
1½ cups lard or vegetable shorening, plus extra for greasing
2 tbsp granulated sugar, plus extra for sprinkling
1 tbsp milk, to glaze

FOR THE FILLING
2¼lb (1kg) tart apples
juice of 1 lemon
2 tbsp all-purpose flour
½ tsp ground cinnamon, or to taste
¼ tsp grated nutmeg, or to taste
½ cup granulated sugar, or to taste

1 To make the dough, sift the flour and salt into a bowl. Add the fat, cutting it in with 2 butter knives, then rub the fat into the flour with your fingertips until the mixture resembles bread crumbs. Add the sugar. Sprinkle with 6–7 tablespoons cold water. Mix with a fork. Press the crumbs into a ball, wrap and chill for 30 minutes. Grease the dish.

2 Roll out two-thirds of the dough on a floured surface to a circle, 2in (5cm) larger than the dish. Using the rolling pin, drape the dough over the dish, then gently push it into the contours. Trim any excess dough, then chill for 15 minutes, until firm.

3 Peel, quarter, and core the apples. Set each quarter, cut-side down, on a cutting board and cut into slices, then put them in a bowl and pour on the lemon juice. Toss to coat. Sprinkle the flour, cinnamon, nutmeg, and sugar over the top and toss to coat. Arrange the apples in the dish so that it is slightly mounded in the center. Brush the edge of the dough with water. Roll the rest of the dough to an 11in (28cm) circle. Drape it over the filling and trim the top crust. Press the edges together to seal, crimping with the back of a knife as you go.

4 Cut an "X" in the top crust. Gently pull back the point of each triangle to reveal the filling. Roll out the trimmings, cut into strips, and moisten. Lay on the pie in a crisscross pattern. Brush the top with the milk, sprinkle the sugar over the top, and chill for 30 minutes. Preheat the oven to 425°F (220°C).

5 Bake for 20 minutes. Reduce to 350°F (180°C) and bake for 30–35 minutes. Insert a skewer to check that the apples are tender. Serve warm.

One of the best known of all desserts, this famous Austrian dish originated in Vienna. It traditionally uses a homemade strudel pastry, although filo dough works just as well and saves time.

APPLE STRUDEL

 SERVES 10–12   PREP 50 MINS PLUS RESTING   COOK 30–40 MINS

EQUIPMENT
baking sheet

INGREDIENTS

FOR THE FILLING
butter, for greasing
2¼lb (1kg) crisp apples,
such as Gala or Braeburn
grated zest of ½ lemon
3 tbsp rum
⅓ cup raisins
½ cup granulated sugar
a few drops of pure vanilla extract
⅓ cup blanched almonds, chopped

FOR THE DOUGH
4 x 10in x 18in (25cm x 45 cm)
sheets filo dough, (or to make your
own strudel pastry, see pp.114–115)
4 tbsp butter, melted
1–1½ cups fresh bread crumbs
confectioners' sugar, for dusting

1 Preheat the oven to 350°F (180°C). Grease a large baking sheet. To prepare the apples, peel, core, and cut the apples into small pieces. Choose crisp apples that are not too ripe, to ensure that the strudel does not turn soggy. Don't cut the fruit too small, since it will soften while baking.

2 Place the apple pieces into a bowl and mix together with the lemon zest, rum, raisins, granulated sugar, vanilla extract, and chopped almonds.

3 Place a sheet of filo on a clean work surface and brush with a little of the melted butter. Lay another filo sheet on top and brush with more melted butter. Repeat with the remaining filo sheets.

4 Sprinkle the bread crumbs over the dough, leaving a ¾in (2cm) border. Spoon the filling over the bread crumbs and fold the edges of the short sides that have been left uncovered over the filling. Roll the dough, starting from one of the longer sides, and press the ends together tightly. Transfer the strudel onto the baking sheet and brush with more butter.

5 Bake for 30–40 minutes, brushing the strudel with the remaining melted butter after the first 20 minutes.

6 Remove the strudel from the oven and set aside to cool on the baking sheet. Sprinkle liberally with confectioners' sugar and serve warm or cold. This strudel is good served with a spoonful of whipped cream.

Named after the French word for a "louvered shutter", the pastry is slashed to resemble a shutter, revealing the sweet, glistening apple filling inside. For variety, use pears instead of apples.

APPLE JALOUSIE

 **SERVES 6–8**   **PREP 1¼–1½ HRS PLUS CHILLING**   **COOK 30–40 MINS**   **FREEZE UP TO 1 MONTH**

1 To make the pastry, coarsely grate the butter into a bowl. Sift over the flour and salt and rub together with your fingertips until the mixture resembles coarse bread crumbs. Pour in ⅓–½ cup water and the lemon juice, and form a rough dough. Turn the dough onto a floured surface, work into a ball, then flatten it slightly. Place the dough in a plastic bag and chill for 20 minutes.

2 Thinly roll out the dough on a floured surface to form a long rectangle, with short sides of 10in (25cm). Take one-third of the dough and fold into the middle. Fold over the remaining third. Turn it over so the seams are easily sealed when it is re-rolled. Turn it by a quarter turn. Roll out again to a similar size as the original rectangle. Keep the short sides even in size.

3 Repeat the folding, turning, and rolling. Return it to the bag and chill for 20 minutes. Roll, fold, and turn the dough twice more, then chill for 20 minutes.

4 Melt the butter in a saucepan. Add the apples, ginger, and all but 2 tablespoons of the sugar and sauté and stir for 15–20 minutes, until the apples are tender and caramelized. Set aside to cool.

5 Roll out the dough on a floured surface to 11in x 13in (28cm x 32cm), then cut lengthwise in half. Fold one half lengthwise and cut across the fold at ¼in (5mm) gaps, leaving a border. Place the uncut dough on the baking sheet and spoon the apple filling along the center. Top with the cut dough and chill for 15 minutes. Preheat the oven to 425°F (220°C). Bake for 20–25 minutes. Brush with the egg white to glaze and sprinkle the remaining sugar over the top. Bake for 10–15 minutes. Serve the slices warm or at room temperature.

EQUIPMENT
baking sheet

INGREDIENTS

FOR THE PASTRY
(For visual step-by-step instructions, see quick puff pastry pp.112–113)
18 tbsp unsalted butter, frozen for 30 minutes
1⅛ cups all-purpose flour, sifted, plus extra for dusting
1 tsp salt
1 tsp lemon juice

FOR THE FILLING
1 tbsp unsalted butter
2¼lb (1kg) tart apples, peeled, cored, and cubed
1in (2.5cm) fresh ginger, finely chopped
½ cup granulated sugar
1 large egg white, beaten, to glaze

An all-time classic tart, this French dish uses a combination of puréed apple as a filling and finely sliced apple as a topping. Serve with vanilla ice cream for a delicious finale to a Sunday lunch.

TARTE AUX POMMES

 SERVES 8   PREP 20 MINS   COOK 1¼ HRS   ❄ FREEZE UP TO
                    PLUS CHILLING   1 MONTH

EQUIPMENT
9in (23cm) fluted tart pan,
baking beans

INGREDIENTS

FOR THE DOUGH
13oz (375g) store-bought sweet pie
dough (or to make your own, see p.105)
all-purpose flour, for dusting
2 tbsp apricot jam, sieved

FOR THE FILLING
4 tbsp butter
1lb 10oz (750g) apples,
peeled, cored, and chopped
½ cup granulated sugar
finely grated zest and juice of ½ lemon
2 tbsp Calvados or brandy
2 sweet apples

1 Roll the dough out on a lightly floured surface and use to line the tart pan. Trim around the top of the pan and prick the bottom of the dough with a fork. Chill the crust for 30 minutes.

2 Preheat the oven to 400°F (200°C). Line the crust with wax paper and fill with baking beans. Bake for 15 minutes. Remove the paper and beans, then return to the oven for another 5 minutes, or until the dough is a light golden color.

3 Melt the butter in a saucepan and add the chopped apples. Cover and cook over low heat, stirring occasionally, for 15 minutes, or until soft and mushy.

4 Push the cooked apple through a sieve to produce a smooth purée, then return it to the pan. Reserve 1 tablespoon granulated sugar and add the rest to the apple purée, then stir in the lemon zest and Calvados. Return the pan to the heat and simmer, stirring constantly until it thickens.

5 Spoon the purée into the crust. Peel, core, and thinly slice the sweet apples and arrange on top of the purée. Brush with the lemon juice and sprinkle with the reserved granulated sugar. Bake for 30–35 minutes, until the apple slices have softened and are starting to turn pale golden. Warm the apricot jam and brush it over the top. Cut into slices and serve.

These light, delicate individual tartlets couldn't be easier to make and can be ready in a matter of minutes. Make sure to coat the apple slices with the lemon juice to prevent them from discoloring.

APPLE AND ALMOND GALETTES

 MAKES 8   PREP 25–30 MINS   COOK 20–30 MINS
                        PLUS CHILLING

1 Roll out half the pastry on a lightly floured surface to a 14in (35cm) square, about ⅛in (3mm) thick. Using a 6in (15cm) plate as a guide, cut out 4 circles.

2 Sprinkle the baking sheets with water. Set the circles on a baking sheet, and prick each with a fork, avoiding the edge. Repeat with the remaining pastry. Chill for 15 minutes. Divide the marzipan into 8 portions and roll each into a ball.

3 Spread a sheet of parchment paper on the work surface. Set a ball of marzipan on the parchment, and cover with another sheet of parchment. Roll out the marzipan to a 5in (12.5cm) circle between the sheets and set on top of a pastry circle, leaving a border of ½in (1cm). Repeat with the remaining marzipan and pastry circles. Chill until ready to bake.

4 Cut the lemon in half, and squeeze the juice from one half into a small bowl. Peel, halve, and core the apples; then cut into thin slices. Drop the slices into the lemon juice and toss until they are coated.

5 Preheat the oven to 425°F (220°C). Arrange the apple slices, overlapping them slightly, in an attractive spiral over the marzipan circles. Leave a thin border of pastry dough around the edge. Bake for 15–20 minutes, until the pastry edges have risen around the marzipan and are light golden. Sprinkle the apples evenly with the granulated sugar.

6 Return to the oven and bake for 5–10 minutes, until the apples are golden brown, caramelized around the edges, and tender when tested with the tip of a small knife. Transfer to warmed serving plates, dust with a little confectioners' sugar, and serve at once.

EQUIPMENT
2 baking sheets

INGREDIENTS

FOR THE PASTRY
1lb 5oz (600g) store-bought puff pastry (or to make your own, see pp.110–113)
all-purpose flour, for dusting
confectioners' sugar, for dusting

FOR THE FILLING
7½oz (215g) marzipan
1 lemon
8 small, tart apples
¼ cup granulated sugar

This upside-down tart is a true French classic. The caramelized apples give a sweet, tangy flavor to the dish, and the rich sweet crust helps soak up any of the escaping juices.

APPLE TARTE TATIN

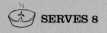 **SERVES 8**　　　**PREP 45–50 MINS PLUS CHILLING**　　　**COOK 35–50 MINS**

EQUIPMENT
9–10in (23–25cm) ovenproof frying pan or tatin dish

INGREDIENTS

FOR THE DOUGH
1⅓ cups all-purpose flour, plus extra for dusting
2 large egg yolks
1½ tbsp granulated sugar
a pinch of salt
5 tbsp unsalted butter, softened

FOR THE FILLING
14–16 apples, total weight about 5½lb (2.4kg)
1 lemon
8 tbsp unsalted butter
¾ cup granulated sugar

1 To make the dough, sift the flour into a bowl and make a well in the center. Add the egg yolks, sugar, salt, butter, and 1 tablespoon of water, and using your fingertips, work until mixed. Work in the flour until coarse bread crumbs form. Press the dough into a ball. On a floured surface, knead the dough for 2 minutes, until smooth. Wrap in plastic wrap, and chill in the refrigerator for 30 minutes, until firm.

2 For the filling, peel the apples, then halve and core them. Cut the lemon in half, and rub the apples all over with it. Melt the butter in the pan. Add the sugar and stir it together. Cook over medium heat, stirring occasionally, until caramelized. Set aside to cool to tepid.

3 Put the apple in concentric circles to fill the pan and cook over high heat for 15–25 minutes until caramelized. Turn once. Set aside to cool for 15 minutes. Preheat the oven to 375°F (190°C). Make the tatin (see below). Spoon some caramel over the apples. Serve with crème fraîche.

Constructing the tarte

1 Roll out the dough to a circle, 1in (2.5cm) larger than the pan. Drape it over the pan.

2 Tuck the edges of the dough down around the apples and bake for 20–25 minutes, until golden.

3 Set aside to cool to tepid, then set a plate on top, hold firmly together, and invert.

A traditional apple and blackberry crumble is given a wholesome twist with the addition of oats to the topping. These help to give the crumble a lovely chewy texture.

OATY BLACKBERRY AND APPLE CRUMBLE

SERVES 6–8   PREP 15–20 MINS   COOK 45 MINS   FREEZE UP TO 1 MONTH

1 Preheat the oven to 350°F (180°C). To make the filling, put the apples in the wide, shallow ovenproof dish and add the blackberries. Sprinkle the sugar over the fruit, then cover with foil and bake for 15 minutes, just to get the fruit to start to soften.

2 To make the crumble, work the butter and flour together with your fingertips until it resembles bread crumbs. Add the sugar, then the oats (you can do this in a food processor, but add the oats last so they don't get chopped too finely).

3 Remove the fruit from the oven, stir it briefly, and spread the crumble all over the top. Bake for another 30 minutes, or until the fruit is oozing out from beneath the golden crumble. Serve immediately with heavy cream or custard.

EQUIPMENT
2 quart ovenproof dish

INGREDIENTS

FOR THE FILLING
2¼lb (1 kg) apples, peeled, cored, and thickly sliced
12oz (350g) blackberries
⅓ cup dark brown sugar

FOR THE CRUMBLE TOPPING
(For visual step-by-step instructions, see crumble topping p.121)
8 tbsp butter, cubed
¾ cup all-purpose flour
⅔ cup dark brown sugar
1½ cups rolled oats

Not strictly a pie, but a popular French "pielike" classic, this recipe is great when eaten as a dessert, warm from the oven with thick cream, but will keep for several days to serve cold.

APPLE TOURTE WITH NUTS AND RAISINS

 SERVES 8   PREP 20 MINS   COOK 30–35 MINS   ❄ FREEZE UP TO 2 MONTHS

EQUIPMENT
8in (20cm) round springform cake pan

INGREDIENTS

7 tbsp unsalted butter, plus extra for greasing
½ cup granulated sugar
1 tsp pure vanilla extract
2 large eggs
1 cup self-rising flour
1 tsp ground cinnamon
2 sweet apples, peeled, cored, and finely sliced
¼ cup raisins
¼ cup coarsely chopped walnuts

1 Preheat the oven to 350°F (180°C). Grease and line the bottom of the cake pan. Melt the butter and set aside to cool.

2 Whisk the sugar, vanilla extract, and eggs together in a large bowl. Whisk in the cooled, melted butter until all the ingredients are thoroughly mixed. Sift in the flour and cinnamon, and fold it together well. Finally, fold in the apples, raisins, and walnuts.

3 Pour the mixture into the prepared cake pan and smooth the top. Bake for 30–35 minutes, until it is well risen and golden brown, and a skewer inserted into the center comes out clean.

4 Set the tourte aside to rest for at least 15 minutes before serving warm with whipped cream, or cold as a cake. Best eaten the same day, but can be stored, well wrapped, for up to 2 days.

Depending on whether you bought your blackberries or gathered them yourself, blackberries can vary in taste from very sweet to supersharp, so taste the filling as you go, adding sugar as required.

BLACKBERRY AND APPLE PIE

SERVES 4–6   PREP 35–40 MINS PLUS CHILLING   COOK 50 MINS – 1 HR   FREEZE UP TO 1 MONTH

EQUIPMENT
9½in (24cm) pie dish,
pie funnel

INGREDIENTS

FOR THE DOUGH
(For visual step-by-step instructions,
see sweet pie dough p.105)
1⅔ cups all-purpose flour,
plus extra for dusting
1½ tbsp granulated sugar
¼ tsp salt
3 tbsp lard or vegetable
shortening, chilled and cubed
4 tbsp unsalted butter,
chilled and cubed

FOR THE FILLING
2lb (875g) Granny Smith apples,
peeled, cored, and cubed
juice of 1 lemon
⅔ cup granulated sugar, or to taste
1lb 2oz (500g) blackberries

1 To make the dough, sift the flour, sugar, and salt into a bowl. Add the lard and butter, and rub together with your fingertips until the mixture resembles bread crumbs. Sprinkle water over the mix, 1 tablespoon at a time, stopping as soon as clumps form; too much water toughens the dough. Press the dough lightly into a ball, wrap in plastic wrap, and chill for 30 minutes.

2 For the filling, put the apples in a bowl, add the lemon juice and all but 2 tablespoons of sugar and toss until coated. Add the blackberries and toss again.

3 Roll out the dough on a lightly floured surface to a shape 3in (7.5cm) larger than the top of the pie dish. Invert the dish onto the dough. Cut a ¾in (2cm) strip off the dough, leaving a shape 1½in (4cm) larger than the dish. Turn the pie dish the right way up, place a pie funnel in the center, and spoon the fruit around.

4 Dampen the edge of the dish with water and transfer the strip of dough, pressing firmly. Brush the strip with cold water and transfer the dough top, pressing down to seal. Cut a hole over the pie funnel and trim the edges. Chill for 15 minutes.

5 Preheat the oven to 375°F (190°C). Bake for 50–60 minutes, until lightly browned and crisp. Sprinkle with the remaining sugar and serve hot or warm. The dough can be made 2 days ahead and stored in the refrigerator, wrapped in plastic wrap.

The classic fall pairing of sweet, soft apples and tart blackberries is given a twist here with a cobbler topping. Add a hint of ground cinnamon or apple pie spice for an additional layer of flavor.

APPLE AND BLACKBERRY COBBLER WITH CINNAMON

 SERVES 6–8   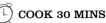 PREP 20 MINS   🕑 COOK 30 MINS

1 Preheat the oven to 375°F (190°C). For the filling, toss the apples and blackberries in the lemon juice, then mix them together with the 2 types of sugar. Put them in the dish and dot with the butter.

2 To make the cobbler topping, sift the flour, granulated sugar, salt, and cinnamon into a bowl. Rub in the butter with your fingertips until the mixture resembles fine bread crumbs. Whisk the egg and buttermilk together in another bowl, then add the liquid to the dry ingredients, and bring it together to form a soft, sticky dough.

3 Drop heaping tablespoonfuls of the dough over the surface of the fruit, leaving a little space between them. Sprinkle with the light brown sugar.

4 Bake for 30 minutes, or until golden and bubbling. The cobbler is ready when a skewer inserted into the center of the topping comes out clean. Set aside to cool for at least 5 minutes before serving with ice cream, custard, or cream.

EQUIPMENT
shallow ovenproof dish

INGREDIENTS

FOR THE FILLING
2¼lb (1kg) apples, peeled, cored, and thinly sliced
9oz (250g) blackberries
juice of ½ lemon
2 tbsp granulated sugar
2 tbsp light brown sugar
2 tbsp unsalted butter, chilled and cubed

FOR THE COBBLER TOPPING
(For visual step-by-step instructions, see cobbler dough pp.118–119)
1½ cups self-rising flour
⅓ cup granulated sugar
a pinch of salt
½–¾ tsp ground cinnamon, to taste
5 tbsp unsalted butter
1 large egg
⅓ cup buttermilk
1 tbsp light brown sugar

For a warm and satisfying dessert, a simple filling of apples, brown sugar, and spices is topped with a crunchy mix of buttery bread crumbs and baked until golden. Serve with whipped cream.

APPLE BROWN BETTY

 **SERVES 4**   **PREP 30 MINS**   **COOK 35–45 MINS**

EQUIPMENT
1 quart baking dish

INGREDIENTS

FOR THE TOPPING
6 tbsp butter
1¾ cups fresh bread crumbs

FOR THE FILLING
2lb (900g) apples, such as
Pink Lady, Granny Smith, or Golden
Delicious (about 4 apples)
¾ cup brown sugar
1 tsp ground cinnamon
½ tsp apple pie spice
zest of 1 lemon
2 tbsp lemon juice
1 tsp pure vanilla extract

1 Preheat the oven to 350°F (180°C). For the topping, melt the butter in a saucepan, add the bread crumbs, and mix well.

2 For the filling, peel, quarter, and core the apples. Cut each quarter into slices and place in a bowl. Add the sugar, cinnamon, apple pie spice, lemon zest and juice, and vanilla extract, and mix well.

3 Put half the apple mixture into the baking dish. Cover with half the bread crumbs, then put in the rest of the apples and top with the remaining bread crumbs.

4 Bake for 35–45 minutes, checking after 35 minutes. If it is getting too brown, reduce the oven temperature to 325°F (170°C) and cover with wax paper. It is cooked when the crumbs are golden brown and the apples are soft. Serve warm.

Here the mellow flavors of pears contrast with the nuttiness of the crust. Adding ground nuts such as walnuts, hazelnuts, or almonds to a sweet pie dough can make an elegant alternative to a simple dessert.

PEAR PIE WITH WALNUT CRUST

 SERVES 6–8   PREP 35–40 MINS   COOK 35–40 MINS
                            PLUS CHILLING

1 To make the dough, finely grind the walnuts with half the sugar in a food processor. Sift the flour onto a surface, add the ground nuts, and make a large well in the center. Put the egg, remaining sugar, butter, salt, and cinnamon into the well, and using your fingertips, work the ingredients until mixed, then work in the flour until coarse bread crumbs form. Press the dough into a ball. On a lightly floured surface, knead the dough for 1–2 minutes until very smooth. Form into a ball, wrap, and chill for 30 minutes until firm.

2 Brush the pan with melted butter, then roll out two-thirds of the dough on a floured surface to an 11in (28cm) circle. Rewrap and chill the unrolled dough. Line the pan with the rolled-out dough. Trim off the excess dough and add the trimmings to the chilled dough. Press the dough up the side of the pan, then chill in the refrigerator for 1 hour.

3 Peel the pears. Using the tip of a knife, cut out the stem and flower ends from each pear. Cut each pear into quarters, then scoop out the central stems and cores, being sure to remove all the hard fibers and working gently to keep the pear quarters intact. Put the pear wedges into a bowl. Add the black pepper and lemon juice, and toss until the pears are coated.

4 Shaking off the excess lemon juice, arrange the pears in a cartwheel pattern on the bottom of the crust. Roll out the dough to a 10in (25cm) circle; stamp out a circle from the center using a cutter and drape it over the pears. Trim the excess dough. Press the dough edges together to seal. Brush with water and sprinkle with sugar. Chill for 15 minutes. Preheat the oven to 375°F (190°C). Heat a baking sheet. Bake the pie on the sheet for 35–40 minutes, until browned.

EQUIPMENT
9in (23cm) tart pan with removable bottom,
2in (5cm) cookie cutter

INGREDIENTS

FOR THE DOUGH
2oz (60g) walnut pieces
⅔ cup granulated sugar
1⅓ cups all-purpose flour,
   plus extra for dusting
1 large egg
11 tbsp unsalted butter, slightly softened,
   plus extra for brushing
½ tsp salt
1 tsp ground cinnamon
1 tbsp granulated sugar, for sprinkling

FOR THE FILLING
2lb (875g) pears
½ tsp freshly ground black pepper
juice of 1 lemon

A classic frangipane-filled tart, this recipe hails from Normandy in northern France, where they grow the most wonderful pears. Best eaten warm or at room temperature the day it is made.

NORMANDY PEAR TART

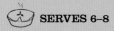 SERVES 6–8   PREP 40–45 MINS PLUS CHILLING   COOK 35–45 MINS   FREEZE UP TO 1 MONTH

1 For the dough, sift 1 cup flour onto a work surface, make a well in the center, add 3 egg yolks, ¼ cup sugar, salt, 5 tbsp butter, and vanilla and mix with your fingertips. Work the flour into the ingredients until the mixture resembles bread crumbs. If dry, add a little water. On a floured surface, knead for 1–2 minutes. Wrap and chill for 30 minutes. Grease the pan. Roll out the dough on a floured surface to a circle, 2in (5cm) larger than the pan, and use to line the pan. Prick the bottom with a fork. Chill for 15 minutes.

2 Preheat the oven to 400°F (200°C). Grind the almonds to a "flour" in a food processor; prepare the frangipane (see below). Toss the pears with the lemon juice. Spread the frangipane over the dough; place the pears in a spiral pattern. Set the pan on a baking sheet. Bake for 12–15 minutes. Reduce the heat to 350°F (180°C). Bake for 25–30 minutes until set. Melt the jam with the kirsch, and work it through a sieve. Cool, unmold, then brush with the glaze. Serve warm.

EQUIPMENT
9–10in (23–25cm) fluted tart pan with removable bottom

INGREDIENTS

FOR THE DOUGH
1 cup all-purpose flour, plus 2 tbsp extra
3 large egg yolks
¾ cup granulated sugar
a pinch of salt
14 tbsp unsalted butter, softened, plus extra for greasing
½ tsp pure vanilla extract

FOR THE FILLING
4½oz (125g) whole blanched almonds
1 large egg, plus 1 egg yolk
3–4 pears, peeled, cored, and cut in wedges
juice of 1 lemon
⅓ cup apricot jam
2–4 tbsp kirsch

For the frangipane

1 With an electric mixer, beat 9 tbsp butter and ½ cup sugar for 2–3 minutes, until fluffy.

2 Gradually add 1 egg and the remaining egg yolk, beating well after each addition.

3 Add 1 tablespoon kirsch, then gently stir in the almonds and remaining flour until well blended.

This may seem like a complicated recipe, but really it's just a few different stages, most of which are prepared ahead. The caramel sauce here is fabulous, and should become a staple recipe of any cook.

FLAKY PEAR TARTLETS

 MAKES 8   PREP 30–40 MINS   COOK 30–40 MINS
                                PLUS CHILLING
                                AND COOLING

EQUIPMENT
2 baking sheets

INGREDIENTS

FOR THE TARTLET BASES
1lb (450g) all-butter puff pastry
(or to make your own, see pp.110–113)
all-purpose flour, for dusting
1 large egg beaten with ½ tsp salt, to glaze
butter or oil, for greasing
4 pears
juice of 1 lemon
¼ cup sugar

FOR THE CARAMEL SAUCE
⅔ cup granulated sugar
½ cup heavy cream

FOR THE CHANTILLY CREAM
½ cup heavy cream
1–2 tsp confectioners' sugar
½ tsp pure vanilla extract

1 Sprinkle the baking sheets with cold water. Roll out the puff pastry on a lightly floured surface, then cut in half lengthwise, then cut diagonally at 4in (10cm) intervals along the length of each piece, to make 8 diamond shapes. Transfer to the prepared baking sheets and brush with the glaze. With the tip of a knife, score a border around each. Chill for 15 minutes.

2 Preheat the oven to 425°F (220°C). Bake the crusts for 15 minutes, until they start to brown, then reduce the temperature to 375°F (190°C) and bake for another 20–25 minutes, until golden and crisp. Transfer to wire racks to cool, then cut out the lid from each crust, and scoop out any undercooked pastry from inside.

3 For the caramel sauce, put ½ cup water in a saucepan, and dissolve the sugar. Boil, without stirring, until golden. Reduce the heat. Remove from the heat and add the cream. Heat gently until the caramel dissolves. Set aside to cool.

4 Pour the cream for the Chantilly cream into a bowl and whip until soft peaks form. Add the confectioners' sugar and vanilla extract, and continue whipping until stiff peaks form. Chill.

5 Grease a baking sheet. Preheat the broiler. Peel and core the pears. Thinly slice, keeping attached at the stalk end. With your fingers, flatten, transfer to the sheet, brush with lemon, and sprinkle with sugar. Broil until caramelized.

6 Place some Chantilly cream and a pear fan in each pastry crust. Pour a little cold caramel sauce over each fan, and partially cover with the pastry lids.

Canned pears are one of the few canned fruits that bake well. Fresh pears can be unpredictable—hard one day, overripe the next. Using a good-quality canned pear means you will have a soft, yielding filling.

PEAR AND ALMOND TART

 SERVES 8    PREP 20 MINS
                                PLUS CHILLING
                                AND COOLING   COOK 50 MINS

1 To make the dough, place the flour, sugar, and orange zest in a food processor. Add the butter and pulse until the mixture resembles bread crumbs. Add the egg and pulse until the dough gathers in a ball. Roll out the dough on a lightly floured surface and use to line the tart pan. Chill for 30 minutes.

2 Preheat the oven to 375°F (190°C). Place the tart pan on a baking sheet, cover the dough with wax paper, and fill with baking beans. Bake for 10 minutes, then remove the paper and beans, and bake for another 10 minutes. Cool on a wire rack.

3 Reduce the oven temperature to 325°F (170°C). Mix the mascarpone, sugar, egg, egg yolk, almond extract, and orange juice together until smooth and pour into the tart crust. Arrange the pears on top, scatter with the almonds, sprinkle with sugar, and bake for 30 minutes, or until just set.

4 Warm the marmalade through by stirring in a little hot water, sieve it, and gently brush it over the tart. Serve cold. Good with whipped cream or ice cream.

EQUIPMENT
9in (23cm) tart pan with removable bottom, baking beans

INGREDIENTS

FOR THE DOUGH
**(For visual step-by-step instructions,
   see sweet pie dough p.105)**
1 cup all-purpose flour, plus
   extra for dusting
¼ cup granulated sugar
1 tbsp grated orange zest
4 tbsp butter, chilled and cubed
1 large egg

FOR THE FILLING
4½oz (125g) mascarpone
½ cup granulated sugar,
   plus extra for sprinkling
1 large egg, plus 1 large egg yolk
1 tsp almond extract
2 tbsp fresh orange juice
4 canned pears, drained and sliced
½ cup sliced almonds, roasted
2 tbsp marmalade

Although apples are the fruit traditionally used for a Tarte Tatin, pears also work well in this recipe for an upside-down tart topped with sumptuous caramelized fruit. Serve with crème fraîche.

PEAR TARTE TATIN

 **SERVES 8**   **PREP 30 MINS PLUS CHILLING AND COOLING**   **COOK 45–55 MINS**

EQUIPMENT
9–10in (23–25cm) ovenproof pan
or tarte tatin dish

INGREDIENTS

FOR THE DOUGH
(For visual step-by-step instructions,
see sweet pie dough p.105)
1 cup all-purpose flour,
plus extra for dusting
2 large egg yolks
1½ tbsp granulated sugar
a pinch of salt
5 tbsp unsalted butter, softened

FOR THE FILLING
8 tbsp unsalted butter
¾ cup granulated sugar
12–14 pears, total weight
5½lb (2.4kg), peeled, halved, cored,
and rubbed with lemon halves

1 To make the dough, sift the flour into a large bowl and make a well in the center. Put the egg yolks, sugar, and salt in the well. Add the butter and 1 tablespoon water. Work the ingredients in the well with your fingertips until mixed. Work the flour into the ingredients until the mixture resembles coarse bread crumbs. Press the dough into a ball. On a floured surface, knead the dough for 2 minutes until smooth. Wrap in plastic wrap and chill for 30 minutes.

2 For the filling, melt the butter in the ovenproof frying pan. Add the sugar and stir together. Cook over medium heat for 3–5 minutes, stirring, until caramelized to a deep golden brown. Remove the pan from the heat, and set aside to cool.

3 Arrange the pears on their sides in the pan, with the tapered ends toward the center of the pan. Cook the pears over a high heat for 20–30 minutes until caramelized. Turn once to caramelize on both sides. The pears should be tender but still retain their shape, and very little juice should remain.

4 Remove the pan from the heat and set aside to cool for 10–15 minutes. Preheat the oven to 375°F (190°C). Roll out the dough on a lightly floured surface to a circle 1in (2.5cm) larger than the pan. Drape it over the pan and tuck the edges around the pears. Bake the tart for 20–25 minutes.

5 Set the tart aside to cool to tepid. Once cooled, set a plate on top, hold together, and invert. Spoon some caramel over the pears. The tart can be baked 6–8 hours ahead and warmed briefly on the stovetop before unmolding.

If you have any mincemeat left over after Christmas, try making this easy dessert. Using little more than a good-quality, store-bought puff pastry, a pear, and a jar of mincemeat, you'll have dessert in minutes.

BOOZY FRUIT AND NUT TURNOVER

 SERVES 8   PREP 15 MINS   COOK 30–40 MINS   FREEZE UP TO
                         PLUS SOAKING   1 MONTH

1 Mix the mincemeat with the cherries, apricots, brandy, and orange and lemon zest together in a bowl. Set aside for 30 minutes to soak.

2 Preheat the oven to 400°F (200°C). Lightly grease the baking sheet.

3 Lay 1 sheet of pastry on the prepared baking sheet, then spoon the mincemeat mixture on top, leaving a ¾in (2cm) border around the edges. Top with the pear slices and walnuts, then brush the border with beaten egg. Carefully place the second sheet of pastry on top of the first. Press the edges together, pinching the sides with your finger and thumb to decorate them.

4 Make a few slashes on the top with a knife for the steam to escape. Brush the pastry with the remaining beaten egg and bake for 30–40 minutes, until the pastry is golden brown and cooked through.

EQUIPMENT
baking sheet

INGREDIENTS

FOR THE FILLING
10oz (300g) mincemeat
2oz (50g) candied cherries,
   finely chopped
2oz (50g) dried apricots,
   finely chopped
2 tbsp brandy
zest of 1 orange
zest of 1 lemon
oil, for greasing
1 ripe pear, quartered, cored,
   peeled, and thinly sliced
½ cup chopped walnuts

FOR THE PASTRY
14oz (425g) store-bought puff pastry,
   rolled out into 2 x 11in x 8in (28cm x
   20cm) sheets (or to make your own,
   see pp.110–113)
1 large egg, beaten, to glaze

This recipe is so handy, because it really does make use of whatever fruit you have available. Try mixing a few of the orchard fruits and the soft fruits together to find your favorite combination.

FALL FRUIT TART

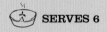 SERVES 6   PREP 20 MINS   COOK 1 HR
                     PLUS CHILLING

EQUIPMENT
8in (20cm) fluted tart pan
with removable bottom, baking beans

INGREDIENTS

FOR THE DOUGH
(For visual step-by-step instructions,
see sweet pie dough p.105)
1 cup all-purpose flour,
plus extra for dusting
1 tbsp granulated sugar
6 tbsp butter, chilled and cubed
1 large egg

FOR THE FILLING
4 sweet apples or pears
3 large egg yolks
¼ cup light brown sugar
¾ cup heavy cream
1 tsp pure vanilla extract
handful of blackberries, pitted,
plums, or blueberries
1 tsp ground cinnamon
2 tbsp granulated sugar

1 To make the dough, place the flour, sugar, and butter in a food processor and process until the mixture resembles bread crumbs. To make by hand, rub the butter into the flour with your fingertips until the mixture resembles bread crumbs. Add the egg and process or bring together with your hands, until it forms a ball. Roll out the dough on a lightly floured surface and use to line the pan. Using a fork, prick the bottom of the dough, and chill for 30 minutes.

2 Preheat the oven to 375°F (190°C). Line the tart crust with wax paper, fill with baking beans, and bake for 10 minutes. Remove the paper and beans and return to the oven for another 10 minutes, then take out and set aside to cool.

3 Meanwhile, for the filling, peel, core, and thinly slice the apples. Whisk together the egg yolks, brown sugar, cream, and vanilla extract. Arrange the apples and other fruits in the tart crust and pour over the cream mixture. Sprinkle the cinnamon and granulated sugar over the top and bake for 40–45 minutes, or until set. Set aside to cool in the pan and serve cold.

Using a mixture of vegetable shortening and butter gives this crust a light, flaky quality. Traditionally, lard or shortening was often the only fat used for pie dough, but use all butter if you prefer.

VICTORIAN PLUM PIE

SERVES 4–6 **PREP 35–40 MINS PLUS CHILLING** **COOK 1 HR 10 MINS** **FREEZE UP TO 1 MONTH**

1 To make the dough, sift the flour, sugar, if using, and salt into a bowl. Add the fat and cut into the mixture with 2 butter knives. Rub in the fat with your fingertips until the mixture resembles bread crumbs. Sprinkle 3–4 tablespoons water over the mixture, 1 tablespoon at a time, and mix with a fork until the crumbs are moist enough to stick together. Press into a ball, wrap, and chill for 30 minutes.

2 Preheat the oven to 350°F (180°C). Spread the walnut pieces evenly on a baking sheet and toast for 8–10 minutes until lightly browned, stirring occasionally so that they color evenly. Increase the oven temperature to 375°F (190°C).

3 Combine the plums, walnuts, and granulated sugar; taste, and add more sugar, if liked. Roll out the dough on a floured surface and trim to an oval 3in (7.5cm) larger than the top of the pie dish. Reserve the trimmings. Invert the pie dish onto the dough and cut a ¾in (2cm) strip from the edge of the dough, leaving an oval 1½in (4cm) larger than the dish. Set the dish, right-side up, on the surface. Place the pie funnel, if using, in the center and spoon the filling around it. With a pastry brush, moisten the edge of the dish with water. Lift the strip from around the oval of dough and transfer it to the edge of the dish, pressing it down firmly. Trim and brush the strip with water.

4 Roll the pie dough around a rolling pin and unroll it over the filling. Press down to seal. Cut a hole in the top of the crust so steam can escape. If using a funnel, cut the hole over the funnel. Trim, re-roll the trimmings, and cut leaves to decorate. Chill for 15 minutes. Meanwhile, preheat the oven to 375°F (190°C). Bake for 50 minutes to 1 hour, until crisp. Sprinkle with sugar while warm.

EQUIPMENT
1 quart oval pie dish,
pie funnel (optional)

INGREDIENTS

FOR THE DOUGH
1½ cups all-purpose flour,
  plus extra for dusting
1½ tbsp granulated sugar
¼ tsp salt
¼ cup vegetable shortening,
  chilled and cut into pieces
4 tbsp unsalted butter,
  chilled and cut into pieces
2 tbsp sugar, for sprinkling

FOR THE FILLING
1 cup walnut pieces
2⅛lb (1.15kg) plums,
  cut in half and pitted
½ cup granulated sugar,
  plus more to taste

Brown sugar and cinnamon add a sweet, dark, and spicy flavor to the plum filling. A cobbler topping can be used to cover any fruit suitable for cooking, making it a year-round favorite.

PLUM AND CINNAMON COBBLER

 SERVES 6–8　　PREP 20 MINS　　COOK 30 MINS

EQUIPMENT
shallow ovenproof dish

INGREDIENTS

FOR THE FILLING
2¼lb (1kg) plums, pitted and halved
¼ cup light brown sugar
1 tsp ground cinnamon
2 tbsp unsalted butter, chilled and cubed

FOR THE COBBLER TOPPING
(For visual step-by-step instructions, see cobbler dough pp.118–119)
1½ cups self-rising flour
2 tsp baking powder
⅓ cup granulated sugar
a pinch of salt
½–¾ tsp ground cinnamon, to taste
5 tbsp unsalted butter
1 large egg
⅓ cup buttermilk
1 tbsp light brown sugar

1 Preheat the oven to 375°F (190°C). For the filling, toss the plums with the light brown sugar and ground cinnamon. Put them in the dish and dot with the cubed butter.

2 To make the cobbler topping, sift the flour, baking powder, granulated sugar, salt, and cinnamon into a bowl. Rub in the butter until the mixture resembles fine bread crumbs. Whisk together the egg and buttermilk, then add the liquid to the dry ingredients, and bring it together to form a soft, sticky dough.

3 Drop heaping tablespoons of the dough over the surface of the fruit, leaving a little space between them. Sprinkle with the light brown sugar.

4 Bake for 30 minutes, or until golden and bubbling. The cobbler is ready when a skewer inserted into the center of the topping comes out clean. Set aside to cool for at least 5 minutes before serving with ice cream, custard, or cream.

Using a quick brioche base rather than the more usual pie dough, this delicious Bavarian specialty rises spectacularly on cooking, so that the soft doughy base encompasses the sweet, ripe plums.

BAVARIAN PLUM TART

🍲 SERVES 8–10   🥣 PREP 35–40 MINS PLUS RISING   ⏰ COOK 50–55 MINS

1 Sprinkle or crumble the yeast over ¼ cup lukewarm water in a bowl. Let stand for 5 minutes, until dissolved. Lightly grease a medium bowl. Sift the flour onto a surface, make a well in the center, and add the sugar, salt, yeast, and eggs. Using your fingertips, work the ingredients until mixed. Work in the flour to form a soft dough; add more flour if it is too sticky. On a floured surface, knead for 10 minutes until elastic. Work in more flour so that the dough is slightly sticky.

2 Add the butter to the dough; pinch and squeeze to mix it in, then knead until smooth. Shape into a ball and put it into the greased bowl. Cover and chill for 1½–2 hours, until doubled in size.

3 Brush the pan with melted butter. Knead the dough to punch down the air, then roll out on a floured surface to a 13in (32cm) circle and use to line the pan. Trim the excess dough. Sprinkle the bread crumbs over the bottom of the crust. Preheat the oven to 425°F (220°C). Put a baking sheet in the oven to heat.

4 Arrange the plums, cut-side up, in concentric circles on the brioche shell. Set aside at room temperature for 30–45 minutes, until the edge of the dough is puffed. Beat the yolks, two-thirds of the sugar, and the cream together. Sprinkle the plums with the remaining sugar and bake the tart on the baking sheet for 5 minutes. Reduce the heat to 350°F (180°C). Ladle the custard over the fruit and bake for another 45–50 minutes until the dough is browned, the fruit is tender, and the custard is set. Serve warm or at room temperature.

EQUIPMENT
11in (28cm) quiche dish

INGREDIENTS

FOR THE DOUGH
1½ tsp dried yeast, or ⅓oz (9g) fresh yeast
oil, for greasing
2¼ cups flour, plus extra for dusting
2 tbsp granulated sugar
1 tsp salt
3 large eggs
9 tbsp unsalted butter, softened, plus extra for brushing

FOR THE FILLING
2 tbsp dried bread crumbs
2lb (875g) purple plums, pitted and cut in half
2 large egg yolks
½ cup granulated sugar
¼ cup heavy cream

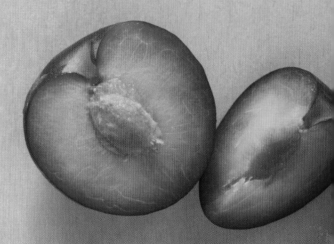

This perennial favorite never fails to delight family and friends. Make double or triple quantity of the crumble topping and store it in a plastic food bag in the freezer for last-minute desserts.

PLUM CRUMBLE

SERVES 4   PREP 10 MINS   COOK 30–40 MINS   FREEZE UP TO 2 MONTHS

EQUIPMENT
medium ovenproof dish

INGREDIENTS

FOR THE CRUMBLE TOPPING
(For visual step-by-step instructions, see crumble topping p.121)
1¼ cups all-purpose flour
7 tbsp butter, chilled, and cubed
½ cup light brown sugar
¾ cup rolled oats

FOR THE FILLING
1lb 5oz (600g) plums, pitted and halved
maple syrup or honey, to drizzle

1 Preheat the oven to 400°F (200°C). To make the crumble topping, place the flour in a large bowl and rub in the butter with your fingertips until the mixture resembles bread crumbs. Do not make the bread crumbs too fine or your crumble will have a soggy top. Stir in the sugar and oats.

2 Place the plums in the ovenproof dish, drizzle the maple syrup over the top, and top with the crumble mixture. Bake for 30–40 minutes, until the top is golden brown and the plum juices are bubbling. Serve hot. The crumble mixture can be made 1 month in advance and stored in the freezer until ready to use.

In France, all types of fruits are used to offset this rich, buttery crust and frangipane filling. Early summer could bring peaches, while fall heralds pear or prune variations.

NORMANDY PEACH TART

 SERVES 6–8   PREP 40–45 MINS PLUS CHILLING   COOK 35–45 MINS

1 Roll the dough out on a lightly floured surface and use to line the tart pan. Trim around the top of the pan and prick the bottom of the dough with a fork. Chill the crust for 30 minutes.

2 Preheat the oven to 400°F (200°C). Line the crust with wax paper and fill with baking beans. Bake for 15 minutes. Remove the paper and beans, then return to the oven for another 5 minutes, or until the dough is a light golden color.

3 Put a baking sheet inside the oven to heat up. For the frangipane, grind the almonds to a "flour" in a food processor. Put the butter and sugar in a large bowl and beat until fluffy. Add the egg and egg yolk and beat well. Add the kirsch, then stir in the almonds and flour. Spoon the mixture into the prepared crust.

4 Immerse the peaches in a saucepan of boiling water, leave for 10 seconds, then transfer to a bowl of cold water. Cut each peach in half, remove the pit, and peel off the skin. Cut each half into thin slices and arrange on the frangipane.

5 Set the pan on the preheated baking sheet and bake for 12–15 minutes. Reduce the oven temperature to 350°F (180°C) and bake for another 25–30 minutes, until the frangipane is puffed up and set. Set aside to cool.

6 Make a glaze by melting the jam with the extra kirsch in a small saucepan, then push the mixture through a sieve. Unmold the tart, then brush with the glaze. The tart is best eaten the same day but can be kept for 2 days in an airtight container.

EQUIPMENT
9–10in (23–25cm) tart pan with removable bottom, baking beans

INGREDIENTS

FOR THE FILLING
1 cup whole blanched almonds
8 tbsp unsalted butter,
  at room temperature
½ cup granulated sugar
1 large egg, plus 1 egg yolk
1 tbsp kirsch
2 tbsp all-purpose flour, sifted
2¼lb (1kg) ripe peaches

FOR THE DOUGH
13oz (375g) store-bought sweet pie dough
  (or to make your own, see p.105)
all-purpose flour, for dusting
⅓ cup apricot jam
2–3 tbsp kirsch, to glaze

Here the peaches are gently poached for a few minutes before assembling the cobbler, which helps to break them down when cooking. Really ripe, juicy peaches will need no such help.

PEACH COBBLER

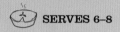 SERVES 6–8   PREP 20 MINS   COOK 30–35 MINS

EQUIPMENT
shallow ovenproof dish

INGREDIENTS

FOR THE FILLING
¼ cup granulated sugar
8 ripe peaches, peeled,
pitted, and quartered
1 tsp cornstarch
juice of ½ lemon

FOR THE COBBLER TOPPING
(For visual step-by-step instructions,
see cobbler dough pp.118–119)
1¼ cup self-rising flour
⅓ cup granulated sugar
a pinch of salt
½–¾ tsp ground cinnamon, to taste
5 tbsp unsalted butter
1 large egg
⅓ cup buttermilk
1 tbsp light brown sugar

1 Preheat the oven to 375°F (190°C). For the filling, heat the sugar and 3–4 tablespoons water in a large, heavy-bottomed saucepan. Once the sugar has dissolved, add the quartered peaches, cover, and cook over medium heat for 2–3 minutes.

2 Mix the cornstarch with the lemon juice to make a paste, then add it to the peaches. Continue to cook uncovered, over low heat, until the liquid thickens around the peaches. Transfer the peaches and syrup to the ovenproof dish.

3 To make the cobbler topping, sift the flour, sugar, salt, and cinnamon into a large bowl. Rub in the butter with your fingertips until the mixture resembles fine bread crumbs. Whisk together the egg and buttermilk in a separate bowl. Add the liquid to the dry ingredients and bring together to form a soft, sticky dough.

4 Drop heaping tablespoons of the dough over the surface of the fruit, leaving a little space between them. Sprinkle with the brown sugar. Bake for 25–30 minutes, until golden and bubbling. It is ready when a skewer inserted into the center of the topping comes out clean. Set aside to cool for 5 minutes before serving with ice cream, custard, or cream.

Choose perfectly ripe peaches to make this classic American pie. Cornstarch is often used to thicken the juices that the fruit yields upon cooking, but all-purpose flour can also be used.

PEACH PIE

 **SERVES 8**   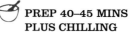 **PREP 40–45 MINS PLUS CHILLING**   **COOK 40–45 MINS**   ❄ **FREEZE UP TO 1 MONTH**

EQUIPMENT
9in (23cm) round pie pan

INGREDIENTS

FOR THE DOUGH
(For visual step-by-step instructions, see pie dough p.104)
1¾ cups all-purpose flour, plus extra for dusting
½ tsp salt
½ cup lard or vegetable shortening, chilled
5 tbsp unsalted butter, chilled
1 large egg, lightly beaten with ½ tsp salt, to glaze

FOR THE FILLING
4–5 ripe peaches
¼ cup all-purpose flour
⅔ cup granulated sugar
salt
1–2 tbsp lemon juice, to taste

1 To make the dough, sift the flour and salt into a bowl. Dice the lard and butter, and rub into the flour with your fingertips until the mixture resembles bread crumbs. Sprinkle with 3 tablespoons water and bring together to form a soft dough. Wrap in plastic wrap and chill in the refrigerator for 30 minutes.

2 Preheat the oven to 400°F (200°C). Put a baking sheet inside to heat. Roll out two-thirds of the dough on a floured surface and use to line the pan, making sure it overlaps the sides. Press the dough into the dish and chill for 15 minutes.

3 Immerse the peaches in boiling water for 10 seconds, then transfer to a bowl of cold water. Halve the peaches, remove the pits, and peel off the skins. Cut into ½in (1cm) slices and put it in a large bowl.

4 Sprinkle the peaches with the flour, sugar, a pinch of salt, and lemon juice, to taste. Carefully stir the peaches until they are coated, then transfer them to the crust, in the pie pan, with their juices.

5 Roll out the remaining dough into a rectangle. Cut out 8 strips, each ½in (1cm) wide and arrange them in a latticelike pattern on top of the pie, then trim the dough. Lightly beat the egg and ½ teaspoon salt together in a small bowl, and use to glaze the pie.

6 Bake for 40–45 minutes, until the dough is golden brown and the peaches are soft and bubbling. Serve warm. The pie can be kept in an airtight container for 2 days, but it is really best eaten on the day it is baked.

When peaches are plentiful, this Almond and Peach Tart is a fabulous dessert for entertaining. Making your own frangipane is easy, and you can vary the soft fruits you use according to the season.

ALMOND AND PEACH TART

 SERVES 8   PREP 20 MINS   COOK 30 MINS

1 Preheat the oven to 400°F (200°C) and put a baking sheet inside to heat up. Roll out the dough on a lightly floured surface to about ¼in (5mm) thick, then use it to line the tart pan. Trim away any excess dough and set the crust aside.

2 To make the filling, place the butter and sugar in a large bowl and beat with an electric hand mixer until creamy, then beat in the eggs. Mix in the ground almonds and flour until well combined, then smooth the mixture into the crust.

3 Press the peach halves cut-side down into the almond mixture. Sit the pan on the hot baking sheet, then bake for 30 minutes, or until the almond mixture is golden brown and cooked through. Serve cold or warm, dusted with confectioners' sugar.

EQUIPMENT
5in x 14½in (12cm x 36cm) rectangular tart pan

INGREDIENTS

FOR THE DOUGH
7oz (250g) store-bought sweet pie dough
  (or to make your own, see p.105)
flour, for dusting
confectioners' sugar, for dusting

FOR THE FILLING
7 tbsp butter, at room temperature
½ cup granulated sugar
2 large eggs
1 cup ground almonds
¼ cup all-purpose flour
4 peaches, halved and pitted

This beautiful fruit tart looks like the kind of thing that's only found in the best pâtisserie shop. However, with some good ingredients and a little patience, it is simple to re-create at home.

EXOTIC FRUIT TART

 SERVES 8　　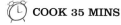 **PREP 30 MINS PLUS COOLING**　　 **COOK 35 MINS**

EQUIPMENT
9½in (24cm) fluted tart pan with removable bottom, baking beans

INGREDIENTS

FOR THE DOUGH
9½oz (270g) store-bought filo dough
(6 x 10in x 17in [26cm x 44cm] sheets)
3 tbsp unsalted butter, melted

FOR THE FILLING
3½oz (100g) dark chocolate with ginger
1¼ cups heavy cream
9oz (250g) mascarpone
7oz (200g) raspberries
1–2 tbsp raspberry liqueur
3 pieces stem ginger,
or 3 pieces candied ginger, finely chopped
1 tbsp stem ginger syrup,
plus extra for drizzling
6oz (150g) fresh pineapple slices
1 kiwi fruit, sliced
2oz (60g) fresh mango pieces

1 Preheat the oven to 400°F (200°C). Place a sheet of filo dough in the tart pan with the edges hanging over the sides. Brush it generously with melted butter and place another sheet of dough across the first, so they form a cross shape in the bottom. Brush with more butter. Repeat the filo layers, until all the filo dough is used up and the bottom of the pan is completely covered. Roughly trim the edges, so they are overhanging by about ½in (1cm).

2 Place the pan on a baking sheet, line with parchment paper, and fill with baking beans. Bake for 20 minutes, then remove the beans and paper and bake for another 5 minutes, or until the dough is cooked and golden brown. Set aside to cool in the pan, then remove from the pan and place on a serving plate.

3 For the filling, melt the chocolate in a heatproof bowl over a saucepan of simmering water. Spoon the melted chocolate into the crust and spread it over the bottom in an even layer with the back of a spoon. Whip the cream in a large bowl and stir in the mascarpone. Add half the raspberries and crush them with the back of a spoon. Stir in the liqueur to taste, chopped ginger, and syrup.

4 Just before serving, spoon the raspberry and ginger cream into the tart crust. Arrange the pineapple slices around the edge of the tart, followed by the kiwi slices, and then the mango pieces. Place a raspberry in the center of the tart and in any spaces between the fruit, in a symmetrical pattern. Drizzle a little ginger syrup over the fruit and serve.

For a tropical twist on a classic Tarte Tatin, try substituting slices of mango for the apples. These delicious tartlets make a quick dessert for entertaining, especially when mangoes are in season.

CARAMELIZED MANGO TARTLETS

 MAKES 6   PREP 40–45 MINS   COOK 30 MINS
PLUS CHILLING
AND COOLING

1 To make the dough, combine the yolks and vanilla. In a food processor, pulse the flour, sugar, and salt for 5 seconds. Add the butter and pulse until the mixture resembles coarse bread crumbs. Add the egg yolks, and work until the mixture resembles peas. If dry, work in 1–2 tablespoons water. On a floured surface, knead the dough until smooth. Chill for 30 minutes.

2 Gently heat the sugar and ½ cup water in a saucepan until dissolved. Boil, without stirring, until the mixture starts to turn golden around the edge. Reduce the heat and cook, swirling the pan once or twice so the syrup colors evenly, until the caramel is medium golden. Immediately plunge the pan into a bowl of cold water. Pour one-sixth of the caramel into the bottom of the baking dishes, tilting the dishes to coat with a thin layer. Set aside to cool.

3 Peel and cut each mango lengthwise on both sides of the pit. Cut the remaining flesh away from each pit in 2 long slices, and set aside. Discard the pits. Cut each large piece of mango into 3 diagonal slices. Arrange 3 slices, cut-side up, on top of the caramel in the dishes.

4 Preheat the oven to 400°F (200°C). On a floured surface, shape the dough into a cylinder about 12in (30cm) long and cut it into 6 equal pieces. Shape each piece into a ball and roll them out to 6 x 5in (12cm) circles. Drape the circles over the dishes and tuck the edge down around the mango slices. Chill for 15 minutes. Bake for 20–25 minutes, until golden.

5 Purée the reserved mango in a food processor. Stir in the lime juice, taste, and add more confectioners' sugar or juice. Chill and serve with the tartlets out of their dishes.

EQUIPMENT
6 x 4in (10cm) baking dishes

INGREDIENTS

FOR THE DOUGH
(For visual step-by-step instructions, see sweet pie dough p.105)
3 large egg yolks
½ tsp pure vanilla extract
1¼ cups all-purpose flour, plus extra for dusting
¼ cup granulated sugar
¼ tsp salt
6 tbsp unsalted butter, cut into pieces

FOR THE FILLING
¾ cup granulated sugar
4 mangoes, total weight about 3½ lb (1.5kg)
juice of ½ lime, or to taste
1–2 tbsp confectioners' sugar (optional)

This classic French tart is filled with a delicate custard and juicy apricots. Canned apricots are often more reliable than fresh ones, but if you have some ripe apricots do use them instead.

APRICOT TART

SERVES 6–8   PREP 30 MINS PLUS CHILLING   COOK 50 MINS – 1 HR   FREEZE CRUST, UP TO 3 MONTHS

1 To make the dough, rub the flour, sugar, and butter together by hand, or in a food processor, until the mixture resembles fine bread crumbs. Add the egg yolk and bring the mixture together to form a soft dough. Add a little more water if needed. Wrap and chill for 30 minutes. Preheat the oven to 350°F (180°C).

2 Roll out the dough on a floured surface to ⅛in (3mm) thick and use to line the tart pan, leaving an overhang of at least ½in (1cm). Trim off any excess dough that hangs down farther than this. Prick the bottom with a fork, brush with the egg white to seal, line the tart crust with a piece of silicone or wax paper, and fill with baking beans. Place the crust on a baking sheet and bake for 20 minutes. Remove the beans and paper, and bake for another 5 minutes, if the center looks uncooked. Trim off any ragged edges from the tart crust while still warm.

3 Whisk the cream, sugar, eggs, egg yolk, and vanilla together in a large bowl. Lay the apricots, face down, evenly over the bottom of the cooked tart crust. Place the tart crust on a baking sheet and pour the cream mixture carefully over the fruit. Bake for 30–35 minutes, until lightly golden and just set. Set the tart aside to cool to room temperature before dusting with confectioners' sugar and serving with fresh cream.

EQUIPMENT
9in (22cm) tart pan with removable bottom, baking beans

INGREDIENTS

FOR THE DOUGH
(For visual step-by-step instructions,
see sweet pie dough p.105)
1½ cups all-purpose flour,
plus extra for dusting
2 tbsp granulated sugar
7 tbsp unsalted butter,
at room temperature, cut into pieces
1 large egg yolk, beaten with 2 tbsp cold
water, plus 1 large egg white, for
brushing

FOR THE FILLING
¾ cup heavy cream
¼ cup granulated sugar
2 large eggs, plus 1 large egg yolk
½ tsp pure vanilla extract
14oz can apricot halves, drained
confectioners' sugar, for dusting

Heady with the aroma of warming spices, these fruity parcels are best eaten warm, or at room temperature. Dust them with some cinnamon-laced confectioners' sugar before serving with vanilla ice cream.

FILO APRICOT TURNOVERS

MAKES 24   PREP 35–40 MINS   COOK 40 MINS   FREEZE UP TO 1 MONTH

EQUIPMENT
baking sheet

INGREDIENTS

FOR THE FILLING
1 lemon
1lb 2oz (500g) apricots, pitted, halved, and cut into 4–5 pieces
¾ cup granulated sugar
1 tsp ground cinnamon
a pinch of ground nutmeg
a pinch of ground cloves

FOR THE DOUGH
1lb 2oz (500g) store-bought filo dough
12 tbsp unsalted butter

1 For the filling, grate the zest from half of the lemon. In a medium saucepan, combine the apricots, lemon zest, ⅔ cup sugar, cinnamon, nutmeg, and cloves. Add 2 tablespoons water and cook gently for 20–25 minutes, stirring occasionally, until the mixture thickens to the consistency of jam. Transfer to a bowl and set aside to cool. Preheat the oven to 400°F (200°C).

2 Lay a dish towel on the work surface and sprinkle it lightly with water. Unroll the filo dough and cut them lengthwise in half. Cover them with a second damp dish towel. Melt the butter in a small pan. Take one half sheet of filo and and lightly brush half of it lengthwise with butter. Fold the other half on top.

3 Brush the strip of dough with more melted butter. Spoon 1–2 teaspoons of the cooled apricot filling onto it, about 1in (2.5cm) from one end. Fold a corner of the filo strip over the filling to meet the other edge of filo, forming a triangle. Continue folding the strip over and over to form a triangle with the filling inside. Set the triangle with the final edge underneath, and cover with a dampened dish towel.

4 Continue making the filo triangles. Brush the top of each triangle with the rest of the melted butter and sprinkle with the remaining sugar. Bake for 12–15 minutes, until golden brown and flaky. Transfer the turnovers to the rack to cool slightly, and serve warm or at room temperature. The filo turnovers can be prepared up to 2 days in advance and kept in the refrigerator. Bake just before serving.

This traditional German tart shares a common base of flavors with the great British classic, the Bakewell Tart. The tart can be stored in an airtight container for up to 2 days; the flavor will mellow.

ALMOND AND RASPBERRY LATTICE TART

SERVES 6–8   **PREP 30–35 MINS PLUS CHILLING**   **COOK 50 MINS – 1 HR**

1 Sift the flour into a bowl. Mix in the spices and nuts, and make a well. Mix the butter, yolk, ½ cup sugar, salt, zest, and juice with your fingertips, add to the well, and work in the flour until bread crumbs form. Shape into a ball, knead, wrap, and chill for 1–2 hours.

2 Cook the rest of the sugar and berries in a saucepan for 10–12 minutes, until thick. Cool. Press half of the fruit through a sieve. Stir in the remaining pulp. Grease the pan. Preheat the oven to 375°F (190°C).

3 Roll out two-thirds of the dough on a floured surface into an 11in (28cm) circle and line the pan. Trim any excess dough and add the filling in the crust. Roll the remaining dough to a 6in x 12in (15cm x 30cm) rectangle for the lattice top (see below). Bake for 15 minutes, reduce to 350°F (180°C), and bake for 25–30 minutes. Cool and dust with confectioners' sugar to serve.

EQUIPMENT
9in (23cm) tart pan with removable bottom, fluted pastry wheel (optional)

INGREDIENTS

FOR THE DOUGH
¾ cup all-purpose flour, plus extra
  for dusting
a pinch of cloves and ½tsp ground cinnamon
1¾ cups ground almonds
8 tbsp butter, plus extra for greasing
1 large egg yolk
1 cup granulated sugar
¼ tsp salt
grated zest of 1 lemon and juice of ½ lemon

FOR THE FILLING
13oz (375g) raspberries

For the lattice top

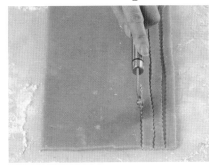

1 Using a fluted wheel for a decorative edge, cut the dough into 12 x ½in (12 x 1cm) strips.

2 Arrange half the strips from left to right over the tart, 1in (2.5cm) apart. Turn the tart 45°.

3 Put strips diagonally on top. Trim, re-roll trimmings, cut 4 strips, fix to edge, and chill for 15 minutes.

This dainty tart is wonderful for a traditional tea. The usual custard filling is replaced by a mixture of cream cheese and sour cream— a perfect foil for the sharp sweetness of the raspberries.

RASPBERRY CREAM CHEESE TART

 SERVES 8   PREP 25 MINS PLUS CHILLING   COOK 35–45 MINS

EQUIPMENT
9in (23cm) tart pan with removable bottom, baking beans

INGREDIENTS

FOR THE DOUGH
(For visual step-by-step instructions, see sweet pie dough p.105)
1 cup all-purpose flour, plus extra for dusting
6 tbsp butter, cubed
2 tbsp granulated sugar
1 large egg yolk

FOR THE FILLING
4oz (115g) cream cheese
¼ cup sour cream
¼ cup granulated sugar
a pinch of grated nutmeg
3 large eggs, beaten
zest of 1 lemon
12oz (350g) raspberries
confectioners' sugar, for dusting

1 To make the dough, place the flour, butter, and sugar in a food processor, and pulse until it resembles bread crumbs. Alternatively, to make by hand, rub the butter into the flour with your fingertips until it resembles bread crumbs, then stir in the sugar.

2 Add the egg yolk to the mixture and mix to a firm dough. Roll out the dough on a lightly floured surface and use to line the pan. Prick the bottom of the crust with a fork and chill for 30 minutes. Preheat the oven to 400°F (200°C).

3 Line the crust with wax paper and fill with baking beans. Bake for 10 minutes, then remove the paper and beans and bake for another 10 minutes, or until pale golden. Remove from the oven and reduce the temperature to 350°F (180°C).

4 For the filling, beat together the cream cheese, sour cream, sugar, nutmeg, eggs, and lemon zest until well combined. Pour into the crust and scatter the raspberries over the surface. Bake for 25–30 minutes, or until just set. Set aside to cool before transferring to a serving plate. Serve warm or cold, dusted with confectioners' sugar.

Fresh raspberries and dark chocolate are a classic combination and here they combine to make the ultimate in luxurious desserts. Try to use the best-quality dark chocolate that you can find.

RASPBERRY TART WITH CHOCOLATE CREAM

 SERVES 6–8   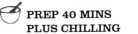 PREP 40 MINS PLUS CHILLING   🕐 COOK 20–25 MINS   ❄ FREEZE CRUST, UP TO 3 MONTHS

1 To make the dough, rub the flour, cocoa, and butter together with your fingertips until they resemble fine bread crumbs. Stir in the sugar. Beat the egg yolk with the vanilla and add to the flour mixture, bringing it together to form a soft dough. Add a little water if it seems too stiff. Wrap and chill for 30 minutes.

2 Preheat the oven to 350°F (180°C). Roll out the dough on a lightly floured surface to ⅛in (3mm) thick and use to line the pan. Leave an overlapping edge of ¾in (2cm), and trim the excess with scissors. Prick the bottom of the dough with a fork, then line the crust with parchment paper and fill with baking beans. Place on a baking sheet and bake for 20 minutes. Remove the beans and paper, and bake for another 5 minutes. Trim the excess dough.

3 For the filling, beat together the sugar, cornstarch, eggs, and vanilla. Put the milk and 4oz (100g) of the chocolate in a saucepan and bring to a boil, whisking constantly. Remove just as it starts to bubble. Pour the milk onto the egg mixture, whisking constantly. Return to the cleaned-out pan and bring to a boil, whisking. When it thickens, reduce the heat to its lowest and cook for 2–3 minutes, whisking. Turn into a bowl, cover with plastic wrap, and cool.

4 Melt the remaining chocolate in a bowl set over a pan of simmering water, and brush the inside of the crust. Put aside to set. Beat the crème pâtissière with a wooden spoon, and spread over the crust. Arrange the raspberries on top and remove from the pan. Dust with confectioners' sugar. Best eaten the same day.

EQUIPMENT
9in (22cm) tart pan with removable bottom, baking beans

INGREDIENTS

FOR THE DOUGH
(For visual step-by-step instructions, see sweet pie dough p.105)
1 cup all-purpose flour, plus extra for dusting
¼ cup cocoa powder
7 tbsp unsalted butter, chilled and cubed
¼ cup granulated sugar
1 large egg yolk
½ tsp pure vanilla extract

FOR THE FILLING
½ cup granulated sugar
½ cup cornstarch, sifted
2 large eggs
1 tsp pure vanilla extract
2 cups whole milk
6oz (175g) good-quality dark chocolate, broken into pieces
14oz (400g) raspberries
confectioners' sugar, for dusting

For a simple yet tasty alternative to a pie crust, try making these cookie-based crusts instead. Make a few extra and freeze the rest for an instant dessert another time.

RASPBERRY TARTLETS WITH CRÈME PÂTISSIÈRE

 MAKES 6   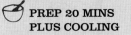 PREP 20 MINS PLUS COOLING   COOK 10 MINS   FREEZE CRUSTS, UP TO 2 MONTHS

1 Preheat the oven to 350°F (180°C). To make the crust, crush the wafers in a food processor, or by hand using a rolling pin, until they resemble fine bread crumbs. Mix the cookie crumbs, sugar, and melted butter, until the mixture resembles wet sand.

2 Divide the cookie mixture between the tartlet pans and press it firmly into the bottom of each pan, allowing it to come up the sides as it spreads out. Bake for 10 minutes, then set aside to cool. Once cooled, store the tart crusts in the refrigerator until needed.

3 For the crème pâtissière, beat together the sugar, cornstarch, eggs, and vanilla extract in a bowl. In a saucepan, bring the milk to a boil, and remove from the heat just as it starts to bubble up. Pour the hot milk onto the egg mixture, whisking constantly. Return the custard to the pan, and bring to a boil, whisking constantly to prevent lumps. As the custard heats it will thicken considerably. At this point reduce the heat to low and cook for another 2–3 minutes.

4 Turn the thickened crème pâtissière out into a bowl, cover the surface of it with plastic wrap (to prevent a skin from forming), and set it aside to cool. Once it is cold, beat it well with a wooden spoon before use.

5 When you are ready to assemble the tartlets, spoon, or pipe, the crème pâtissière into the crusts. Top with raspberries, and dust with confectioners' sugar to serve. The tart crusts can be chilled for up to 3 days, and the crème pâtissière for up to 2 days, well covered.

EQUIPMENT
6 x 4in (10cm) loose-bottomed tartlet pans

INGREDIENTS

FOR THE COOKIE CRUST
(For visual step-by-step instructions, see cookie crust p.120)
7oz (200g) vanilla wafers
¼ cup granulated sugar
7 tbsp butter, melted and cooled

FOR THE FILLING
½ cup granulated sugar
⅓ cup cornstarch
2 large eggs
1 tsp pure vanilla extract
1¾ cup whole milk
raspberries
confectioners' sugar, for dusting

A great standby dessert, this Italian favorite is little more than a large jam tart decorated with a crust top. Use whatever jam you have available, and try making individual ones for children.

CROSTATA DI MARMELLATA

🍲 SERVES 6–8   🥄 PREP 30 MINS   🕐 COOK 50 MINS   ❄ FREEZE CRUST,
                              PLUS CHILLING   UP TO 3 MONTHS

EQUIPMENT
9in (22cm) tart pan with
removable bottom, baking beans

INGREDIENTS

FOR THE DOUGH
(For visual step-by-step instructions,
see sweet pie dough p.105)
1⅓ cups all-purpose flour,
plus extra for dusting
7 tbsp unsalted butter,
chilled and cubed
¼ cup granulated sugar
1 large egg yolk, plus 1 large egg,
beaten, to glaze
2 tbsp milk, plus extra if needed
½ tsp pure vanilla extract

FOR THE FILLING
14oz jar good-quality raspberry,
cherry, or apricot jam

1 To make the dough, rub the flour and butter together with your fingertips until fine bread crumbs form. Stir in the sugar. Beat the egg yolk with the milk and vanilla extract, and add it to the dry ingredients, bringing the mixture together to form a soft dough. Use an extra tablespoon of milk if the mixture seems a little dry. Wrap in plastic wrap and chill for 30 minutes.

2 Preheat the oven to 350°F (180°C). Roll out the dough on a well-floured surface to ⅛in (3mm) thick. If it begins to crumble, bring it together again with your hands and gently knead to get rid of any cracks. Line the pan with dough, leaving an overlapping edge of ¾in (2cm) and trim away any excess dough. Prick the bottom of the dough with a fork, then roll up the excess and chill for later use.

3 Line the crust with parchment paper and fill with baking beans. Place it on a baking sheet and bake for 20 minutes. Remove the beans and paper, and bake for another 5 minutes if the center still looks uncooked. Increase the heat to 400°F (200°C).

4 Spread the jam in a ½–¾in (1–2cm) layer over the crust. Roll out the remaining dough into a square just larger than the tart and ⅛in (3mm) thick. Cut the dough into 12 strips, each ½in (1cm) wide, and use these to top the tart in a latticelike pattern.

5 Use beaten egg to secure the strips to the sides of the tart and to gently brush the lattice. Bake for 20–25 minutes until the lattice is cooked through and golden brown on top. Cool for 10 minutes before eating. Serve while still warm or at room temperature. The tart will keep in an airtight container for 2 days.

Strawberry shortbread is another favorite dessert, but by making the shortbread into a tart the filling is better contained for a more elegant finish. Try this with raspberries when they are in season.

STRAWBERRIES AND CREAM SHORTBREAD TARTLETS

 MAKES 4   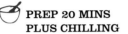 PREP 20 MINS PLUS CHILLING   COOK 15–20 MINS   FREEZE UP TO 2 MONTHS

1 To make the dough, mix the flour, cornstarch, and granulated sugar together in a large bowl until well combined. Rub in the butter with your fingertips until the mixture resembles bread crumbs, then bring the mixture together to form a soft dough. Wrap in plastic wrap and chill for 30 minutes.

2 Preheat the oven to 325°F (170°C). Roll out the dough on a well-floured surface to about ¼in (5mm) thick. This dough is very delicate, so if you find it hard to roll out, divide it equally between the tartlet pans and use your fingers to press it into the bottom and sides of the pans to form the tartlet crusts. Cut out 6 circles and use to line the bottom and the sides of the tartlet pans. Prick the bottom of the dough with a fork and place them on a baking sheet.

3 Bake the tartlet crusts for 15–20 minutes until they start to brown at the edges. Remove them from the oven and set aside to cool completely before carefully removing them from the pans.

4 Fill the tartlet crusts with the whipped heavy cream and top with the strawberry slices, layered over each other to cover the cream filling. Dust with confectioners' sugar to serve within 30 minutes of assembling. The cooked crusts can be stored in an airtight container for up to 3 days. These tartlets are best eaten on the same day they are made.

EQUIPMENT
4 x 4in (10cm) fluted tartlet pans with removable bottoms

INGREDIENTS

FOR THE DOUGH
(For visual step-by-step instructions, see sweet pie dough p.105)
¾ cup all-purpose flour, plus extra for dusting
2 tbsp cornstarch
¼ cup granulated sugar
7 tbsp butter, at room temperature

FOR THE FILLING
⅔ cup heavy cream (crème pâtissière can be used, see p.260)
8–10 large ripe strawberries, thinly sliced, or raspberries can be used
confectioners' sugar, for dusting

This sumptuous Strawberry Tart would take center stage at any meal. Master the art of the delicate crust and the crème pâtissière, then use whatever soft fruits are in season. Eat on the day it is made.

STRAWBERRY TART

SERVES 6–8   **PREP 40 MINS PLUS CHILLING**   **COOK 25 MINS**   **FREEZE CRUST, UP TO 3 MONTHS**

EQUIPMENT
9in (22cm) tart pan with removable bottom, baking beans

INGREDIENTS

FOR THE DOUGH
(For visual step-by-step instructions, see sweet pie dough p.105)
1¼ cups all-purpose flour, plus extra for dusting
7 tbsp butter, chilled and cubed
⅔ cup granulated sugar
2 large eggs, plus 1 large egg yolk
½ tsp pure vanilla extract
6 tbsp red currant or sour cherry jelly, to glaze

FOR THE CRÈME PÂTISSIÈRE
⅓ cup cornstarch
1 tsp pure vanilla extract
1¾ cups whole milk
10oz (300g) strawberries, thickly sliced

1 For the dough, rub the flour and butter together with your fingertips until the mixture resembles bread crumbs. Stir in ¼ cup sugar. Whisk the yolk and vanilla, and add to the flour. Bring together to form a dough. Wrap and chill for 30 minutes.

2 Preheat the oven to 350°F (180°C). Roll out the dough on a floured surface to ⅛in (3mm) thick and use to line the pan, leaving an overlapping edge of ¾in (2cm). Trim away any excess dough. Prick the bottom of the dough, line with parchment paper, and fill with baking beans. Put on a baking sheet and bake for 20 minutes. Remove the beans and paper and bake for another 5 minutes. Trim off excess dough. Melt the jelly with 1 tablespoon water and brush a little over the crust. Set aside to cool.

3 Make the crème pâtissière (see below), then spread over the crust. Top with strawberries. Reheat the jelly glaze, brush over the strawberries, then set.

Making crème pâtissière

1 Whisk rest of sugar, cornstarch, eggs, and vanilla. Bring milk to a boil; take off heat just as it bubbles.

2 Pour the milk into the egg mix, whisking. Return to the pan and boil over medium heat, whisking.

3 When it thickens, reduce the heat to low, and cook for 2–3 minutes. Put in a bowl, cover, and cool, then beat.

This is a great recipe for any cook who is lucky enough to grow both of these in the garden. This homey double-crusted pie is best served with vanilla ice cream or thick whipped cream.

RHUBARB AND STRAWBERRY PIE

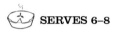 SERVES 6–8   PREP 30–35 MINS   COOK 50–55 MINS
                              PLUS CHILLING

1 To make the dough, sift the flour and salt into a bowl. Add the shortening and cut it into the flour mixture with 2 butter knives or a dough blender. Rub the shortening into the flour with your fingertips until the mixture forms coarse bread crumbs. Sprinkle 6–7 tablespoons water over the mixture, 1 tablespoon at a time, and mix lightly with a fork. When the crumbs are moist enough to start sticking together, press the dough lightly into a ball, wrap it tightly, and chill for about 30 minutes, or until firm.

2 Combine the rhubarb, orange zest, sugar, salt, and flour in a bowl and stir to mix. Add the strawberries and toss until coated. Spoon the fruit mixture into the dough-lined pie dish, doming the mixture slightly. Dot the pieces of butter all over the filling.

3 Brush the edge of the crust with water. Roll out the remaining dough on a floured surface into an 11in (28cm) circle. Drape the dough over the filling, trim it to be even with the bottom crust, and, using your thumb and finger, press the edges together to seal.

4 Cut a steam vent in the center of the pie. Brush with milk and sprinkle with the sugar. Chill for 15 minutes. Preheat the oven to 425°F (220°C) and put a baking sheet inside to heat up.

5 Bake the pie on the baking sheet for 20 minutes. Reduce the temperature to 350°F (180°C) and bake for another 30–35 minutes, until the crust is browned. Test the fruit with a skewer and if it needs longer but the top could burn, cover with foil. Transfer to a wire rack, and set aside to cool. The dough can be made 2 days ahead and kept in the refrigerator.

EQUIPMENT
9in (23cm) shallow pie dish

INGREDIENTS

FOR THE DOUGH
2 cups all-purpose flour
½ tsp salt
¾ cup vegetable shortening
1 tbsp milk, to glaze

FOR THE FILLING
2¼lb (1kg) rhubarb, sliced
finely grated zest of 1 orange
1 cup granulated sugar,
  plus 1 tbsp to sprinkle
¼ tsp salt
¼ cup all-purpose flour
13oz (375g) strawberries, hulled,
  and halved or quartered
1 tbsp unsalted butter, cubed

It's hard to beat the smooth, creamy vanilla flavor of custard matched with the sharp fruitiness of rhubarb. Here they come together in a very British tart that looks as good as it tastes.

RHUBARB AND CUSTARD TART

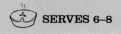 **SERVES 6–8**　　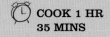 **PREP 30 MINS PLUS CHILLING**　　**COOK 1 HR 35 MINS**　　**FREEZE CRUST, UP TO 3 MONTHS**

EQUIPMENT
9in (22cm) fluted tart pan with removable bottom, baking beans

INGREDIENTS

FOR THE DOUGH
(For visual step-by-step instructions, see sweet pie dough p.105)
1 cup all-purpose flour, plus extra for dusting
2 tbsp granulated sugar
7 tbsp unsalted butter, at room temperature, cut into pieces
1 large egg yolk, beaten with 2 tbsp cold water, plus leftover egg white for brushing

FOR THE FILLING
1lb (450g) rhubarb, prepared weight, cut into ¾in (2cm) chunks
⅓ cup granulated sugar
¾ cup heavy cream
2 large eggs, plus 1 egg yolk
½ tsp pure vanilla extract
confectioners' sugar, for dusting

1 To make the dough, rub the flour, sugar, and butter together by hand, or in a food processor, until they resemble fine bread crumbs. Add the egg yolk and bring the mixture together to form a soft dough. Add a little more water if necessary. Wrap and chill for 30 minutes.

2 Preheat the oven to 350°F (180°C). Toss the rhubarb with 2 tbsp of the sugar and roast in the oven, in a single layer, for 30 minutes. When cooked, gently remove the fruit and drain in a sieve, taking care not to break up the pieces.

3 Roll out the dough on a floured surface to ⅛in (3mm) thick and use to line the tart pan, leaving an overhang of at least ½in (1cm). Trim off any excess dough that hangs down farther than this. Prick the bottom of the dough with a fork, brush with the egg white to seal, line with a piece of silicone or wax paper, and fill with baking beans. Place the crust on a baking sheet and bake for 20 minutes. Remove the beans and paper, and bake for another 5 minutes, if the center still looks uncooked. Trim off any ragged edges from the dough crust while it is still warm.

4 Whisk together the cream, the remaining ¼ cup of sugar, eggs, egg yolk, and vanilla extract. Spread the cooked rhubarb evenly over the bottom of the tart crust. Place the tart crust on a baking sheet and pour the cream mixture carefully over the fruit.

5 Bake for 30–40 minutes, until lightly golden and just set. Set aside to cool to room temperature before dusting with confectioners' sugar and serving with fresh cream. Best eaten the day it is made. The cooked tart crust can be stored in an airtight container for up to 3 days.

Very similar to a classic crumble, this Swedish dessert is simply
a shallow layer of fruit topped with a delicious oaty crumble mix.
The cornstarch helps to thicken the fruit juices.

RHUBARB SMULPAJ

 SERVES 4   PREP 10 MINS   COOK 30 MINS   ✳ FREEZE TOPPING,
                                                                            UP TO 1 MONTH

EQUIPMENT
8in (20cm) round ovenproof dish

INGREDIENTS

FOR THE FILLING
10oz (300g) rhubarb, trimmed weight,
chopped into ¾in (2cm) chunks
4 tbsp granulated sugar
1 tsp cornstarch

FOR THE CRUMBLE TOPPING
(For visual step-by-step instructions,
see crumble topping p.121)
⅓ cup all-purpose flour
⅓ cup light brown sugar
5 tbsp softened unsalted butter
1 cup oats
½ tsp ground cinnamon

1 Preheat the oven to 375°F (190°C). For the filling,
put the chopped rhubarb, granulated sugar, and
cornstarch in a large bowl and toss together, making
sure that the fruit is well covered. Transfer the rhubarb
into the ovenproof dish, packing the fruit down well.

2 For the crumble topping, mix the flour and light
brown sugar together in a separate bowl. Add the
butter and rub it in with your fingertips, making sure
that there are a few pea-sized lumps of butter left. Stir
in the oats and cinnamon, and mix together well.

3 Pile the crumble topping onto the rhubarb and
spread it out, taking care not to pack it down too
firmly. Place the ovenproof dish on a baking sheet and
bake for 30 minutes, until the fruit is soft and the
crumble is golden brown on top.

4 Set aside to rest for 5–10 minutes before serving hot
or warm with thick cream. This is best eaten the
day it is made, or stored overnight in the refrigerator.

Despite it's impressive appearance, a large millefeuilles is really just a good assembly job. Once you are confident with the basic dough and construction, you can use whatever soft fruits are available.

SUMMER FRUIT MILLEFEUILLES

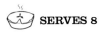 **SERVES 8**   **PREP 45–50 MINS PLUS CHILLING**   **COOK 25–30 MINS**

1 Heat the milk in a saucepan over medium heat until it just comes to a boil. Remove from the heat. Whisk the egg yolks and granulated sugar for 2–3 minutes until thick. Whisk in the flour and gradually whisk the milk into the egg mixture until smooth. Return to a clean pan. Bring to a boil, whisking until thickened. Reduce the heat to low and whisk again for 2 minutes. If lumps form, remove from the heat and whisk until smooth again. Set aside.

2 Preheat the oven to 400°F (200°C). Sprinkle a baking sheet evenly with cold water. Roll out the pastry on a lightly floured surface to a rectangle larger than the baking sheet and about ⅛in (3mm) thick. Roll the dough around a rolling pin, then unroll it onto the baking sheet, letting the edges overhang. Press the dough down. Chill for about 15 minutes.

3 Prick the dough with a fork. Cover with parchment paper, then set a wire rack on top. Bake for 15–20 minutes, until it just begins to brown. Gripping the sheet and rack, invert the pastry. Slide the baking sheet back under and bake for another 10 minutes until both sides are browned. Remove from the oven and slide the pastry onto a cutting board. While still warm, trim the edges, then cut lengthwise into 3 equal strips. Return to the wire rack and set aside to cool.

4 Whip the heavy cream until firm and fold into the pastry cream. Spread half the pastry cream filling over 1 pastry strip. Sprinkle with half the fruit. Repeat with another pastry strip to make 2 layers. Put the last pastry strip on top and press down gently. Sift the confectioners' sugar thickly over the millefeuilles. The dish can be made ahead and chilled for up to 6 hours.

EQUIPMENT
baking sheet

INGREDIENTS

FOR THE FILLING
1½ cups milk
4 large egg yolks
¼ cup granulated sugar
3 tbsp all-purpose flour
1 cup heavy cream
14oz (400g) mixed summer fruits, such as strawberries, cubed, and raspberries

FOR THE PASTRY
1lb 5oz (600g) store-bought puff pastry (or to make your own, see pp.110–113)
flour, for dusting
confectioners' sugar, for dusting

Once you have perfected the art of making a sweet pie dough, you will always have dessert. For a quicker version, these little tartlet crusts can be filled with whipped cream and whatever soft fruit is in season.

FRESH FRUIT TARTLETS

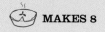 **MAKES 8**   **PREP 40–45 MINS PLUS CHILLING AND COOLING**   **COOK 30 MINS**   **FREEZE CRUST, UP TO 3 MONTHS**

EQUIPMENT
8 x 4in (10cm) tartlet pans

INGREDIENTS

FOR THE DOUGH
1 cup all-purpose flour, plus extra for dusting
4 large egg yolks
⅓ cup granulated sugar
½ tsp salt
½ tsp vanilla extract
6 tbsp unsalted butter, cubed, plus extra for greasing

FOR THE FILLING
1½ cups milk
1 vanilla bean, split, or 2 tsp pure vanilla extract
5 large egg yolks
¼ cup granulated sugar
2 tbsp all-purpose flour
1lb 2oz (500g) mixed fresh fruit, such as kiwi fruit, raspberries, grapes, peaches, peeled and sliced
⅓ cup apricot jam or red currant jelly, to glaze

1 To make the dough, sift the flour onto a work surface and make a well in the center. Add the egg yolks, sugar, salt, vanilla, and butter. Work with your fingertips until mixed, then draw in the flour until bread crumbs form. Press into a ball, and knead for 1–2 minutes, until smooth. Wrap and chill for 30 minutes.

2 Bring the milk to a boil in a saucepan with the vanilla bean. Remove from the heat, cover, and leave for 10–15 minutes. Whisk the egg yolks, sugar, and flour together in a bowl. Beat in the hot milk. Return the mixture to the cleaned-out pan and cook gently, whisking, until the cream has thickened. Simmer over low heat for 2 minutes. Transfer the pastry cream to a bowl and remove the vanilla bean (if using) or stir in the extract. Press plastic wrap over the surface and cool.

3 Grease the pans. Roll out the dough on a floured surface to ⅛in (3mm) thick. Group the pans with their edges nearly touching. Roll the dough around the rolling pin and drape it over the pans. Roll the rolling pin over the tops to remove excess dough, then press the dough into each pan. Set the pans on a baking sheet and prick the dough with a fork. Chill for 30 minutes.

4 Preheat the oven to 400°F (200°C). Line each tartlet crust with foil, pressing it down well. Bake for 6–8 minutes, then remove the foil and bake for another 5 minutes. Cool on a wire rack, then turn out.

5 Melt the jam with 2–3 tablespoons water in a small pan, and work it through a sieve, then use to brush the inside of each crust. Half-fill each crust with the pastry cream, smoothing the top. Arrange the fruit on top, and brush with jam. Best eaten right away.

When blueberries and peaches are in season, be sure to make this delicious summer dessert, which is perfect for any special occasion. It is good served with a spoonful of custard or heavy cream.

BLUEBERRY COBBLER

SERVES 4   PREP 15 MINS   COOK 30 MINS

1 Preheat the oven to 375°F (190°C). Spread the blueberries and peaches over the bottom of the ovenproof dish, and sprinkle with lemon zest and sugar.

2 For the topping, sift the flour, sugar, and salt into a bowl. Add the butter and work together with your fingertips until the mixture resembles bread crumbs.

3 Break the egg into the buttermilk and beat well. Add to the dry ingredients and mix together to form a soft, sticky dough. Drop walnut-sized spoonfuls of the mixture over the top of the fruit, leaving a little space between them. Press them down lightly with your fingers, then sprinkle the sliced almonds and 1 tablespoon of sugar over the top.

4 Bake for 30 minutes, or until golden and bubbling, covering it loosely with foil if it is browning too quickly. It is done when a skewer pushed into the middle comes out clean. Cool briefly before serving.

EQUIPMENT
shallow ovenproof dish

INGREDIENTS

FOR THE FILLING
1lb (450g) blueberries
2 large peaches or 2 apples, sliced
grated zest of ½ lemon
2 tbsp granulated sugar

FOR THE TOPPING
(For visual step-by-step instructions, see cobbler topping pp.118–119)
1½ cups self-rising flour
¼ cup granulated sugar, plus 1 tbsp for sprinkling
a pinch of salt
5 tbsp butter, chilled and cubed
1 large egg
½ cup buttermilk
handful of sliced almonds

Here, the sweetness of the ripe blueberries is balanced by a tangy mix of sour cream and cream cheese. The perfect end to a dinner party, serve this tart with thick cream or a berry compote.

BLUEBERRY CREAM CHEESE TART

 SERVES 8

 PREP 25 MINS
PLUS CHILLING

COOK 45–50 MINS

EQUIPMENT
9in (23cm) tart pan with removable bottom, baking beans

INGREDIENTS

FOR THE DOUGH
(For visual step-by-step instructions, see sweet pie dough p.105)
1 cup all-purpose flour, plus extra for dusting
6 tbsp butter, cubed
2 tbsp granulated sugar
1 large egg yolk

FOR THE FILLING
4oz (115g) cream cheese
2oz (60g) sour cream
½ cup granulated sugar
a pinch of grated nutmeg
3 large eggs, beaten
zest of 1 lemon
12oz (350g) blueberries
confectioners' sugar, for dusting

1 To make the dough, rub the flour and butter together with your fingertips, or pulse in a food processor, until the mixture resembles bread crumbs. Stir in the sugar, add the egg yolk, and mix to form a firm dough. Roll out the dough on a lightly floured surface and use to line the tart pan. Prick the bottom with a fork. Wrap in plastic wrap and chill for 30 minutes. Preheat the oven to 400°F (200°C).

2 Line the dough crust with wax paper and fill with baking beans. Bake for 10 minutes, then remove the paper and beans, and bake for another 10 minutes, or until pale golden. Remove from the oven, and reduce the heat to 350°F (180°C).

3 To make the filling, beat together the cream cheese, sour cream, sugar, nutmeg, eggs, and lemon zest until well combined. Pour into the tart crust and scatter the blueberries over the surface. Bake for 25–30 minutes, until just set. Set aside to cool before transferring to a serving plate. Serve warm or cold, dusted with confectioners' sugar. The tart crust can be made several days in advance and kept in the refrigerator.

One of the best-known American desserts, this classic Cherry Pie is a great recipe to make when cherries are at their ripe, succulent best. Here, cornstarch helps to thicken the juices of the finished pie.

CHERRY PIE

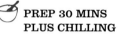 SERVES 4–6   PREP 30 MINS PLUS CHILLING   COOK 50 MINS – 1 HR   FREEZE UP TO 1 MONTH

EQUIPMENT
8in (20cm) metal pie dish with a lip

INGREDIENTS

FOR THE DOUGH
(For visual step-by-step instructions, see sweet pie dough p.105)
1½ cups all-purpose flour, plus extra for dusting
8 tbsp unsalted butter, chilled and cubed
¼ cup granulated sugar
2 tbsp milk
1 large egg, beaten, to glaze

FOR THE FILLING
¼ cup granulated sugar
1lb 2oz (500g) fresh cherries, pitted
juice of 1 small or ½ large lemon
1 tbsp cornstarch

1 To make the dough, rub the flour and butter with your fingertips until the mixture resembles bread crumbs. Stir in the sugar. Add the milk and mix to form a dough. Wrap in plastic wrap and chill for 30 minutes. Preheat the oven to 350°F (180°C).

2 For the filling, melt the sugar in 3½ tablespoons of water in a saucepan. Once the sugar has dissolved, add the cherries and lemon juice. Bring to a boil, cover, reduce the heat, and simmer for 5 minutes. Mix the cornstarch with 1 tablespoon of water to make a paste. Add it to the cherries and cook over low heat until the mixture thickens. Set the cherries aside to cool.

3 Roll out the dough on a floured surface to ⅛–¼in (3–5mm) thick. Lift it over the pie dish and line the bottom and the sides of the dish. Trim off the excess dough, leaving an overhang of ¾in (2cm). Brush the edge with beaten egg.

4 Re-roll the excess dough to make a circle just bigger than the dish. Fill the pie crust with the cherries, then place the remaining dough carefully on top, pressing it down firmly around the edges to create a seal. Trim off the overhanging dough with a sharp knife, and brush with beaten egg. Cut 2 small slits in the top of the pie to allow steam to escape.

5 Bake the pie for 45–50 minutes, until the top is golden brown. Set aside to cool for 10–15 minutes but serve when still warm. The pie will keep in an airtight container for 1 day. The filling can be made 3 days ahead and refrigerated. The dough can be made 1 day ahead and refrigerated.

You can make the dough for these individual tartlets using the old-fashioned method, or in a food processor. Either way, use cherries when they are at their juiciest for a truly luscious dessert.

CHERRY TARTLETS

 MAKES 8   PREP 40–45 MINS   COOK 20–25 MINS
                     PLUS CHILLING

1 To make the dough, sift the flour onto a work surface and make a well in the center. Put the sugar, butter, vanilla, salt, and yolks into the well and work the ingredients with your fingertips until mixed. Work in the flour until coarse bread crumbs form. Press the bread crumbs firmly together to form a dough. On a floured surface, knead the dough for 1–2 minutes, then shape into a ball, wrap, and chill for 30 minutes.

2 Melt the butter for greasing, then use to brush 4 of the molds. Roll out two-thirds of the dough on a floured surface to ⅛in (3mm) thick. Chill the remaining dough. Cut out 4 circles with the cutter; they should be large enough to line the molds. Press 1 circle into the bottom and up the side of a mold to form a tartlet crust. Repeat for the rest of the circles. Prick the bottom of each crust with a fork and chill for 15 minutes. Preheat the oven to 400°F (200°C). Put a baking sheet in the oven. Line each of the tartlet crusts with a second mold and bake on the baking sheet for 6–8 minutes. Remove the lining molds, and reduce the heat to 375°F (190°C). Bake for 3–5 minutes. Unmold and cool each crust on a wire rack. Roll out the remaining dough, line the molds, chill, and bake 4 more tart crusts in the same way.

3 Beat the cream cheese until soft. Add the vanilla, sugar, and lemon zest and beat for 2–3 minutes, until light and fluffy. Pour the cream into a chilled bowl and whip until soft peaks form. Add the cream to the cream cheese mix and fold together until well mixed. Cover and chill. Heat the jelly and kirsch in a small saucepan until melted, then use to brush the inside of each tartlet crust. Pipe the filling into the crusts three-quarters full. Put the cherries in a circle on top and brush them with the remaining glaze.

EQUIPMENT
8 x 3in (7.5cm) diameter brioche molds or tartlet pans, 4in (10cm) round cookie cutter, piping bag, star nozzle

INGREDIENTS

FOR THE DOUGH
1½ cups all-purpose flour,
   plus extra for dusting
¼ cup granulated sugar
6 tbsp unsalted butter, softened,
   plus extra for greasing
½ tsp pure vanilla extract
¼ tsp salt
3 large egg yolks

FOR THE FILLING
9oz (250g) cream cheese
½ tsp pure vanilla extract
3 tsp sugar
grated zest of 1 lemon
½ cup heavy cream
12oz (375g) cherries, pitted

FOR THE GLAZE
¼ cup red currant or sour cherry jelly
1 tbsp kirsch

When fresh cherries are in season, take advantage of the plentiful supply to make this delicious dessert for any special occasion. Serve hot with lots of custard or a scoop of vanilla ice cream.

CHERRY CRUMBLE

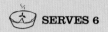 **SERVES 6** 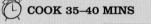 **PREP 15 MINS** ⏰ **COOK 35–40 MINS** ❄ **FREEZE UP TO 1 MONTH**

EQUIPMENT
2 quart ovenproof dish

INGREDIENTS

FOR THE CRUMBLE TOPPING
(For visual step-by-step instructions, see crumble topping p.121)
¾ cup all-purpose flour
1 cup ground almonds
8 tbsp butter, cubed
¼ cup granulated sugar

FOR THE FILLING
1¼lb (550g) cherries, pitted
2 tbsp granulated sugar
2 tbsp apple juice

1 Preheat the oven to 350°F (180°C). To make the crumble topping, put the flour and ground almonds in a large bowl, then rub in the butter with your fingertips until the mixture resembles rough bread crumbs. Stir in the granulated sugar.

2 Place the cherries in the ovenproof dish and scatter over the sugar and apple juice. Sprinkle the crumble mixture over the cherries and bake for 35–40 minutes, or until golden brown.

A classic strudel is given a modern twist by replacing the apples with a fresh cherry and walnut filling. Serve warm with creamy vanilla ice cream or a spoonful of thick whipped cream or crème fraîche.

CHERRY STRUDEL

SERVES 6–8   **PREP 45–50 MINS**   **COOK 30–40 MINS**

1 To make the dough, sift the flour onto a work surface and make a well in the center. Beat the egg with ½ cup water, lemon juice, and salt in a bowl, then pour into the well. Work the ingredients with your fingertips, gradually drawing in the flour. Knead in just enough flour so the dough forms a ball; it should be quite soft. On a floured surface, knead the dough for 10 minutes until shiny and smooth. Shape into a ball, cover with a bowl, and set aside to rest for 30 minutes.

2 Cover a work surface with an old, clean bedsheet. Lightly and evenly flour it. Roll out the dough to a very large square. Cover with damp dish towels for 15 minutes. Preheat the oven to 375°F (190°C). Grease a baking sheet and melt the butter.

3 Make the strudel (see below). Brush the top of the strudel with the remaining melted butter and bake for 30–40 minutes until crisp. Leave for a few minutes before moving to a wire rack with a metal spatula. Sprinkle with confectioners' sugar and serve.

EQUIPMENT
baking sheet

INGREDIENTS

FOR THE PASTRY
(For visual step-by-step instructions,
   see strudel pastry pp.114–115)
1¾ cups all-purpose flour,
   plus extra for dusting
1 large egg
½ tsp lemon juice
a pinch of salt
8 tbsp unsalted butter,
   plus extra for greasing

FOR THE FILLING
1lb 2oz (500g) cherries, pitted
grated zest of 1 lemon
3oz (75g) walnuts, coarsely chopped
½ cup light brown sugar
1 tsp ground cinnamon
confectioners' sugar, to sprinkle

Constructing the strudel

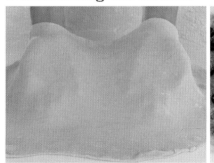

1 Stretch dough, starting at center and working outward until very thin. Brush with most of the butter.

2 Sprinkle the dough with the filling. Trim off the thicker edges, pulling them out and pinching them off.

3 Roll up the strudel using a bed sheet. Transfer to the baking sheet and shape into a crescent or circle.

The classic American Cherry Pie is given a delicate, decorative lattice topping, making it just the thing to serve after a summer dinner party. Best served warm with vanilla ice cream.

CHERRY LATTICE PIE

 **SERVES 8**   **PREP 40–45 MINS PLUS CHILLING**   **COOK 40–45 MINS**   **FREEZE UP TO 1 MONTH**

EQUIPMENT
9in (23cm) pie dish

INGREDIENTS

FOR THE DOUGH
(For visual step-by-step instructions, see sweet pie dough p.105)
1¼ cups all-purpose flour, plus extra for dusting
1 tsp salt
½ cup lard or vegetable shortening, chilled and cubed
5 tbsp unsalted butter, chilled and cubed
1 large egg, to glaze

FOR THE FILLING
1lb 2oz (500g) cherries, pitted
¾ cup granulated sugar
3 tbsp all-purpose flour
¼ tsp almond extract (optional)

1 To make the dough, sift the flour and ½ teaspoon salt into a bowl. Rub the lard and butter into the flour with your fingertips until the mixture resembles bread crumbs. Sprinkle with 3 tablespoons water, and mix until the dough forms a ball. Wrap in plastic wrap and chill for 30 minutes.

2 Preheat the oven to 400°F (200°C), and put in a baking sheet. Roll out two-thirds of the dough on a lightly floured surface and use to line the dish with some dough hanging over the edge. Press the dough into the dish and chill for 15 minutes.

3 For the filling, place the cherries in a bowl and add the sugar, flour, and almond extract, if using. Stir until well mixed, then spoon into the pan.

4 Roll out the remaining dough into a rectangle. Cut out 8 strips, each ½in (1cm) wide, and arrange them in a latticelike pattern on top of the pie, then trim the dough. Beat the egg with ½ teaspoon of salt, and use this to glaze the lattice. Secure the strips to the edge of the pie. Bake for 40–45 minutes, until the dough is golden brown. Serve at room temperature or chilled. The pie can be kept in an airtight container for 2 days, but is really best eaten on the day it is baked.

A true sign of summer, this Gooseberry Tart is a British favorite. The light, crisp dough, just set custard, and sharp gooseberries work best when they are smothered with thick, cold cream.

GOOSEBERRY TART

 SERVES 6–8   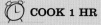 PREP 30 MINS PLUS CHILLING   COOK 1 HR

EQUIPMENT
10in (24cm) tart pan with removable bottom, baking beans

INGREDIENTS

FOR THE DOUGH
(For visual step-by-step instructions, see sweet pie dough p.105)
1¼ cups all-purpose flour, plus extra for dusting
2 tbsp granulated sugar
5 tbsp butter
1 large egg yolk
or 9oz (250g) store-bought pie dough

FOR THE FILLING
14oz (400g) gooseberries
1 cup heavy cream
2 large eggs
¼ cup granulated sugar

1 To make the dough, combine the flour, sugar, and butter and mix in a food processor to form fine bread crumbs, or if making by hand, rub with your fingertips. Add the egg yolk and process or mix by hand, until the mixture forms a ball, adding a little cold water, a tablespoon at a time, if necessary. Wrap in plastic wrap and chill for 30 minutes.

2 Preheat the oven to 350°F (180°C). Trim the gooseberries and set aside. To make the custard, beat the cream, eggs, and sugar together in a bowl. Put the custard in the refrigerator.

3 Roll out the dough on a lightly floured surface to a circle a little larger than the tart pan and use to line the pan. Line the crust with wax paper and fill with baking beans. Bake for 15 minutes, then remove the beans and paper, and bake for another 10 minutes, until cooked through but still pale.

4 Remove the pan from the oven and put a single layer of gooseberries in the bottom of the crust. Pour the custard in and return it to the oven for another 35 minutes, until the custard is set and golden at the edges. Set aside to cool slightly before serving with thick cream or custard.

The unusual addition of rosemary is used in this tart to delicately flavor the dough and the filling. Serve as part of a special occasion lunch with a scoop or two of vanilla ice cream or crème fraîche.

ORANGE AND ROSEMARY TART

🥧 SERVES 6–8   🥄 PREP 30 MINS   ⏰ COOK 1 HR
                          PLUS CHILLING

1 Preheat the oven to 350°F (180°C). To make the dough, place the flour, butter, and rosemary into a food processor, then pulse briefly until it resembles bread crumbs. Alternatively, to make by hand, rub the butter into the flour and rosemary with your fingertips until the mixture resembles bread crumbs. Add the sugar and egg, and briefly process, or bring together by hand, until the dough forms a ball. If a ball does not form, add a little water. Wrap in plastic wrap and chill in the refrigerator for 30 minutes.

2 Roll out the dough on a lightly floured surface and use to line the pan. Line the crust with wax paper and fill with baking beans. Bake for 10 minutes, then remove the paper and beans and bake for another 10–15 minutes or until golden. Remove the pan from the oven and reduce the oven temperature to 325°F (170°C).

3 For the filling, place the orange juice and rosemary in a saucepan. Bring to a boil, then reduce the heat, and simmer until the liquid has thickened and reduced. Set aside to cool, then strain through a sieve, and discard the rosemary.

4 Beat the strained juice, orange zest, sugar, eggs, and cream together until combined, then pour into the crust. Bake the tart for 35 minutes or until just set. Set aside to cool, then chill until required. Serve decorated with orange zest.

EQUIPMENT
8in (20cm) tart pan with removable bottom, baking beans

INGREDIENTS

FOR THE DOUGH
(For visual step-by-step instructions, see sweet pie dough p.105)
1¼ cups all-purpose flour, plus extra for dusting
8 tbsp unsalted butter, chilled
2 tbsp chopped rosemary
2 tbsp confectioners' sugar
1 large egg, lightly beaten

FOR THE FILLING
2 cups fresh orange juice
2 sprigs of rosemary
grated zest of 2 oranges
⅔ cup granulated sugar
4 large eggs
½ cup heavy cream
orange zest, to decorate

A family favorite, the flavors of this pie are made to be together—sharp lemon and sweet vanilla meringue. Spread the meringue all the way to the edge of the crust to make sure it doesn't shrink on cooking.

LEMON MERINGUE PIE

 SERVES 8   PREP 30 MINS   COOK 40–50 MINS

EQUIPMENT
9in (23cm) tart pan with removable bottom, baking beans

INGREDIENTS

FOR THE DOUGH
butter, for greasing
14oz (400g) store-bought sweet pie dough (or to make your own see p.105)
flour, for dusting

FOR THE FILLING
6 large eggs, at room temperature, separated
3 tbsp cornstarch
3 tbsp all-purpose flour
1¾ cups granulated sugar
juice of 3 lemons
1 tbsp finely grated lemon zest
3 tbsp butter, cubed
½ tsp cream of tartar
½ tsp vanilla extract

1 Preheat the oven to 400°F (200°C). Grease the tart pan. Roll out the dough on a floured surface and use it to line the pan. Line the crust with parchment paper and fill with baking beans. Place on a baking sheet and bake for 10–15 minutes, until pale golden. Remove the paper and beans and bake for 3–5 minutes more, until golden. Reduce the heat to 350°F (180°C). Set aside to cool slightly in the pan.

2 Lightly beat the egg yolks. Combine the cornstarch, flour, and 1 cup of the sugar in a saucepan. Slowly add 1½ cups water and heat gently, stirring, until the sugar dissolves and there are no lumps. Increase the heat slightly and cook, stirring, for 3–5 minutes, until the mixture starts to thicken.

3 Beat several spoonfuls of the hot mixture into the yolks. Pour the mixture back into the pan and slowly bring to a boil, stirring. Boil for 3 minutes, then stir in the lemon juice, zest, and butter. Boil for another 2 minutes until the mix is thick and glossy, stirring and scraping down the sides of the pan as necessary. Remove from the heat and cover.

4 Whisk the egg whites in a large clean bowl until foamy. Sprinkle over the cream of tartar and whisk. Continue whisking, adding the remaining sugar, 1 tablespoon at a time. Add the vanilla with the last tablespoon of sugar, whisking until thick and glossy.

5 Place the crust on a baking sheet, pour in the filling, then top with the meringue, spreading it so it covers the filling. Bake for 12–15 minutes, until the meringue is golden. Cool on a wire rack before serving. The unfilled crust can be made 3 days ahead and stored in an airtight container.

This classic American pie benefits from using an easy cookie crust, rather than a pastry one. Experiment with different cookies, such as gingersnaps, for a new twist on an old favorite.

KEY LIME PIE

SERVES 8　　　PREP 20–25 MINS　　　COOK 20–30 MINS

1 Preheat the oven to 350°F (180°C). To make the cookie crust, melt the butter in a saucepan over low heat. Add the vanilla wafer cookie crumbs and stir until well combined. Remove from the heat and pour the mixture into the tart pan, then use the bottom of a metal spoon to press it evenly and firmly all over the bottom and sides of the pan. Place on a baking sheet and bake for 5–10 minutes.

2 Meanwhile, grate the zest of 3 of the limes into a bowl. Juice all 5 of the limes, and set aside.

3 Place the egg yolks into the bowl with the lime zest, and beat until the egg has thickened. Pour in the condensed milk and continue beating for 5 minutes, if using an electric mixer, or for 6–7 minutes if whisking by hand. Add the lime juice, and beat again until it is incorporated. Pour the mixture into the pan and bake for 20–30 minutes until set. The filling will be very loose, but will firm up as it cools.

4 Remove the pie from the oven and set aside to cool completely. Serve the pie decorated with the lime slices and whipped cream.

EQUIPMENT
9in (23cm) tart pan with removable bottom

INGREDIENTS

FOR THE COOKIE CRUST
(For visual step-by-step instructions, see cookie crust p.120)
7 tbsp butter
8oz (225g) vanilla wafers, crushed

FOR THE FILLING
5 limes, plus 1 extra, cut into thin slices, to decorate
3 large egg yolks
14oz can condensed milk

When entertaining, there is nothing that seems to finish a meal quite as well as this classic French tart. The sharpness of the lemon filling encrusted in a rich dough makes a fantastic end to any meal.

TARTE AU CITRON

 **SERVES 8**   **PREP 35 MINS PLUS CHILLING**   **COOK 45 MINS**

1 To make the dough, place the flour, butter, and sugar into a food processor and pulse until it resembles bread crumbs. Add the egg and process until the dough draws together into a ball. To make the dough by hand, rub the flour and butter together with your fingertips until the mixture resembles bread crumbs. Stir in the sugar, then add the egg and bring the mixture together to form a soft dough.

2 Roll out the dough on a lightly floured surface and use it to line the tart pan. Wrap in plastic wrap and chill for at least 30 minutes.

3 To make the filling, beat the eggs and sugar together until combined. Beat in the lemon zest and juice, then whisk in the cream. Chill for 1 hour.

4 Preheat the oven to 375°F (190°C). Line the tart crust with wax paper, fill with baking beans, and bake for 10 minutes. Remove the paper and beans, and bake for another 5 minutes, or until the bottom is crisp.

5 Reduce the oven temperature to 275°F (140°C). Place the tart pan on a baking sheet and pour in the lemon filling, being careful not to allow the filling to spill over the edges. Bake for 30 minutes, or until just set. Remove from the oven and set aside to cool. Dust with confectioners' sugar, sprinkle with grated lemon zest, and serve with a spoonful of whipped cream.

EQUIPMENT
10in (24cm) tart pan with removable bottom, baking beans

INGREDIENTS

FOR THE DOUGH
(For visual step-by-step instructions, see sweet pie dough p.105)
1 cup all-purpose flour, plus extra for dusting
6 tbsp butter, chilled
¼ cup granulated sugar
1 large egg

FOR THE FILLING
5 large eggs
¾ cup granulated sugar
zest and juice of 4 lemons
1 cup heavy cream
confectioners' sugar, for dusting
lemon zest, to sprinkle

For a perfect result, chill the bottom two layers until they firm up, but take care to remove the pie from the refrigerator 30 minutes before serving, and top with the bananas and cream at the last minute.

BANOFFEE PIE

🍚 SERVES 6–8　　🥣 PREP 20 MINS PLUS CHILLING　　⏰ 5–10 MINS　　❄ FREEZE UP TO 2 MONTHS

EQUIPMENT
9in (22cm) round springform pan or tart pan with removable bottom

INGREDIENTS

FOR THE COOKIE CRUST
(For visual step-by-step instructions, see cookie crust p.120)
9oz (250g) vanilla wafers
7 tbsp unsalted butter, melted and cooled

FOR THE CARAMEL
4 tbsp unsalted butter
⅓ cup light brown sugar
14oz can condensed milk

FOR THE TOPPING
2 large, ripe bananas
1 cup heavy cream, whipped
a little dark chocolate, to decorate

1 Line the tart pan with parchment paper. To make the cookie crust, put the cookies into a sturdy plastic bag, and use a rolling pin to crush them finely; you should have about 2½ cups of crushed cookies. Mix the cookies with the melted butter, and pour them into the prepared pan. Press them down firmly to create a compressed, even layer. Cover and chill.

2 To make the caramel, melt the butter and sugar in a small, heavy saucepan over medium heat. Add the condensed milk and bring to a boil. Reduce the heat and simmer for 2–3 minutes, stirring constantly. It will thicken and take on a light caramel color. Pour the caramel over the cookie crust and let set.

3 Once set, remove the cookie and caramel crust from the pan and transfer to a serving plate. Peel and slice the bananas thinly into ¼in (5mm) disks, cut slightly on a diagonal, and use them to cover the surface of the caramel.

4 Spread the cream over the bananas using a spatula until smooth, then decorate with finely grated chocolate and larger chocolate curls made by grating the chocolate with a vegetable peeler. The pie will keep in an airtight container in the refrigerator for 2 days.

Using good-quality store-bought pie dough is perfectly acceptable when time is short, but try to use one made purely with butter, for a better bake and flavor, rather than the margarine-based pastries.

BANANA SHUTTLES

 MAKES 6   PREP 1¼–1½ HRS PLUS CHILLING   COOK 30–40 MINS   FREEZE UNCOOKED, UP TO 1 MONTH

1 Mix the sugar, cloves, and cinnamon together in a bowl. Pour the rum into another bowl. Peel the bananas and cut each in half. Dip in the rum, then add to the sugar mixture and toss until coated.

2 Sprinkle a baking sheet with water. Roll out the pastry on a lightly floured surface and trim it to a 12in–15in (30cm–37cm) rectangle. Cut the dough into twelve 3in–5in (7.5cm–12cm) rectangles. Fold 6 of the rectangles in half lengthwise, and make three ½in (1cm) cuts across the fold of each. Set the remaining rectangles on the baking sheet, pressing lightly.

3 Cut each banana half into thin slices; then set the slices in the center of each pastry rectangle, leaving a ½in (1cm) border around the edge. Brush the borders with water.

4 Line up and unfold the slashed rectangles over the filled bases. Press the edges with your fingers to seal. Trim one end of each rectangle to a blunt point, then scallop the edges of the shuttles with the back of a small knife. Chill the shuttles for 15 minutes.

5 Preheat the oven to 425°F (220°C). Bake for 15–20 minutes. Brush with the egg white and sprinkle over the remaining sugar. Bake for another 10–15 minutes, until crisp and golden. Carefully transfer to a wire rack and set aside to cool. Serve the shuttles warm or at room temperature. They can be frozen at the chilling stage.

EQUIPMENT
baking sheet

INGREDIENTS

FOR THE FILLING
¼ cup granulated sugar, plus 2 tbsp to sprinkle
¼ tsp cloves
¼ tsp cinnamon
3 tbsp dark rum
3 bananas

FOR THE PASTRY
1lb 5oz (600g) store-bought puff pastry (or to make your own, see pp.110–113)
all-purpose flour, for dusting
1 large egg white, beaten, to glaze

This classic American pie is a sophisticated version of the childhood staple of bananas and cream. To save time, use a store-bought pastry crust and custard, although it is well worth it to make your own.

BANANA CREAM PIE

 **SERVES 8**   **PREP 20 MINS PLUS CHILLING**   **COOK 25–30 MINS**

EQUIPMENT
9in (23cm) deep pie plate
with a flat rim, baking beans

INGREDIENTS

FOR THE DOUGH
1lb 2oz (500g) store-bought pie dough
(or to make your own, see p.104)
all-purpose flour, for dusting

FOR THE FILLING
4 large egg yolks
⅓ cup granulated sugar
4 tbsp cornstarch
¼ tsp salt
2 cups whole milk
1 tsp pure vanilla extract
3 ripe bananas
½ tbsp lemon juice
1½ cups heavy cream
3 tbsp confectioners' sugar

1 Preheat the oven to 400°F (200°C). Roll out the dough on a lightly floured surface to a 12in (30cm) circle, use to line the pie plate, and trim off the excess. Prick the bottom of the dough with a fork.

2 Line the dough with wax paper, fill with baking beans, and place the plate on a baking sheet. Bake for 15 minutes, or until the dough looks pale golden. Lift off the paper and beans, and prick the bottom of the dough again. Return to the oven and bake for another 5–10 minutes, or until the dough is golden and dry. Transfer the pie plate to a wire rack and set aside to cool completely.

3 Meanwhile, for the filling, beat the egg yolks, sugar, cornstarch, and salt until the sugar dissolves and the mixture is pale yellow. Beat in the milk and vanilla. Transfer the mixture to a saucepan over medium-high heat and bring to just below a boil, stirring until a smooth, thick custard forms. Reduce the heat and stir for 2 minutes. Strain through a fine sieve into a bowl and set aside to cool.

4 Peel and thinly slice the bananas and toss with the lemon juice. Spread them out in the pie crust, then top with the custard. Cover the pie with plastic wrap and chill for at least 2 hours.

5 Beat the cream until soft peaks form, then sift the confectioners' sugar over the top, and continue beating until stiff. Spoon over the custard just before serving. The dough crust can be baked a day in advance and wrapped in foil.

variation

CHOCOLATE BANANA CREAM PIE
Add 2 tablespoons cocoa powder to the egg yolk mixture with the cornstarch, and add 2 teaspoons cocoa powder to the cream with the confectioners' sugar. To decorate, dust with cocoa, sprinkle with grated chocolate, or drizzle melted dark chocolate on top.

A variation on the classic Tarte Tatin, use slightly underripe bananas for this upside-down tart, since once the tart is turned out, you will want the banana slices to retain their shape for an impressive result.

CARAMEL BANANA TART

SERVES 6   PREP 15 MINS   COOK 30–35 MINS

1 Preheat the oven to 400°F (200°C). Put the butter and syrup in a small, heavy-bottomed saucepan and heat until the butter has melted and the mixture is smooth, then allow to boil for 1 minute. Pour into the tart dish or pan. Arrange the banana slices on top of the syrup mixture—this will be the top of the tart when it is turned out. Place the pan on a baking sheet and bake for 10 minutes.

2 Meanwhile, roll out the pastry on a lightly floured surface to a circle about 9in (23cm) in diameter and ½in (5mm) thick. Trim off any excess pastry.

3 Carefully remove the tart from the oven and place the pastry circle on top. Use the handle of a small knife to tuck the edge down into the pan, being very careful of the hot caramel, since it will burn.

4 Return the tart to the oven and bake for another 20–25 minutes, until the pastry is golden brown. Set aside for 5–10 minutes, then place a serving plate on top and turn the tart upside down. It is good served with vanilla ice cream.

EQUIPMENT
8in (20cm) tart dish or pan
(not with a removable bottom)

INGREDIENTS

FOR THE FILLING
5 tbsp butter
⅔ cup corn syrup
4 medium bananas, peeled
  and sliced ½in (1cm) thick

FOR THE PASTRY
7oz (200g) store-bought puff pastry
  (or to make your own, see pp.110–113)
all-purpose flour, for dusting

These delicious, little, fried pastries are found all over Brazil, stuffed with both sweet and savory fillings. A small amount of alcohol is used in the dough, which could be omitted, if preferred.

BANANA AND CINNAMON PASTELS

 MAKES 10   PREP 35 MINS   COOK 10 MINS
                     PLUS CHILLING

EQUIPMENT
medium, heavy-bottomed saucepan

INGREDIENTS

FOR THE DOUGH
1¾ cups all-purpose flour,
plus extra for dusting
½ tsp salt
2 tbsp sunflower or vegetable oil
1 tbsp Cachaça or vodka
1 tbsp white vinegar

FOR THE FILLING
1 large banana
2 tbsp brown sugar
1 tsp ground cinnamon
vegetable oil, for deep frying
confectioners' sugar, for dusting

1 To make the dough, mix the flour and salt in a bowl. Stir in the sunflower oil, Cachaça, and vinegar. Then gradually add ½ cup warm water, stirring well to form a smooth dough. On a well-floured surface, knead the dough very lightly. Wrap in plastic wrap and chill for 1 hour.

2 For the filling, mash the banana in a small dish and stir in the sugar and cinnamon.

3 Divide the dough into 2 equal pieces. On a well-floured surface, roll out one piece of the dough to form a rectangle 7in x 12in (18cm x 30cm). Cut the dough into 5 rectangles measuring 2½in x 7in (6cm x 18cm). Put a little filling on one half of each rectangle, brush the edges with water, fold, and press firmly together, to seal, using the tines of a fork. Repeat to use up the remaining dough and filling.

4 Heat the vegetable oil in the saucepan to 350°F (180°C). Cook the pastels, two at a time, for about 1½–2 minutes, until golden brown. Transfer the cooked pastels to a plate lined with paper towels to drain. Serve hot, dusted with confectioners' sugar.

When passion fruit are in plentiful supply, try baking this delicate tart. The sweet sharpness of the fruit really shines through, making it an unusual alternative to a classic lemon tart.

PASSION FRUIT TART

 SERVES 6–8   PREP 30 MINS   COOK 45–55 MINS   ✳ FREEZE CRUST,
                           PLUS CHILLING   UP TO 3 MONTHS

EQUIPMENT
9in (22cm) fluted tart pan with removable bottom, baking beans

INGREDIENTS

FOR THE DOUGH
(For visual step-by-step instructions, see sweet pie dough p.105)
1 cup all-purpose flour, plus extra for dusting
2 tbsp granulated sugar
7 tbsp unsalted butter, softened
1 large egg yolk

FOR THE FILLING
½ cup passion fruit juice, from 6–8 passion fruit
juice and grated rind of 1 lime
½ cup granulated sugar
1 cup heavy cream
3 large eggs, plus 1 large egg yolk

1 To make the dough, rub the flour, granulated sugar, and butter together with your fingertips until the mixture resembles fine bread crumbs. Beat the egg yolk together with 2 tablespoons of water and add it to the dry ingredients, bringing the mixture together to form a soft dough. Add a little more water if needed. Wrap in plastic wrap and chill for 30 minutes.

2 Preheat the oven to 350°F (180°C). Roll out the dough on a well-floured surface to ⅛in (3mm) thick and use to line the tart pan, leaving an overlapping edge of at least ½in (1cm). Trim away any excess. Prick the bottom, line with wax paper, and fill with baking beans. Put the crust on a baking sheet and bake for 20 minutes. Remove the beans and paper and bake for another 5 minutes if the center still looks a little uncooked. Trim away any ragged edges from the crust while it is still warm.

3 For the filling, cut open the passion fruit and scrape the insides into a sieve. Use the back of a spoon to push as much juice through as possible, until just the black seeds are left in the sieve.

4 Whisk together the passion fruit juice, lime rind and juice, sugar, cream, eggs, and egg yolk until well combined. Pour the filling into a measuring cup.

5 Place the crust on a baking sheet and pour the filling into the crust. The best way to do this is to rest the baking sheet half on the oven shelf with the oven door open, then pour the filling in and slide the crust into the oven. Bake for 25–30 minutes until just set. Set aside to cool for 30 minutes before serving. Best served on the day, but can be chilled overnight.

This impressive-looking tart uses almonds both in the frangipane and scattered on top to create layers of texture. Steeping the prunes in brandy is optional (otherwise use black tea), but highly recommended.

PRUNE AND ALMOND TART

 **SERVES 8**   **PREP 20 MINS PLUS CHILLING**   **COOK 50 MINS**

1 To make the dough, place the flour, sugar, and butter into a food processor and pulse until it resembles bread crumbs. Add the egg, and process until the dough forms a ball. To make by hand, rub the butter into the flour until it resembles bread crumbs. Stir in the sugar, then add the egg. Bring it together into a dough using first a spoon and then your hands. Roll out on a floured surface and use to line the tart pan. Chill for 30 minutes.

2 Preheat the oven to 375°F (190°C). Line the crust with wax paper and baking beans. Bake for 10 minutes, then remove the paper and beans, and bake for another 5 minutes. Set the crust aside to cool on a wire rack.

3 Reduce the oven temperature to 350°F (180°C). For the filling, place the prunes in a saucepan, cover with water, and add the brandy. Simmer for 5 minutes, then remove from the heat and set aside. Place half the sliced almonds with the granulated sugar in a food processor, and pulse until finely ground. Add the eggs, egg yolk, orange zest, almond extract, butter, and cream, and process until smooth.

4 Drain the prunes, and cut any large ones in half. Pour the almond cream into the tart, and arrange the prunes on top. Scatter the remaining sliced almonds on top, and bake for 30 minutes, or until just set. The tart can be made and chilled 2 days in advance.

EQUIPMENT
9in (23cm) tart pan with removable bottom, baking beans

INGREDIENTS

FOR THE DOUGH
(For visual step-by-step instructions, see sweet pie dough p.105)
1⅓ cups all-purpose flour, plus extra for dusting
1 tbsp sugar
6 tbsp butter, chilled
1 small egg

FOR THE FILLING
7oz (200g) pitted prunes
2 tbsp brandy
1 cup sliced almonds, toasted
⅓ cup granulated sugar
2 large eggs, plus 1 large egg yolk
1 tbsp grated orange zest
a few drops of almond extract
2 tbsp butter, softened
½ cup heavy cream

This rich, fruity strudel makes an ideal finale to a festive meal. Dusted with confectioners' sugar and stuffed with dried fruit soaked in rum, it makes an impressive Christmas dessert.

DRIED FRUIT STRUDEL

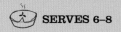 SERVES 6–8   PREP 45–50 MINS   COOK 30–40 MINS   ❄ FREEZE UP TO 1 MONTH

EQUIPMENT
baking sheet

INGREDIENTS

FOR THE FILLING
1lb 2oz (500g) mixed dried fruit (apricots, prunes, dates, raisins, figs)
½ cup dark rum
⅔ cup coarsely chopped walnuts
½ cup light brown sugar
1 tsp ground cinnamon

FOR THE DOUGH
4 x 10in x 18in (25cm x 45cm) sheets filo dough, or to make your own strudel pastry, see pp.114–115)
8 tbsp unsalted butter, melted, plus extra for greasing
confectioners' sugar, for dusting

1 Put the dried fruit into a saucepan with the rum and ½ cup water. Place over low heat for 5 minutes, stirring constantly. Remove from the heat and set aside to cool. The fruit will plump up. Preheat the oven to 375°F (190°C). Grease a baking sheet.

2 If using filo dough, place a sheet on a clean surface and brush with a little melted butter. Lay another sheet on top and brush with melted butter. Repeat with the remaining filo sheets.

3 Drain the dried fruit and sprinkle over the filo dough or strudel pastry, leaving a ¾in (2cm) border around the edge. Sprinkle the chopped walnuts, light brown sugar, and cinnamon over the top.

4 Roll the dough, starting from one of the longer sides, and press the ends together tightly. Transfer the strudel to the baking sheet and brush with a little more melted butter.

5 Bake for 30–40 minutes, until crisp and golden brown. Set aside to cool before transferring to a wire rack using a metal spatula. Dust with confectioners' sugar and serve warm. The uncooked strudel can be stored in the refrigerator a few hours before baking. The cooked strudel can be warmed in the oven 1 day later.

A twist on the classic British Mince Pie, here the filling is kept extra moist with the addition of finely chopped banana. Freeze pies in their pans, uncooked, to bake at the last minute during the holiday season.

MINCE PIES

 MAKES 18   PREP 20 MINS
                                        PLUS CHILLING   COOK 10–12 MINS   FREEZE UP TO
                                                                                          1 MONTH

1 Preheat the oven to 375°F (190°C). Grate the apple (including the peel), and place in a large bowl. Add the melted butter, golden raisins, raisins, currants, mixed peel, nuts, lemon zest, apple pie spice, brandy, and sugar, and mix. Peel and chop the banana into small cubes, and add to the bowl. Mix well.

2 Roll out the dough on a lightly floured surface to ⅛in (2mm) thick. Cut out 18 circles using the larger round cookie cutter. Re-roll the dough, and cut another 18 smaller circles or shapes.

3 Line the muffin pans with the larger dough circles, and place a heaping teaspoon of mincemeat in each crust. Top with the smaller circles or shapes. Chill for 10 minutes, and then bake for 10–12 minutes, until the crust is golden. Carefully remove from the pans, and set aside to cool on a wire rack. Dust with confectioners' sugar. The pies can be baked up to 3 days in advance and stored in an airtight container.

EQUIPMENT
muffin pans, 3in (7.5cm) and 2½in (6cm) round cookie cutters

INGREDIENTS

FOR THE FILLING
1 small apple
2 tbsp butter, melted
½ cup golden raisins
½ cup raisins
¼ cup currants
¼ cup mixed peel, chopped
⅓ cup chopped almonds
   or hazelnuts
finely grated zest of 1 lemon
1 tsp apple pie spice
1 tbsp brandy or whiskey
2 tbsp dark brown sugar
1 small banana

FOR THE DOUGH
1lb 2oz (500g) store-bought pie dough
   (or to make your own, see p.104)
all-purpose flour, for dusting
confectioners' sugar, for dusting

CHOCOLATE PIES AND TARTS

A rich dark chocolate tart such as this one is a wonderful way to finish a meal, but remember, a little goes a long way. Best served just-set and still warm from the oven, with thick, cold cream.

CHOCOLATE TART

SERVES 8–10   **PREP 30 MINS PLUS CHILLING**   **COOK 35–40 MINS**   **FREEZE CRUST, UP TO 3 MONTHS**

EQUIPMENT
9in (22cm) tart pan with removable bottom, baking beans

INGREDIENTS

FOR THE DOUGH
(For visual step-by-step instructions, see sweet pie dough p.105)
1 cup all-purpose flour, plus extra for dusting
7 tbsp butter, chilled and cubed
¼ cup granulated sugar
1 large egg yolk
½ tsp pure vanilla extract

FOR THE FILLING
11 tbsp unsalted butter, cubed
7oz (200g) dark chocolate, chopped
3 large eggs
2 tbsp granulated sugar
½ cup heavy cream

1 For the pastry, rub the flour and butter together in a large bowl with your fingertips until the mixture resembles bread crumbs. Stir in the sugar. Beat the egg yolk and vanilla, add to the bowl, and bring together to form a dough; add water if dry. Wrap and chill for 30 minutes. Preheat the oven to 350°F (180°C).

2 Roll out the dough on a floured surface to ⅛in (3mm) thick and use to line the tart pan, leaving an overlapping edge of ¾in (2cm). Trim off any excess dough that hangs down farther than this. Prick the bottom with a fork, line with parchment paper, and fill with baking beans. Place on a baking sheet and bake for 20 minutes. Remove the beans and paper and return to the oven for another 5 minutes. Trim off excess crust.

3 Prepare the chocolate filling (see below), and assemble the tart. Bake for 10–15 minutes, until just set. Cool for 5 minutes and serve. The tart can be chilled for two days in an airtight container.

For the chocolate filling

1 Melt butter and chocolate in a bowl set over a pan of simmering water. Cool. Whisk eggs and sugar to mix.

2 Pour in the cooled chocolate mixture and whisk gently, but thoroughly, to combine.

3 Mix in the cream. Pour the filling into a measuring cup. Put the crust on a baking sheet; pour in the filling.

This recipe will have your children begging for more, and most likely the adults, too. This delicious pie is best if it is served still warm, with vanilla ice cream or a spoonful of whipped cream.

CHOCOLATE CHIP COOKIE PIE

 SERVES 6   **PREP 20 MINS PLUS CHILLING**   **COOK 1¼ HRS – 1 HR 20 MINS**   **FREEZE CRUST, UP TO 1 MONTH**

1 To make the dough, rub the flour and butter together in a bowl with your fingertips until the mixture resembles fine bread crumbs. Stir in the sugar. Add the egg yolk to the flour mixture and bring the mixture together to form a smooth dough, adding 1–2 teaspoons cold water if needed. Wrap in plastic wrap and chill in the refrigerator for 30 minutes.

2 Preheat the oven to 350°F (180°C). Roll out the dough on a floured surface to a circle large enough to line the tart pan. Place the dough in the pan, pressing down firmly into the bottom and around the edges. Trim off any excess dough, prick the bottom with a fork, and line with parchment paper. Place the pan on a baking sheet and fill with baking beans. Bake for 20 minutes. Remove the beans and paper and bake for another 5 minutes. Reduce the oven temperature to 325°F (160°C).

3 For the filling, place the eggs in a large bowl and, using an electric mixer, beat for 2–3 minutes, or until they are foamy. Beat in the flour and sugars. Add the butter and beat until the mixture is smooth.

4 Sprinkle the chocolate chips over the bottom of the tart crust and spoon in the filling in an even layer. Bake for 50–55 minutes, until the filling is set. Set aside to cool on a wire rack.

EQUIPMENT
8in (20cm) straight-sided tart pan with removable bottom, baking beans

INGREDIENTS

FOR THE DOUGH
(For visual step-by-step instructions, see sweet pie dough p.105)
1 cup all-purpose flour, plus extra for dusting
7 tbsp unsalted butter
¼ cup granulated sugar
1 large egg yolk

FOR THE FILLING
2 large eggs
¼ cup all-purpose flour
⅓ cup granulated sugar
⅓ cup dark brown sugar
8 tbsp butter, chilled and cubed
2oz (50g) milk chocolate chips
2oz (50g) white chocolate chips

Using a good-quality, store-bought crust is a great time-saver for this truly decadent dessert. Use ripe, fresh raspberries and the best quality white and dark chocolate that you can find.

DOUBLE CHOCOLATE RASPBERRY TART

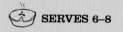 SERVES 6–8   PREP 20 MINS
PLUS COOLING   COOK 5–10 MINS   FREEZE CRUST,
UP TO 3 MONTHS

EQUIPMENT
9in (22cm) tart pan with removable bottom, baking beans

INGREDIENTS

FOR THE FILLING
3½oz (100g) good-quality white chocolate, broken into pieces
2½oz (75g) good-quality dark chocolate, broken into pieces
1 cup heavy cream
14oz (400g) raspberries
confectioners' sugar, for dusting

FOR THE PASTRY
store-bought chocolate crust
(or to make your own,
see p.105 and pp.122–123)

1 Melt the white chocolate in a heatproof bowl, set over a saucepan of barely simmering water. Set the chocolate aside to cool.

2 Melt the dark chocolate in the same way, then use a pastry brush to paint the inside of the tart crust with a layer of the chocolate. This will stop the crust from becoming soggy once it is filled with the creamy filling. Set the crust aside until the chocolate has set.

3 Whip the cream stiffly. Fold the cooled white chocolate into the whipped cream. Crush half the raspberries and fold them through the cream mixture. Pile the filling into the crust evenly. Decorate with the remaining raspberries, dust with confectioners' sugar, and serve. The tart will keep in an airtight container in the refrigerator for 2 days. The unfilled, cooked crust can be kept in an airtight container for 3 days.

Chocolate and pears are a classic combination, and here they come together to form these delicious tartlets, which are good served either hot or at room temperature with a scoop of vanilla ice cream.

CHOCOLATE AND PEAR TARTLETS

 MAKES 8   PREP 30–35 MINS   COOK 25–30 MINS
                                     PLUS CHILLING

EQUIPMENT
3 x 4in (8 x 10cm) tartlet pans

INGREDIENTS

FOR THE DOUGH
1 cup all-purpose flour,
plus extra for dusting
¼ cup granulated sugar
½ tsp salt
½ tsp pure vanilla extract
6 tbsp unsalted butter, softened,
plus extra for greasing
3 large egg yolks

FOR THE FILLING
5½oz (150g) bittersweet chocolate,
finely chopped
1 large egg
½ cup half-and-half
1 tbsp kirsch (optional)
2 large, ripe pears
1–2 tbsp granulated sugar, to sprinkle

1 To make the dough, sift the flour onto a work surface and make a well in the center. Put the sugar, salt, vanilla, and butter into the well and, with your fingertips, work the ingredients together until mixed. Work in the yolks, then work in the flour until the mixture resembles bread crumbs. Press the dough into a ball and knead for 1–2 minutes, until smooth. Shape into a ball, wrap, and chill for 30 minutes.

2 Melt the butter for greasing in a saucepan and use to brush the insides of the tartlet pans. Group 4 of the tartlet pans together, with their edges nearly touching. On a lightly floured surface, divide the dough in half, and roll 1 piece out to ⅛in (3mm) thick. Roll the dough loosely around the rolling pin, and drape it over the 4 pans to cover. Push the dough into the pans, then roll the rolling pin over the tops of the pans to cut off the excess dough. Repeat with the 4 remaining pans and the second piece of dough.

3 Preheat the oven to 400°F (200°C). Put a baking sheet into the oven. Sprinkle the finely chopped chocolate into each tartlet crust. Whisk the egg, half-and-half, and kirsch, if using, together until thoroughly mixed. For an extra-smooth custard, rub the mixture through a sieve. Spoon 2–3 tablespoons of the kirsch custard over the chocolate in each crust.

4 Peel the pears, cut them in half, and remove the cores. Cut each pear half across into thin slices. Arrange the slices on the custard so that they overlap. Press them down lightly into the custard, then sprinkle each tartlet evenly with the sugar. Place the pans on a baking sheet and bake for 10 minutes. Reduce the heat to 350°F (180°C) and bake for 15–20 minutes until set. Cool slightly, unmold, and serve.

The sweet Italian *pasta frolla* dough is used here to contain a rich, truffled chocolate filling. Roasting the walnuts first intensifies their flavor and gives them added texture. Serve at room temperature.

CHOCOLATE WALNUT TRUFFLE TART

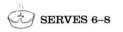 SERVES 6–8   PREP 45–50 MINS   COOK 40–50 MINS
                                    PLUS CHILLING

1 To make the dough, sift the flour onto a work surface and make a well in the center. Put the butter, sugar, salt, and egg into the well and mix. Mix in the flour, then rub with your fingertips until the mixture resembles bread crumbs. Press into a ball. Knead for 1–2 minutes, wrap, and chill for 30 minutes.

2 Grease the pan. Roll out the dough on a floured surface into an 11in (28cm) circle and press it into the pan, sealing any cracks. Prick the bottom of the dough with a fork and chill for 15 minutes.

3 Preheat the oven to 350°F (180°C). Spread out the nuts on a baking sheet and roast for 5–10 minutes, until lightly browned. Cool. Return the baking sheet to the oven. Reserve 8 walnut halves. Grind the remaining nuts with the sugar in a food processor.

4 Beat the butter until creamy. Add the flour and walnut mix and beat for 2–3 minutes, until fluffy. Add the yolks and egg, one at a time, beating after each addition. Mix in the chocolate and vanilla. Spread the filling over the crust and smooth the top. Bake on the baking sheet for 35–40 minutes. Cool on a wire rack.

5 Put the chocolate for the glaze in a bowl, set over a saucepan of simmering water. Stir until melted. Dip the reserved walnuts in the chocolate to coat, then set aside. Cut the butter into pieces and stir it into the chocolate. Add the Grand Marnier. Set aside to cool.

6 Remove the tart from the pan. Pour the glaze on the tart and spread it on top. Cool and set. Dust with cocoa and arrange the walnuts on top to serve.

EQUIPMENT
9in (23cm) springform cake pan

INGREDIENTS

FOR THE DOUGH
1 cup all-purpose flour,
  plus extra for dusting
5 tbsp unsalted butter, softened,
  plus extra for greasing
¼ cup granulated sugar
¼ tsp salt
1 large egg

FOR THE FILLING
5½oz (150g) walnuts
½ cup granulated sugar
11 tbsp unsalted butter
2 tsp all-purpose flour
2 large egg yolks, plus 1 whole large egg
2oz (60g) good-quality dark chocolate,
  finely chopped
1 tsp pure vanilla extract

FOR THE CHOCOLATE GLAZE
6oz (175g) good-quality dark chocolate,
  broken into pieces
5 tbsp unsalted butter
2 tsp Grand Marnier
cocoa powder, sifted, for dusting

In this classic American recipe, a crunchy cookie crust is filled
with a light mousse and topped with thick whipped cream.
Baking the cookie crust briefly helps to hold the crust together.

CHOCOLATE CHIFFON PIE

 **SERVES 8**   **PREP 30 MINS PLUS CHILLING**   **COOK 15 MINS**

EQUIPMENT
9in (23cm) tart pan with removable bottom

INGREDIENTS

FOR THE COOKIE CRUST
**(For visual step-by-step instructions,
see cookie crust p.120)**
6oz (175g) gingersnaps, coarsely broken
¼ cup granulated sugar
5 tbsp butter, melted

FOR THE FILLING
**2oz (50g) dark chocolate, chopped,
plus extra to decorate**
**1½ cups heavy cream,
plus ¾ cup to decorate**
**2 sheets leaf gelatin or 2½ tsp powdered,
unflavored gelatin**
3 large egg yolks, plus 2 large egg whites
⅔ cup granulated sugar
a pinch of salt
**2 tbsp ginger syrup, plus 3 pieces stem,
ginger, or 3 pieces candied ginger, chopped**
¼ tsp cream of tartar
2 tbsp sugar, to decorate

1 Preheat the oven to 375°F (190°C). To make the
crust, put the cookies in a food processor and
pulse until fine crumbs form. Add the sugar and pulse
to mix. Pour in the butter and pulse until blended.
Or, crush the cookies in a plastic bag with a rolling
pin, then mix in the sugar and butter. Press the crumbs
over the bottom of the pan. Bake for 8–10 minutes,
until browned at the edge. Cool on a wire rack.

2 Melt the chocolate in ⅔ cup cream in a saucepan,
without letting the cream boil, stirring until
smooth. Remove from the heat. Add the gelatin and
let stand for several minutes, then stir until dissolved.

3 Meanwhile, using an electric mixer, beat the egg
yolks with ½ cup of the granulated sugar until the
sugar dissolves and the mixture is thick and creamy.
Add the salt, then slowly add the cream mixture and
ginger syrup, beating for 1 minute until the mixture
is well blended. Cover with plastic wrap and chill for
15 minutes, or until firm.

4 Whisk the egg whites in a large bowl until soft
peaks start to form. Sprinkle in the cream of tartar,
then add the remaining sugar, 1 tablespoon at a time,
whisking until stiff peaks form. Set aside. Beat the
chocolate mixture for 2 minutes. Beat in a little of the
egg white, then fold in the remainder. Spoon the
chocolate mixture into the crust and smooth the surface.
Whip the cream for the decoration until thick. Sprinkle
in the sugar and whip until stiff, then use to cover the
pie. Grate the dark chocolate over the top and sprinkle
in the chopped ginger. Chill for 2 hours before serving.

variation

CHOCOLATE COCONUT CHIFFON PIE

Replace the gingersnaps with coconut
cookies, and the ginger syrup with
1 teaspoon coconut extract. Sprinkle
¼ cup toasted, unsweetened coconut
over the finished pie, instead of the
chocolate and ginger.

An all-time favorite, whip a little of the ginger syrup into heavy cream to serve. This tart will keep for a week in the refrigerator or in an airtight container in a cool place, if it lasts that long!

DOUBLE CHOCOLATE AND GINGER TRUFFLE TART

 SERVES 4–6   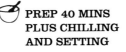 PREP 40 MINS PLUS CHILLING AND SETTING    COOK 30 MINS

1 Preheat the oven to 350°F (180°C). Roll out the dough to the thickness of about ¼in (7mm), then use it to line the tart pan. Prick the bottom of the dough with a fork, line with parchment paper, and fill with baking beans. Bake for 10–15 minutes, until the sides are starting to brown lightly. Remove the beans and paper, cover the sides of the dough with foil and bake for another 10 minutes, or until the bottom is golden and sandy to the touch. Set aside to cool.

2 For the filling, melt 3½oz (100g) of the white chocolate in a small bowl over a saucepan of simmering water, stirring occasionally. Pour the melted white chocolate over the bottom of the tart crust. Set aside to set for about 15–20 minutes.

3 Melt the corn syrup and dark chocolate together in a medium bowl over a pan of simmering water, stirring occasionally. Set aside to cool slightly.

4 Put the cream into a large bowl, fold in the melted dark chocolate mixture, then add the chopped ginger and ginger syrup. Spoon the mixture into the tart crust. Chill in the refrigerator until set for 2–3 hours, or overnight. Roll the rolling pin over the top of the pan, pressing down to cut off the excess crust.

5 To decorate, melt the remaining white chocolate as above, and use a spoon to drizzle the melted white chocolate over the tart to decorate (or use a piping bag with a small round nozzle). Chill again for 30 minutes–1 hour, until the decorative white chocolate swirls have set, then serve.

EQUIPMENT
9in (23cm) tart pan with removable bottom, baking beans, piping bag and small round nozzle (optional)

INGREDIENTS

FOR THE DOUGH
13oz (375g) store-bought pie dough or sweet pie dough (or to make your own, see p.105)

FOR THE FILLING
5½ oz (150g) white chocolate
3 tbsp corn syrup
7oz (200g) 70% dark chocolate
1¼ cups heavy cream
4 pieces stem ginger, finely chopped, or 4 pieces candied ginger, finely chopped
3 tbsp ginger syrup

variation

CHOCOLATE AND PEANUT BUTTER TART
Replace half the dark chocolate with 5 tablespoons crunchy or smooth peanut butter. Add the peanut butter to the bowl with the syrup and remaining dark chocolate. Omit the stem ginger and syrup from the cream.

These unusual little tartlets have to be tasted to be believed and will be a hit with adults and children alike. Serve warm or at room temperature with cream and eat on the day they are made.

BANANA AND NUTELLA CRUMBLE TARTLETS

 MAKES 6   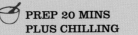 **PREP 20 MINS PLUS CHILLING**   **COOK 35 MINS**   **FREEZE CRUST, UP TO 2 MONTHS**

1 To make the dough, rub the flour, granulated sugar, and butter together, by hand or in a food processor, until they resemble fine bread crumbs. Add the egg yolk and bring the mixture together to form a soft dough; add a little water if needed. Wrap and chill in the refrigerator for 30 minutes.

2 Preheat the oven to 350°F (180°C). Roll out the dough on a floured surface to ⅛in (3mm) thick and use to line the tart pans, leaving an overlapping edge of ½in (1cm). Trim off any excess dough that hangs down farther than this. Prick the bottom with a fork, line with wax paper, and fill with baking beans. Place on a baking sheet and bake for 15 minutes. Remove the beans and paper and return to the oven for another 5 minutes if the centers look uncooked. Trim off any ragged edges from the crusts while still warm. Increase the temperature to 400°F (200°C).

3 For the filling, mix together the flour, light brown sugar, and coconut in a large bowl. Rub in the butter by hand, making sure that the mixture isn't too well mixed, and that there are some larger lumps of butter remaining.

4 Peel and slice the bananas into ½in (1cm) slices across on a diagonal slant, and use pieces to create a single layer on the bottom of the tart crusts, breaking them to fit if needed. Spread 1 tablespoon Nutella over the banana to cover. Divide the crumble mix between the tarts and loosely spread it over, making sure not to pack it down. Bake for 15 minutes, until the crumble has started to brown.

EQUIPMENT
6 x 4in (10cm) fluted tart pans with removable bottoms, baking beans

INGREDIENTS

FOR THE DOUGH
(For visual step-by-step instructions, see sweet pie dough p.105)
1 cup all-purpose flour, plus extra for dusting
2 tbsp granulated sugar
7 tbsp unsalted butter, softened
1 large egg yolk, beaten with 2 tbsp cold water

FOR THE FILLING
2 tbsp all-purpose flour
2 tbsp light brown sugar
½ cup unsweetened coconut
2 tbsp butter, softened
2–3 bananas, not too ripe
¼ cup Nutella

The rich chocolate filling used here contrasts beautifully with a delicate sweet dough made of finely ground almonds. If short on time, use almond meal or almond flour. The tart can be made a day ahead and chilled.

CHOCOLATE PIE WITH A CRUNCHY CRUST

SERVES 8 **PREP 30–35 MINS PLUS CHILLING** **COOK 25–30 MINS**

EQUIPMENT
10in (25cm) tart pan with removable bottom

INGREDIENTS

FOR THE CRUST
¼ cup granulated sugar
6oz (175g) blanched almonds
1 large egg white
butter, for greasing
all-purpose flour, for dusting

FOR THE FILLING
9oz (270g) bittersweet chocolate, finely chopped
1½ cups heavy cream
2 large eggs, plus 1 large egg yolk

1 For the crust, grind the sugar and blanched almonds finely in a food processor. Whisk the egg white in a medium bowl just until it is frothy. Add the ground almond and sugar mixture to the beaten egg white and stir with a wooden spoon to form a stiff paste. Shape it into a ball, wrap in plastic wrap and chill for 30 minutes.

2 Melt the butter in a small saucepan and use to brush the tart pan. On a lightly floured surface, gently pound out the crust mixture with a rolling pin until flattened. Transfer the crust mixture to the pan and press the mixture into the bottom, then push it well up the side. Chill for 15 minutes.

3 Preheat the oven to 350°F (180°C). Put a baking sheet into the oven. Put the crust on the baking sheet and bake for 8–10 minutes, until lightly browned. Slide the tart pan off the baking sheet onto the wire rack and cool in the pan. Leave the oven on.

4 Put the chocolate into a bowl. Bring the cream just to a boil in a pan, then pour in the chocolate and whisk until the chocolate has melted. Set aside to cool to tepid. Put the eggs and yolk into another bowl and whisk until mixed. Whisk the tepid chocolate mix into the eggs just to combine. Pour the filling into the crust. Put the tart on the baking sheet and bake for 15–20 minutes, until the filling begins to set, but is still soft in the center. Cool slightly on a wire rack, then remove from the pan onto the wire rack to cool.

Piled high with luscious summer fruits, these delicate little creamy tartlets are perfect for a special afternoon tea or garden party. Use the best-quality white chocolate that you can find.

WHITE CHOCOLATE AND MASCARPONE TARTS

 MAKES 6   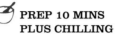 **PREP 10 MINS PLUS CHILLING**   🕐 **COOK 15–20 MINS**

1 Preheat the oven to 400°F (200°C). To make the dough, place the flour, butter, and sugar into a food processor and pulse until the mixture resembles bread crumbs. To make by hand, rub the butter into the flour with your fingertips until the mixture resembles bread crumbs. Mix in the sugar. Add the egg and process or bring together with your hands until the dough draws together in a ball. Roll out the dough on a lightly floured surface and use to line the tart pans. Chill the pans in the refrigerator for 30 minutes.

2 Line the tart crusts with wax paper and fill with baking beans. Bake for 10 minutes, then remove the paper and beans, and bake for another 5 minutes. Set aside to cool.

3 To make the filling, place the white chocolate and 5oz (125g) of the mascarpone into a heatproof bowl set over a saucepan of simmering water, and stir until melted. Add the remaining mascarpone to the bowl, whisk briskly until it is smooth, then whisk in the heavy cream.

4 Pour the mixture into the tart crusts and chill for 3 hours, or until softly set. To serve, arrange the berries on top of the tart, and decorate with mint leaves and a sprinkle of confectioners' sugar.

EQUIPMENT
6 x 4in (10cm) tart pans with removable bottoms, baking beans

INGREDIENTS

FOR THE DOUGH
(For visual step-by-step instructions, see sweet pie dough p.105)
1⅛ cups all-purpose flour, plus extra for dusting
8 tbsp butter, chilled
3 tbsp granulated sugar
1 large egg

FOR THE FILLING
7oz (200g) white chocolate, broken into pieces
1lb (450g) mascarpone
⅔ cup heavy cream
7oz (200g) strawberries, hulled
7oz (200g) raspberries
mint leaves, to decorate
confectioners' sugar, sifted, to decorate

A chocolate-lover's delight, this very sweet traditional American dessert will be a crowd-pleaser whatever the occasion. Serve the pie in small slices, since it is extremely rich, and a little goes a long way.

MISSISSIPPI MUD PIE

SERVES 8–10   PREP 25 MINS
                 PLUS CHILLING   COOK 15 MINS

EQUIPMENT
9in (23cm) springform pan

INGREDIENTS

FOR THE FILLING
7oz (200g) marshmallows
¼ cup milk
12oz (350g) milk chocolate,
roughly broken
1¾ cups heavy cream,
lightly whipped
mini marshmallows and chocolate
flakes, to decorate

FOR THE COOKIE CRUST
(For visual step-by-step instructions,
see cookie crust p.120)
5 tbsp unsalted butter,
plus extra for greasing
9oz (250g) vanilla wafers,
crushed to a fine crumb

1 Grease and line the bottom of the pan with parchment paper. Place the marshmallows and milk in a small saucepan over low heat to melt the marshmallows, stirring occasionally. Set aside to cool.

2 Melt the chocolate in a large heatproof bowl over a pan of simmering water. Remove the bowl from the heat and set aside to cool.

3 Melt the butter in a small pan and mix in the crushed wafers. (You should have about 2½ cups crushed wafers.) Turn into the prepared pan and press down with the back of a metal tablespoon.

4 Pour the cooled marshmallow mixture into the cooled melted chocolate and stir well. Fold in the whipped cream until well combined and pour the mixture over the cookie crust. Smooth and chill for 2–3 hours until ready to serve.

5 To serve, place the pie on a serving plate and remove the pan. Decorate with mini marshmallows and chocolate flakes before serving.

A delicious chocolate variation of a classic Millefeuilles, this is
a great entertaining dessert. The pastry and filling can be made
the day before and assembled at the last minute.

CHOCOLATE MILLEFEUILLES

 SERVES 8   **PREP 35–40 MINS**   **COOK 25–30 MINS**
                PLUS CHILLING

1 Heat the milk in a saucepan over medium heat until
it just comes to a boil. Remove from the heat and
whisk the egg yolks and granulated sugar for 2–3
minutes, until thick. Whisk in the flour. Gradually
whisk the milk into the egg mix until smooth and
return to a clean pan. Bring to a boil, whisking, until
thick. Reduce the heat to low and whisk for 2 minutes.
Set aside to cool, then stir in the rum. Transfer to a
bowl, cover with a plastic wrap, and chill for 1 hour.

2 Stir the brandy into the heavy cream, cover with
plastic wrap, and chill for 1 hour. Preheat the oven
to 400°F (200°C). Sprinkle a baking sheet with water.

3 Roll out the pastry to a rectangle larger than the
baking sheet. Transfer to the baking sheet, letting
the edges overhang. Press the dough down. Chill for 15
minutes. Prick all over with a fork. Cover with parchment
paper, then set a wire rack on top. Bake for 15–20
minutes, until it just begins to brown. Gripping the
sheet and rack, invert the pastry, slide the baking sheet
back under and bake for 10 minutes, until both sides are
browned. Remove from the oven and slide the pastry
onto a cutting board. Trim the edges while still warm,
then cut lengthwise into 3 equal strips. Set aside to cool.

4 Whip the heavy cream until stiff. Stir it into the
pastry cream with two-thirds of the dark chocolate.
Cover and chill. Spread the remaining melted chocolate
over one of the pastry strips to cover it. Put aside to set.
Place another pastry strip on a plate, spread with half
the cream, top with the remaining strip, and spread
with cream. Cover with the chocolate-coated strip. Put
the white chocolate into one corner of a plastic bag.
Twist the bag to enclose the chocolate and snip off the
tip of the corner. Pipe chocolate over the millefeuilles.

EQUIPMENT
baking sheet

INGREDIENTS

FOR THE FILLING
1⅔ cups milk
4 large egg yolks
¼ cup granulated sugar
3 tbsp all-purpose flour, sifted
2 tbsp dark rum
2 tbsp brandy
1⅔ cups heavy cream
2oz (50g) dark chocolate,
   melted and cooled
1oz (30g) white chocolate,
   melted and cooled

FOR THE PASTRY
1lb 5oz (600g) store-bought puff pastry
   (or to make your own, see pp.110–113)

The dough used in this tart is called *pasta frolla*, the classic Italian sweet dough. The gentle hint of orange zest in the crust sets off the rich dark chocolate and orange filling. Serve with whipped cream.

HAZELNUT, CHOCOLATE, AND ORANGE TART

🍲 SERVES 6–8   🥣 PREP 45–50 MINS PLUS CHILLING AND COOLING   ⏰ COOK 55 MINS – 1 HR 10 MINS

EQUIPMENT
9in (23cm) springform pan

INGREDIENTS

FOR THE DOUGH
1 cup all-purpose flour, plus extra for dusting
5 tbsp unsalted butter, softened, plus extra for brushing
¼ cup granulated sugar
½ tsp salt
grated zest of 1 orange
1 large egg

FOR THE FILLING
pared zest of 2 oranges, cut into very fine julienne strips
5oz (125g) hazelnuts
⅔ cup granulated sugar
11 tbsp unsalted butter
2 tsp all-purpose flour
2 large egg yolks, plus 1 large egg
2oz (60g) all-purpose chocolate, chopped into chunks

FOR THE CHOCOLATE GLAZE
5 tbsp unsalted butter, cut into small pieces
5oz (125g) bittersweet chocolate, melted
2 tsp Grand Marnier

1 For the dough, sift the flour onto a surface and make a well in the center. Add the remaining ingredients and mix. Work the flour until bread crumbs form. Press the dough into a ball. On a floured surface, knead until smooth, wrap, and chill for 30 minutes.

2 Brush the pan with melted butter. Roll the dough out on a lightly floured surface to an 11in (28cm) circle and use to line the pan. Trim off excess dough. Prick the bottom with a fork and chill for 15 minutes.

3 Bring a saucepan of water to a boil, add the zest, reduce the heat, and simmer for 2 minutes. Drain. Preheat the oven to 350°F (180°C). Roast the nuts for 5–15 minutes until browned. Rub the nuts in a dish towel while still hot to remove the skins. Cool.

4 Put one-third of the sugar into a pan, add ¼ cup water, and heat gently until dissolved. Add the zest and simmer for 8–10 minutes, until the water has evaporated and the strips are tender. Transfer the zest to parchment paper and cool slightly. Chop two-thirds.

5 Heat a baking sheet. Grind the remaining sugar and nuts in a food processor. Beat the butter until creamy. Add the flour and nuts and beat until light and fluffy. Add the yolks and egg, one at a time, beating after each addition. Mix in the chocolate and chopped zest. Spread over the crust and level. Bake on the baking sheet for 35–40 minutes. Cool. Stir the butter into the warm chocolate in 2–3 batches. Add the Grand Marnier and cool to tepid. Spread the glaze over the top of the tart and decorate with candied zest.

This impressive tart is perfect to serve at a dinner party or special event, yet is easily assembled from pantry essentials. Use a prebaked sweet tart crust to make it even quicker.

DARK CHOCOLATE, APRICOT, AND ALMOND TART

 **SERVES 6–8**   **PREP 20 MINS PLUS CHILLING**   **COOK 1 HR – 1 HR 10 MINS**

1 To make the dough, combine the flour, sugar, and butter and mix in a food processor to form fine bread crumbs, or if making by hand, rub with your fingertips. Add the egg yolk and process or mix by hand, until the mixture forms a ball, adding a little cold water, a tablespoon at a time, if necessary. Wrap in plastic wrap and chill for 30 minutes.

2 Roll out the dough on a lightly floured surface to a circle a little larger than the tart pan and use to line the pan. Line the crust with wax paper and fill with baking beans. Bake for 15 minutes, then remove the beans and paper, and bake for another 10 minutes, until cooked through but still pale.

3 Put the well-drained apricots cut-side down in the crust and scatter over the chocolate chunks.

4 For the filling, cream the butter with the sugar in a large bowl, using an electric mixer, until light and fluffy. Slowly beat in the eggs, one at a time, making sure not to curdle the mixture.

5 Fold in the almond and crumb mixture, then spoon it over the chocolate and apricots, and smooth down lightly. Bake for 40 minutes, or until the tart is firm and golden. Serve warm.

EQUIPMENT
9in (23cm) tart pan, baking beans

INGREDIENTS

FOR THE DOUGH
(For visual step-by-step instructions, see sweet pie dough p.105)
1 cup all-purpose flour, plus extra for dusting
2 tbsp granulated sugar
5 tbsp butter
1 large egg yolk
or 9oz (250g) store-bought pie dough

FOR THE FILLING
14oz can apricot halves, well drained
4oz (100g) dark chocolate, broken into chunks
8 tbsp butter
½ cup granulated sugar
2 large eggs
¾ cup ground almonds, mixed with ¾ cup Madeira or yellow cake crumbs

OTHER SWEET PIES AND TARTS

An ice cream pie is the perfect dessert to serve in hot weather. Use good-quality chocolate ice cream and your favorite types of nuts for the ultimate sweet treat. Serve chilled.

ROCKY ROAD ICE CREAM PIE

 SERVES 8   PREP 20 MINS
PLUS FREEZING,
CHILLING,
AND COOLING   COOK 10 MINS   FREEZE UP TO
2 MONTHS

EQUIPMENT
9in (22cm) fluted tart pan with
removable bottom

INGREDIENTS

FOR THE COOKIE CRUST
(For visual step-by-step instructions,
see cookie crust p.120)
9oz (250g) vanilla wafers
¼ cup granulated sugar
8 tbsp unsalted butter,
melted and cooled

FOR THE FILLING
1 quart good-quality chocolate ice cream
1oz (30g) mini marshmallows
2oz (50g) pecans, coarsely chopped
2oz (50g) blanched almonds,
coarsely chopped

1 Preheat the oven to 350°F (180°C). To make the cookie crust, crush the cookies by hand, or in a food processor until they resemble fine bread crumbs. (You should have about 2½ cups crushed cookies.) Mix the cookie crumbs with the sugar, and the melted butter until the mixture resembles wet sand.

2 Pour the cookie mixture into the tart pan, and press it firmly into the bottom and sides of the pan. Make sure the mixture is as packed as possible, and that there is a good side to the crust (it should go at least 1¼in [3cm] up the sides of the pan). Bake the tart crust for 10 minutes, then set aside to cool. Once cold, store the tart crust in the refrigerator until needed.

3 For the filling, take the ice cream out of the freezer at least 15 minutes before needed, to allow it to soften in the refrigerator. Scoop the ice cream into a food processor with a large spoon. Don't just tip the whole block in as it will be too difficult to break down quickly. Process the ice cream until it is thick and creamy, but entirely smooth. Quickly scrape it into a large bowl, and fold in the mini marshmallows and chopped nuts. Pour the mixture into the prepared crust and freeze for 1 hour, or until firm.

4 To serve the ice cream pie, remove it from the freezer and leave it in the refrigerator for about 20–30 minutes to soften before serving.

The crisp butter-based crust and homemade frangipane makes for a truly English teatime classic, especially when served warm with cream.

BAKEWELL TART

SERVES 6–8

PREP 30 MINS PLUS CHILLING

COOK 1 HR – 1 HR 10 MINS

FREEZE CRUST, UP TO 3 MONTHS

EQUIPMENT
9in (22cm) tart pan with removable bottom, baking beans

INGREDIENTS

FOR THE DOUGH
(For visual step-by-step instructions, see sweet pie dough p.105)
1¼ cups all-purpose flour, sifted, plus extra for dusting
7 tbsp unsalted butter, chilled and cubed
¼ cup granulated sugar
finely grated zest of ½ lemon
1 large egg yolk
½ tsp pure vanilla extract

FOR THE FILLING
8 tbsp unsalted butter, softened
½ cup granulated sugar
3 large eggs
½ tsp almond extract
1 cup ground almonds
⅓ cup good-quality raspberry jam
1oz (25g) sliced almonds
confectioners' sugar, for dusting

1 To make the dough, rub the flour and butter together with your fingertips until the mixture resembles bread crumbs. Stir in the sugar and lemon zest. Beat the egg yolk with the vanilla and mix into the crumbs, bringing the mixture together to form a soft dough; add a little water, if needed. Wrap in plastic wrap and chill for 30 minutes.

2 Preheat the oven to 350°F (180°C). Roll the dough out on a floured surface to about ⅛in (3mm) thick and use to line the pan, leaving an overlapping edge of at least ¾in (2cm). Prick the bottom all over with a fork. Line the crust with parchment paper and fill with baking beans. Place it on a baking sheet and bake for 20 minutes. Remove the beans and the paper, and bake for another 5 minutes, if the center still looks a little uncooked.

3 For the filling, cream the butter and sugar together in a bowl until pale and fluffy. Beat in the eggs and almond extract until well combined. Fold in the ground almonds to form a thick paste.

4 Spread the jam evenly over the bottom of the cooked tart crust. Pour the frangipane over the jam layer and use a palette knife to spread it out evenly. Scatter the sliced almonds over the top.

5 Bake for 40 minutes, until golden brown. Set aside to cool for 5 minutes, then trim the excess crust from the edges and set the tart aside to cool before dusting with confectioners' sugar to serve. The baked tart will keep in an airtight container for up to 2 days. The unfilled crust can be prepared in advance and stored in an airtight container for up to 3 days.

There are only a few ingredients in this simple dessert, so make sure they are of the best quality. The pastry slices can be made in advance and stored for up to 2 days, to be filled at the last minute.

VANILLA MILLEFEUILLES SLICES

 MAKES 6   PREP 35–40 MINS
PLUS CHILLING   COOK 35–40 MINS

1 Heat the milk in a saucepan until it just comes to a boil. Remove from the heat. Whisk the egg yolks and granulated sugar for 2–3 minutes until thick. Whisk in the flour. Gradually whisk the milk into the egg mix until smooth. Return to a clean pan. Bring to a boil, whisking until thickened. Reduce the heat to low and whisk for 2 minutes. If lumps form in the dough cream, remove from the heat and whisk until smooth. Cool, then stir in the rum. Transfer to a bowl, cover with plastic wrap, and chill for 1 hour.

2 Whip the heavy cream until stiff peaks form. Fold it into the dough cream and chill. Preheat the oven to 400°F (200°C). Sprinkle the baking sheet with water. Roll out the dough to a rectangle larger than the baking sheet and transfer to the baking sheet, letting the edges overhang. Press down and chill for 15 minutes.

3 Prick the dough with a fork. Cover with parchment paper, then set a wire rack on top. Bake for 15–20 minutes, until just brown. Gripping the baking sheet and rack, invert the dough and bake for 10 minutes, until both sides are browned. While still warm, cut it into 2in x 4in (5cm x 10cm) rectangles, in multiples of 3.

4 Mix the confectioners' sugar with 1–1½ tablespoons water, then 2 tablespoons of the icing with the cocoa. Place the chocolate icing in the piping bag. Take one-third of the dough pieces and spread with white icing, then pipe horizontal lines across it with chocolate icing. Drag a skewer through the lines vertically to produce a striped effect; dry. Spread a layer of jam over the remaining dough pieces. Spread a ½in (1cm) layer of cream on top of the jam; trim the edges. Take a piece of dough with jam and cream, and place another on top. Press down before topping with a third iced pastry piece.

EQUIPMENT
baking sheet, small piping bag
with thin nozzle

INGREDIENTS

FOR THE FILLING
1½ cups milk
4 large egg yolks
¼ cup granulated sugar
3 tbsp all-purpose flour, sifted
2 tbsp dark rum
1 cup heavy cream
½ x 16oz jar smooth strawberry
  or raspberry jam

FOR THE PASTRY
1lb 5oz (600g) puff pastry
  (or to make your own, see pp.110–113)
¾ cup confectioners' sugar
1 tsp cocoa powder

This traditional Italian tart is really a variation on a cheesecake baked in a pie crust. Use very fresh ricotta for a perfect result and the best-quality pure vanilla extract you can afford.

CROSTATA DI RICOTTA

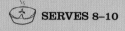 SERVES 8–10   PREP 35–40 MINS   COOK 1–1¼ HRS
                     PLUS CHILLING

EQUIPMENT
9–10in (23–25cm) round
springform cake pan

INGREDIENTS

FOR THE DOUGH
1¾ cups all-purpose flour,
plus extra for dusting
finely grated zest of 1 lemon
¼ cup granulated sugar
12 tbsp unsalted butter, softened,
plus extra for greasing
4 large egg yolks, plus one large egg,
beaten, to glaze
a pinch of salt

FOR THE FILLING
2¾lb (1.25kg) ricotta cheese
½ cup granulated sugar
1 tbsp all-purpose flour
a pinch of salt
finely grated zest of 1 orange
2 tbsp chopped candied orange peel
1 tsp pure vanilla extract
⅓ cup golden raisins
1oz (30g) sliced almonds
4 large egg yolks

1 To make the dough, sift the flour onto a work surface and make a well in the center. Put the lemon zest, sugar, butter, egg yolks, and salt into the well and work together with your fingertips until mixed. Draw in the flour and press the dough into a ball. On a floured surface, knead the dough for 1–2 minutes, until smooth. Shape into a ball, wrap in plastic wrap, and chill for 30 minutes.

2 Grease the pan. Roll out three-quarters of the dough on a floured surface to make a 14–15in (35–37cm) circle and use to line the pan. Trim the excess dough. Chill, with the dough and trimmings, for 15 minutes.

3 Place the ricotta in a bowl and beat in the sugar, flour, and salt. Add the orange zest, candied peel, vanilla, golden raisins, almonds, and egg yolks and beat to combine. Spoon the filling into the crust. Tap the pan on the surface to remove any bubbles. Smooth the top of the filling with the back of a wooden spoon.

4 Press the trimmings into the remaining dough and roll out on a floured surface to a 10in (25cm) circle. Cut it into strips, about ½in (1cm) wide, and place them on the top in a crisscross fashion. Trim off the hanging ends. Moisten the ends of the strips with the beaten egg, then seal them to the edge. Brush the lattice with egg and chill for 15–30 minutes, until firm.

5 Preheat the oven to 350°F (180°C), and put a baking sheet inside to heat up. Place the tart on the baking sheet and bake for 1–1¼ hours, until firm and golden brown. Set aside to cool in its pan until warm, then remove the sides of the pan and cool completely. The crostata can be made 1 day ahead and kept chilled.

Using ground hazelnuts in the dough for this tart makes it quite delicate and hard to handle. However, the results are worth it, and the rich flavors of this dessert make it a decidedly adult affair.

MOCHA TART WITH A HAZELNUT CRUST

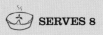 SERVES 8   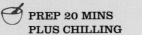 PREP 20 MINS   🕐 COOK 40 MINS   ❄ FREEZE CRUST,
                                          PLUS CHILLING   UP TO 2 MONTHS

1 To make the dough, pulse the hazelnuts and granulated sugar in a food processor to a fine powder. Pour it into a large bowl and mix well with the flour. Rub in the butter with your fingertips until the mixture resembles loose bread crumbs. Add the egg yolk and bring the mixture together to form a soft dough. Wrap in plastic wrap and chill for 30 minutes.

2 Preheat the oven to 325°F (170°C). Roll the dough out on a well-floured surface to ¼in (7mm) thick and use to line the tart pan. Trim away excess dough, leaving a ½in (1cm) overhang. Prick the bottom of the dough with a fork, line the tart with wax paper, and fill with baking beans. Bake for 15 minutes. Remove the beans and paper and bake for another 5 minutes, until the crust is lightly cooked. Trim any excess crust from around the edges.

3 Place the chocolate and the butter in a heatproof bowl and melt it over a saucepan of simmering water. The level of the water should not touch the bottom of the bowl. Set aside to cool. In a large bowl or food processor, whisk together the eggs and granulated sugar until they are light, thick, and frothy.

4 Fold the cooled chocolate mixture into the eggs, then fold in the cooled coffee mixture, mixing well. Pour the filling into the crust and bake for 15–20 minutes, until the center is just set. Remove and set aside for 20 minutes before serving warm or at room temperature with cream. The baked crust can be stored in a container for up to 2 days. Best eaten the same day, but can be chilled overnight.

EQUIPMENT
9in (22cm) fluted tart pan with removable bottom, baking beans

INGREDIENTS

FOR THE DOUGH
(For visual step-by-step instructions, see sweet pie dough p.105)
2oz (50g) hazelnuts, skinned
2 tbsp granulated sugar
¾ cup all-purpose flour, plus extra for dusting
5 tbsp butter, at room temperature
1 large egg yolk

FOR THE FILLING
7oz (200g) good-quality dark chocolate, broken up
7 tbsp unsalted butter, cubed
3 large eggs
¼ cup granulated sugar
1 tbsp strong espresso powder dissolved in 3 tbsp boiling water and cooled

Traditionally, this classic British recipe was made using fresh curds, a by-product of the cheese-making business. Today, you will have to make them from scratch, but it is a simple yet pleasing procedure.

YORKSHIRE CURD TART

 SERVES 6–8

PREP 30 MINS
PLUS CHILLING
OVERNIGHT

COOK 40–45 MINS

EQUIPMENT
9in (22cm) tart pan with
removable bottom

INGREDIENTS

FOR THE CURDS
4 cups whole milk
¼ cup lemon juice

FOR THE DOUGH
(For visual step-by-step instructions,
see sweet pie dough p.105)
1 cup all-purpose flour,
plus extra for dusting
7 tbsp unsalted butter
¼ cup granulated sugar
1 large egg yolk

FOR THE FILLING
5 tbsp butter, at room temperature
⅓ cup granulated sugar
1 large egg
zest of 1 lemon
½ tsp freshly grated nutmeg
⅓ cup currants
⅓ cup raisins

1 Prepare the curd for the filling a day in advance. Heat the milk in a medium saucepan until just boiling. Remove from the heat, stir in the lemon juice, and set aside to cool for an hour, stirring occasionally. Line a sieve or colander with clean cheesecloth, or a dish towel, and place over a large bowl. Pour the milk mixture into the cheesecloth and chill overnight.

2 To make the dough, rub the flour and butter together in a bowl with your fingertips until the mixture resembles fine bread crumbs. Stir in the sugar. Add the egg yolk to the flour mixture and bring it together to form a smooth dough; add 1–2 tablespoons cold water if needed. Wrap and chill for 30 minutes.

3 For the filling, place the butter and sugar in a large bowl and cream them together, using an electric mixer, until pale and fluffy. Add the egg and beat until combined. Spoon in the curd (from the cheesecloth or dish towel), lemon zest, and nutmeg. Stir well. Set aside.

4 Preheat the oven to 350°F (180°C). Roll out the dough on a floured surface to a circle large enough to line the tart pan. Place the dough in the pan, pressing down firmly into the bottom and around the edges. Trim off any excess dough and prick the bottom with a fork. Place the pan on a baking sheet.

5 Evenly scatter the currants and raisins over the dough. Spoon the curd mixture over the fruit and spread it out in an even layer. Bake for 25–30 minutes, until the filling is golden brown. Cool in the pan for 30 minutes before serving warm or chilled.

A great British sweet tart, here a traditional Treacle Tart recipe is given a more sophisticated touch with the addition of cream and eggs to the filling. Serve warm with thick cream.

TREACLE TART

SERVES 4–6   PREP 30 MINS   COOK 1 HR 20 MINS
                    PLUS CHILLING

1 To make the dough, rub the flour and butter together with your fingertips until the mixture resembles bread crumbs. Stir in the sugar. Beat together the egg yolk and vanilla. Add them to the bowl and bring the mixture together to form a soft dough; add a little water if needed. Wrap and chill for 30 minutes. Preheat the oven to 350°F (180°C).

2 Roll out the dough on a well-floured surface to ⅛in (3mm) thick and use to line the pan, leaving an overlapping edge of at least ¾in (2cm). Prick the bottom of the dough with a fork, line with parchment paper, and fill with baking beans. Place the tart crust on a baking sheet and bake for 20 minutes. Remove the beans and paper, and return to the oven for another 5 minutes if the center still looks uncooked. Reduce the heat to 340°F (170°C).

3 For the filling, measure the corn syrup in a large liquid measuring cup. Measure the cream on top of it (the density of the syrup will keep the two separate, making measuring easy). Add the eggs and orange zest and blend together, using a handheld blender, until well combined. Alternatively, transfer to a bowl and whisk. Gently fold in the brioche crumbs.

4 Place the tart crust on a baking sheet and put on an oven rack. Pour the filling into the crust and carefully slide the rack back into the oven. Bake for 30 minutes, until just set, but before the filling starts to bubble up. Trim the crust edge with a small, sharp knife while still warm, then set aside to cool in its pan for at least 15 minutes before turning out. Serve warm with thick cream or ice cream.

EQUIPMENT
9in (22cm) tart pan with removable bottom, baking beans

INGREDIENTS

FOR THE DOUGH
(For visual step-by-step instructions, see sweet pie dough p.105)
1 cup all-purpose flour, plus extra for dusting
7 tbsp unsalted butter, chilled and cubed
¼ cup granulated sugar
1 large egg yolk
½ tsp pure vanilla extract

FOR THE FILLING
¾ cup corn syrup
¾ cup heavy cream
2 large eggs
finely grated zest of 1 orange
1½ cups brioche or croissant crumbs

This pie heralds from Pennsylvania. It uses a lot of molasses and supposedly got its name from the fact that it was so sweet you had to "shoo" the flies away to keep them from gathering around it!

SHOO FLY PIE

SERVES 6–8   PREP 20 MINS   COOK 50–55 MINS   FREEZE CRUST,
                    PLUS CHILLING   UP TO 3 MONTHS
                    AND COOLING

EQUIPMENT
9in (22cm) tart pan with
loose bottom, baking beans

INGREDIENTS

FOR THE DOUGH
(For visual step-by-step instructions,
see sweet pie dough p.105)
1 cup all-purpose flour,
plus extra for dusting
2 tbsp granulated sugar
7 tbsp unsalted butter, at room
temperature, cut into pieces
1 large egg yolk, beaten with
2 tbsp cold water

FOR THE FILLING
1 cup all-purpose flour
½ cup light brown sugar
1 tsp mixed spice
4 tbsp unsalted butter, softened
⅔ cup molasses
½ tsp baking soda
1 large egg

1 To make the dough, rub the flour, sugar, and butter together with your fingertips until the mixture resembles fine bread crumbs. Add the egg yolk and bring the mixture together to form a soft dough; add a little water if needed. Wrap and chill for 30 minutes.

2 Preheat the oven to 350°F (180°C). Roll out the dough on a floured surface to ⅛in (3mm) thick and use to line the tart pan, leaving an overlapping edge of at least ½in (1cm). Trim off any excess dough. Prick the bottom with a fork, line with a piece of wax paper, and fill with baking beans. Place the crust on a baking sheet and bake for 20 minutes. Remove the beans and paper, and bake for another 5 minutes if the center still looks a little uncooked. Trim off any ragged edges from the crust while it is still warm. Increase the heat to 375°F (190°C).

3 For the filling, mix the flour, light brown sugar, and mixed spice together by hand, or in a food processor. Rub in the butter until the mixture resembles fine bread crumbs. Pour the molasses into a large bowl. Mix ½ cup boiling water with the baking soda and whisk it into the molasses until dissolved. Set aside to cool.

4 When the pie crust is ready, whisk the egg into the cooled molasses mixture. Set aside 4 heaping tablespoons of the crumb mixture, and whisk the rest into the molasses. Place the pie crust on a baking sheet and carefully pour in the filling. Scatter the remaining crumbs over the top and bake for 30 minutes, until it is puffed up and just set. Serve warm or at room temperature with thick cream or vanilla ice cream. Best eaten the day it is made.

A simple tart, this classic custard filling is flavored with a hint of nutmeg. To prevent overcooking, remove from the oven while the center is gently wobbling, since it will continue to set.

CUSTARD TART

 SERVES 8   PREP 20 MINS PLUS CHILLING   COOK 45–50 MINS   ❄ FREEZE CRUST, UP TO 3 MONTHS

EQUIPMENT
9in (22cm) tart pan with removable bottom, baking beans

INGREDIENTS

FOR THE DOUGH
(For visual step-by-step instructions see sweet pie dough p.105)
1 cup all-purpose flour, plus extra for dusting
7 tbsp butter, chilled and cubed
¼ cup granulated sugar
2 large egg yolks
1 tsp pure vanilla extract

FOR THE FILLING
1 cup milk
⅔ cup heavy cream
2 large eggs
2 tbsp granulated sugar
¼ tsp freshly grated nutmeg

1 To make the dough, mix the flour and butter together with your fingertips until the mixture resembles fine bread crumbs. Stir in the sugar. Beat the 2 egg yolks with ½ teaspoon vanilla, add them to the bowl, and bring the mixture together to form a soft dough. Wrap in plastic wrap and chill for 30 minutes.

2 Preheat the oven to 350°F (180°C). Roll the dough out on a floured surface to ⅛in (3mm) thick and use to line the pan, leaving an overlapping edge of at least ¾in (2cm). Prick the bottom of the dough with a fork, line with parchment paper, and fill with baking beans. Bake for 20 minutes. Remove the beans and paper and bake for another 5 minutes. Trim off excess dough. Reduce the heat to 325°F (170°C).

3 Make the custard filling (see below). Place the tart case on a baking sheet. Pour the filling into the case and bake for 20–25 minutes, until just set but still with a slight wobble in the center. Set aside to cool.

For the custard filling

1 Put the milk and the cream in a heavy saucepan and bring gently to a boil over medium heat.

2 Meanwhile, whisk 2 eggs, sugar, remaining vanilla, and nutmeg together in a heatproof bowl.

3 Once the milk and cream have come to a boil, pour them over the egg mixture, whisking constantly.

This classic French tart is a deep-dish custard tart, which is best served chilled. Using a cake pan with a removable bottom gives the requisite depth, and the low baking temperature helps the custard to set.

FLAN NATURE

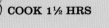

SERVES 6–8   PREP 20 MINS   COOK 1½ HRS   FREEZE CRUST,
                    PLUS CHILLING   UP TO 3 MONTHS

1 To make the dough, rub the flour, granulated sugar, and butter together with your fingertips until the mixture resembles fine bread crumbs. Beat the egg yolk and vanilla together, and add it to the dry ingredients, bringing the mixture together to form a soft dough; adding a little water if needed. Wrap in plastic wrap and chill in the refrigerator for 30 minutes.

2 Preheat the oven to 325°F (170°C). Roll out the dough on a well-floured surface to ⅛in (3mm) thick and use to line the cake pan, leaving an overlapping edge of ¾in (2cm). Trim off any excess dough that hangs down farther than this. Line the crust with a piece of wax paper and fill with baking beans. Place the case on a baking sheet and bake for 25 minutes. Remove the beans and paper and return to the oven for another 5 minutes if the center still looks a little uncooked. Reduce the oven temperature to 300°F (150°C).

3 For the filling, whisk the flour, sugar, eggs, butter, and vanilla together in a bowl to a thick, smooth paste. Whisk in the milk and pour into a liquid measuring cup. Rest the baking sheet with the tart crust on the edge of the middle oven shelf. Holding it with one hand, pour the filling carefully into the tart crust with the other, then gently push the tart onto the oven shelf and bake for 50 minutes–1 hour, until the tart is just set, but has not puffed up at all. The surface should be golden brown. At this point, trim off the excess crust from the sides.

4 Set the tart aside to cool completely in its pan before eating. The tart crust can be prepared up to 3 days before and stored in an airtight container.

EQUIPMENT
7in (18cm) cake pan with removable bottom, 1½in (4cm) deep, baking beans

INGREDIENTS

FOR THE DOUGH
(For visual step-by-step instructions, see sweet pie dough p.105)
1 cup all-purpose flour, plus extra for dusting
¼ cup granulated sugar
7 tbsp unsalted butter, softened
1 large egg yolk
½ tsp pure vanilla extract

FOR THE FILLING
¾ cup all-purpose flour
½ cup granulated sugar
3 large eggs
4 tbsp unsalted butter, melted and cooled
½ tsp pure vanilla extract
¾ cup milk

One of the most celebrated pastries to come out of Portugal, these ambrosial custard tarts are well worth the effort of baking at home. Rolling the pastry is quite tricky at first, but it is easily mastered.

PASTEIS DE NATA

MAKES 16   PREP 30 MINS   COOK 35–40 MINS

EQUIPMENT
16-hole muffin pan

INGREDIENTS

FOR THE PASTRY
1lb 2oz (500g) store-bought puff pastry (or to make your own, see pp.110–113)
all-purpose flour, for dusting

FOR THE FILLING
2 cups milk
1 cinnamon stick
1 large piece lemon zest
4 large egg yolks
½ cup granulated sugar
¼ cup all-purpose flour
1 tbsp cornstarch

1 Preheat the oven to 425°F (220°C). Roll out the pastry on a floured surface to a 16in x 12in (40cm x 30cm) rectangle. Roll up the pastry from the long end nearest you to make a log and trim the ends. Cut the pastry into 16 equal-sized slices.

2 Take a piece of rolled pastry and tuck the loose end underneath it. Lay it down and lightly roll into a thin circle, about 4in (10cm) in diameter, turning it over only once to ensure a natural curve to the finished pastry. You will be left with a pastry that resembles a shallow bowl. Press it into a muffin pan with your thumb, ensuring it is well-shaped to the pan. Lightly prick the bottom and chill while you make the filling.

3 Heat the milk, cinnamon stick, and lemon zest in a heavy saucepan. Remove when the milk starts to boil. Whisk the egg yolks, sugar, flour, and cornstarch together in a bowl until it forms a thick paste. Remove the cinnamon stick and lemon zest from the hot milk, and pour the milk gradually over the egg yolk mixture, whisking constantly. Return the custard to the cleaned-out pan and place over medium heat, whisking constantly, until it thickens. Remove from the heat.

4 Fill each crust, two-thirds full, with the custard and bake at the top of the oven for 20–25 minutes until the custards are puffed and blackened in places. Set aside to cool. The custards will deflate slightly, but this is normal. Set aside for at least 10–15 minutes before eating warm or cold. The tarts will keep in an airtight container for 1 day. The custard and the pastry crusts can be prepared ahead and stored separately in the refrigerator overnight before using.

Traditionally prepared in France for Epiphany, on January 6,
to celebrate the arrival of the three kings, a rich buttery pie
pastry is filled with frangipane and baked until golden brown.

GALETTE DES ROIS

🍲 SERVES 6–8   🥣 PREP 25 MINS   🕐 COOK 30 MINS   ❄️ FREEZE UP TO
                                                                              2 MONTHS

1 Preheat the oven to 400°F (200°C). Cream the
sugar and butter together in a bowl with an
electric mixer. Beat in the egg and blend well. Mix
in the ground almonds, almond extract, and rum,
brandy, or milk, to make a thick paste.

2 Roll out the pastry on a well-floured surface
to a 20in x 10in (50cm x 25cm) rectangle. The
measurements do not have to be exact, but the pastry
should be ⅛–¼in (3–5mm) thick. Fold the pastry in
half and use a 10in (25cm) dinner plate, or similar,
to cut out 2 disks.

3 Lay 1 disk out on the baking sheet. Use a little
beaten egg to brush around the edge of the disk.
Spoon the frangipane filling on the pastry disk,
spreading it out smoothly to within ½in (1cm) of the
edge. Put the other pastry disk on top of the filling,
and use your fingers or the back of a fork to press
down and seal the 2 disks together.

4 Use a small, sharp knife to score a series of thin
slivers on the top of the pastry, in a spiral design,
being careful not to allow them to meet in the center
or the pastry will pull apart when cooking. If you
are feeling artistic, cut the edges of the pastry into
a scalloped edge before cooking.

5 Brush the top of the pastry with the beaten egg,
and bake at the top of the oven for 30 minutes,
until golden brown and puffed up. Set aside to cool for
5 minutes on its sheet before removing to a wire rack.
Serve either warm or cold. The galette will keep in an
airtight container for 3 days. The frangipane can be
prepared 3 days ahead and stored in the refrigerator.

EQUIPMENT
baking sheet

INGREDIENTS

FOR THE FILLING
½ cup granulated sugar
7 tbsp unsalted butter, softened
1 large egg, plus 1 extra, beaten, to glaze
1 cup ground almonds
1 tsp almond extract
1 tbsp brandy, rum, or milk

FOR THE PASTRY
1lb 2oz (500g) store-bought puff pastry
  (or to make your own, see pp.110–113)
all-purpose flour, for dusting

These crisp, crunchy filo crusts are full of just-set delicately spiced custard, and are the perfect way to end a Middle Eastern feast. These little tartlets are best eaten on the day they are made.

CARDAMOM CUSTARD FILO TARTLETS

 MAKES 6   PREP 15 MINS   COOK 20–25 MINS

EQUIPMENT
6-hole deep (2½in[6cm]) muffin pan

INGREDIENTS

FOR THE FILLING
1 cup whole milk
⅔ cup heavy cream
6 cardamom pods, crushed
all-purpose flour, for dusting
2 large eggs
2 tbsp granulated sugar
confectioners' sugar, for dusting

FOR THE DOUGH
3 sheets store-bought filo dough
2 tbsp unsalted butter, melted

1 Preheat the oven to 375°F (190°C). Heat the milk, cream, and cardamom pods in a heavy-bottomed saucepan to boiling point. Turn off the heat and leave the cardamom to infuse.

2 On a well-floured surface, lay out 1 sheet of the filo dough, covering the rest in a clean, damp dish towel. Brush the surface of the dough with a little melted butter, and cover with a second layer. Brush the second layer with more melted butter and cover with a third layer. Cut the dough into 6 equal pieces.

3 Brush the insides of the muffin pan with a little melted butter. Take a piece of the layered filo and use it to line the muffin mold, pushing it into the sides. The dough should be ruffled and stick up over the edges in places. Do this with all 6 pieces of dough. Repeat the layering process with the remaining sheets of dough until you have 6 filo crusts. Brush the dough edges with any remaining butter and cover the pan with the damp dish towel.

4 For the custard, reheat the milk mixture gently over medium heat, but do not allow it to boil. Whisk together the eggs and granulated sugar in a large bowl. Pour the milk mixture into the whisked eggs and cream through a sieve to remove the cardamom. Whisk the mixture together and transfer it to a measuring cup.

5 Pour the custard into the tart crusts and bake for 15–20 minutes, until the dough is crisp at the edges and the custard is just set in the middle. Set the tarts aside to cool in their pans for 10 minutes before removing to cool completely on a wire rack. Dust the tartlets with a little confectioners' sugar before serving.

This rich Middle Eastern confection is baked until crisp, then drenched in a honey syrup for the ultimate after-dinner treat with a strong coffee. Any leftovers can be stored in an airtight container.

BAKLAVA

 MAKES 36   PREP 50–55 MINS   COOK 1½–2HRS

EQUIPMENT
12in x 16in (30cm x 40cm) baking sheet with deep sides, sugar thermometer (optional)

INGREDIENTS

FOR THE FILLING
9oz (250g) unsalted pistachio nuts, shelled and coarsely chopped
9oz (250g) walnut pieces, coarsely chopped
¼ cup granulated sugar
2 tsp ground cinnamon
a large pinch of ground cloves

FOR THE DOUGH
1lb 2oz (500g) filo dough
18 tbsp unsalted butter, melted

FOR THE SYRUP
¾ cup granulated sugar
1 cup honey
juice of 1 lemon
3 tbsp orange flower water

1 Set aside 3–4 tablespoons of the pistachios. Put the remainder in a bowl with the walnuts, sugar, cinnamon, and cloves and stir to mix.

2 Preheat the oven to 350°F (180°C). Unroll the filo onto a damp dish towel and cover with a second damp towel. Brush the baking sheet with butter. Take a sheet of filo and use to line the pan, folding over one end to fit. Brush the filo with butter, and press it into the corners and sides of the pan. Lay another sheet on top, brush with butter, and press into the pan. Continue layering, buttering each sheet, until one-third has been used. Scatter half the filling over the top.

3 Layer another third of the filo sheets as before, then sprinkle the remaining filling over the top. Layer the remaining sheets in the same way. Trim away excess. Brush with butter and pour remaining butter on top. Cut diagonal lines, ½in (1cm) deep, in the filo to mark out 1½in (4cm) diamond shapes. Bake on a low shelf for 1¼–1½ hours, until golden. A skewer inserted in the center for 30 seconds should come out clean.

4 To make the syrup, heat the sugar and 1 cup water in a pan until dissolved. Stir in the honey. Boil for 25 minutes without stirring, until the syrup reaches the soft ball stage, 239°F (115°C) on a thermometer. Or, remove from the heat and dip a teaspoon in the syrup. Cool slightly, then take some between your finger and thumb; a soft ball should form. Cool to lukewarm. Add the lemon juice and orange flower water.

5 Remove from the oven and pour the syrup over the pastries. Cut along the marked lines, almost to the bottom. Cool, then cut through the marked lines. Sprinkle the pastries with the pistachios. The pastries can be made 5 days before serving.

Originating in the American South, where pecans are widely grown, a little of this traditional, rich pie goes a long way. It is best served warm with crème fraîche or whipped cream.

PECAN PIE

 SERVES 6–8   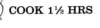 PREP 15 MINS PLUS CHILLING   COOK 1½ HRS   FREEZE CRUST, UP TO 3 MONTHS

1 To make the dough, rub the flour and butter together with your fingertips until the mixture resembles fine bread crumbs. Stir in the sugar. Beat the egg yolk with the vanilla extract and mix them into the dry ingredients, bringing the mixture together to form a soft dough; add a little water to bring the dough together, if necessary. Wrap in plastic wrap and chill in the refrigerator for 30 minutes.

2 Preheat the oven to 350°F (180°C). Roll out the dough on a well-floured surface to ⅛in (3mm) thick and use it to line the pan, leaving an overlapping edge of at least ¾in (2cm). Prick the bottom all over with a fork, line with parchment paper, and fill with baking beans. Place on a baking sheet and bake for 20 minutes. Remove the beans and paper, and bake for another 5 minutes, if the center looks uncooked.

3 Pour the maple syrup into a pan, and add the butter, sugar, vanilla extract, and salt. Place the pan over low heat and stir constantly until the butter has melted and the sugar dissolved.

4 Set the mixture aside to cool until it feels just tepid, then beat in the eggs, one at a time. Stir in the pecans, then pour the mixture into the crust.

5 Bake for 40–50 minutes, until just set. Cover with foil if it is browning too quickly. Remove the pie, transfer it to a wire rack, and set aside to cool for 15–20 minutes. Remove from the pan and serve warm or leave it on the wire rack to cool completely. The pie will keep in an airtight container for 2 days. The unfilled crust can be prepared ahead and stored in an airtight container for up to 3 days.

EQUIPMENT
9in (22cm) tart pan with removable bottom, baking beans

INGREDIENTS

FOR THE DOUGH
(For visual step-by-step instructions, see sweet pie dough p.105)
1 cup all-purpose flour, plus extra for dusting
7 tbsp unsalted butter, chilled and cubed
¼ cup granulated sugar
1 large egg yolk
½ tsp pure vanilla extract

FOR THE FILLING
⅔ cup maple syrup
4 tbsp butter
1 cup light brown sugar
a few drops of vanilla extract
a pinch of salt
3 large eggs
7oz (200g) pecans

Recipes using these seeds are popular all over Eastern Europe, and this German tart is a fantastic showcase for a classic combination of tangy cottage cheese and poppy seeds. Serve either warm or cold.

SILESIAN POPPY SEED TART

 SERVES 8   PREP 35 MINS PLUS COOLING   COOK 1½ HRS

EQUIPMENT
9in (22cm) fluted tart pan with removable bottom

INGREDIENTS

FOR THE DOUGH
(For visual step-by-step instructions, see sweet pie dough p.105)
1⅓ cups all-purpose flour
2 tsp baking powder
½ cup granulated sugar
2–3 drops pure vanilla extract
a pinch of salt
1 large egg
8 tbsp butter, softened, plus extra for greasing

FOR THE FILLING
3½ cups milk
11 tbsp butter
1 cup semolina
1 cup poppy seeds
¾ cup granulated sugar
1 tsp pure vanilla extract
2 large eggs
4oz (100g) cottage or cream cheese
½ cup ground almonds
⅓ cup raisins
1 pear, peeled, cored, and grated
confectioners' sugar, for dusting

1 To make the dough, sift the flour and baking powder into a large bowl. Add the sugar, vanilla, salt, egg, butter, and a little water and mix together to make a dough, roll into a ball, and set aside.

2 Place the milk and butter in a saucepan and bring to a boil. Gradually stir in the semolina and poppy seeds. Simmer over low heat for 20 minutes, stirring occasionally, then remove from the heat and set aside to cool for 10 minutes.

3 Preheat the oven to 350°F (180°C) and grease the bottom of the pan. Roll out half of the dough and fit it into the bottom of the pan. Roll out the remaining dough into a long strip and press it to the side of the pan to form an edge 1¼in (3cm) high.

4 Stir together the sugar, vanilla extract, eggs, cottage cheese, almonds, and raisins into the cooled poppy seed and semolina mixture. Stir in the pear. Pour the mixture evenly into the crust, and bake for 1 hour.

5 Place the pan on a wire rack to cool, loosen the edge of the tart with a knife, and remove the ring. Dust with confectioners' sugar before serving.

Some walnut tart recipes use halved walnuts to decorate the top, but try this alternative. Half a walnut can be difficult to tackle with a fork, so grinding them gives a smooth texture that's easier to handle.

WALNUT TART

 SERVES 8   PREP 20 MINS PLUS CHILLING   COOK 50 MINS   FREEZE CRUST, UP TO 2 MONTHS

1 To make the dough, rub the flour, sugar, and butter together with your fingertips until the mixture resembles fine bread crumbs. Beat the egg yolk together with 2 tablespoons of cold water and add it to the dry ingredients, bringing the mixture together to form a soft dough. Add a little more water if the dough seems dry. Wrap the dough in plastic wrap and chill for 30 minutes to make it easier to handle when rolling out.

2 Preheat the oven to 350°F (180°C). Roll out the dough on a well-floured surface to ¼in (5mm) thick and use to line the tart pan, leaving an overlapping edge of at least ½in (1cm). Trim any excess dough using a pair of scissors. Prick the bottom of the dough with a fork, line with wax paper, and fill with baking beans. Place the pan on a baking sheet and bake for 20 minutes. Remove the beans and the paper, and bake for another 5 minutes if the center looks uncooked. Trim off any ragged edges while it is still warm.

3 For the filling, grind the shelled walnuts and sugar together in a food processor to a fairly fine texture. Whisk together the eggs, half-and-half, and vanilla extract, then whisk in the nut and sugar mixture. Pour the filling into the crust and bake for 20–25 minutes, until the filling has just set.

4 Remove and set aside for at least 10 minutes before serving warm or at room temperature with thick cream. The cooked crust can be stored in an airtight container for up to 3 days.

EQUIPMENT
9in (22cm) tart pan with removable bottom, baking beans

INGREDIENTS

FOR THE DOUGH
(For visual step-by-step instructions, see sweet pie dough p.105)
1 cup all-purpose flour, plus extra for dusting
2 tbsp granulated sugar
7 tbsp unsalted butter, softened
1 large egg yolk

FOR THE FILLING
7oz (200g) walnuts, shelled
½ cup granulated sugar
2 large eggs
¾ cup half-and-half
½ tsp pure vanilla extract

This large, decorative Millefeuilles is a perfect way to end a Christmas meal. When ready to serve, carefully cut the pastry into even portions so as not to disrupt its delicate structure.

CHESTNUT MILLEFEUILLES

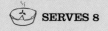 **SERVES 8**   **PREP 35–40 MINS PLUS CHILLING**   **COOK 25–35 MINS**

EQUIPMENT
baking sheet

INGREDIENTS

FOR THE FILLING
1⅔ cups milk
4 large egg yolks
¼ cup granulated sugar
3 tbsp all-purpose flour, sifted
2 tbsp dark rum
1 cup heavy cream
1lb 2oz (500g) candied chestnuts, coarsely crumbled
⅓ confectioners' sugar, plus extra if needed

FOR THE PASTRY
1lb 5oz (600g) store-bought puff pastry
(or to make your own, see pp.110–113)

1 Heat the milk in a saucepan until it just boils. Whisk the yolks and granulated sugar for 2–3 minutes, until thick. Whisk in the flour, then gradually whisk in the milk until smooth. Return to a clean pan, bring to a boil, whisking, until thick. Reduce the heat to low and whisk for 2 minutes. Cool, then stir in the rum. Transfer to a bowl, cover, and chill for 1 hour.

2 Preheat the oven to 400°F (200°C). Sprinkle a baking sheet with water. Roll out the pastry to a rectangle a little larger than the sheet, ⅛in (3mm) thick, and put it on the sheet. Let the edges overhang. Press the dough down. Chill for 15 minutes, then prick with a fork. Cover with parchment paper. Set a wire rack on top. Bake for 15–20 minutes. Grip the baking sheet and rack; invert the pastry. Slide the sheet back under the pastry. Bake for 10 minutes. Prepare the pastry layers (see below). Whip the cream until fairly firm, then fold into the pastry cream. Spread half the cream over 1 pastry strip and sprinkle with half the chestnuts. Repeat to make 2 layers; top with the last strip. Sift over confectioners' sugar.

Preparing the pastry layers

1 Remove the pastry from the oven and carefully slide the pastry onto a cutting board.

2 While still warm, trim around the edges with a large, sharp knife to neaten.

3 Cut the trimmed sheet lengthwise into 3 equal strips. Set the pastry aside to cool.

This Baklava has a crisp yet chewy texture. Serve this delicious treat as a sweet snack or after dinner with a cup of tea or coffee. If you can't find Chilean honey, any variety of honey will do.

MIXED NUT BAKLAVA WITH HONEY AND ORANGE

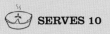 SERVES 10   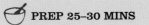 PREP 25–30 MINS   COOK 1 HR

1 Preheat the oven to 350°F (180°C). Chop the nuts in a food processor until coarse, then stir in the ground cinnamon and set aside.

2 Brush the baking pan with melted butter to prevent it from drying.

3 Start layering sheets of filo into the prepared pan, brushing each one with a little of the melted butter before placing the next neatly on top of the last layer. After 6 layers, scatter half of the nut mixture over the top. Repeat, then add a final 6 layers. Brush the top with melted butter and trim off any overlapping filo dough. Cut the filo into 1½–2in (4–5cm) diamonds, making sure that the knife cuts all the way through the filo layers to the bottom of the pan.

4 Bake for 40–45 minutes, until golden and crisp. Reduce the heat to 325°F (160°C) if the baklava is browning too quickly.

5 To make the syrup, place the granulated sugar, honey, cinnamon, orange zest, and cloves with 1¼ cups water in a saucepan and bring to a simmer. Simmer, stirring occasionally, for 15 minutes, or until the liquid has reduced by a third. Set aside to cool.

6 Remove the pastries from the oven and spoon half the syrup on top. Leave for 5 minutes, then spoon the remaining syrup over the top. Set aside to cool completely before removing the pieces from the pan with a palette knife. Store in the pan. The baklava will keep for 3–4 days, but will become increasingly soggy.

EQUIPMENT
9½in x 9½in (24cm x 24cm) baking dish

INGREDIENTS

FOR THE FILLING
5½oz (150g) Brazil nuts
5½oz (150g) cashew nuts
1½ tsp ground cinnamon

FOR THE DOUGH
11 tbsp butter, melted,
   plus extra for greasing
18 sheets of 10in x 9½in (25cm x 24cm)
   store-bought filo dough

FOR THE SYRUP
1½ cup unrefined granulated sugar
½ cup Chilean honey
1 tsp ground cinnamon
grated zest of ½ orange
1 tsp whole cloves

Iranian nibbed pistachios are the best type of nuts to use for this tart, since they give a vivid, bright green color to the finished dish. They are expensive, so normal shelled and peeled pistachios can be used.

PISTACHIO AND ORANGE FLOWER TART

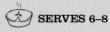 SERVES 6–8   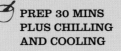 PREP 30 MINS PLUS CHILLING AND COOLING   COOK 50–55 MINS   FREEZE CRUST, UP TO 3 MONTHS

1 To make the dough, rub the flour, sugar, and butter together with your fingertips until the mixture resembles fine bread crumbs. Add the egg yolk and bring the mixture together to form a soft dough. If the dough is too dry, add a little water. Wrap the dough in plastic wrap and chill for 30 minutes.

2 Preheat the oven to 350°F (180°C). Roll out the dough on a floured surface to ⅛in (3mm) thick and use to line the tart pan, leaving an overlapping edge of at least ½in (1cm). Trim off any excess dough that hangs down farther than this. Prick the bottom of the dough with a fork, line with wax paper, and fill with baking beans. Place the crust on a baking sheet and bake for 20 minutes. Remove the beans and paper, and return to the oven for another 5 minutes if the center still looks a little uncooked. Trim off any ragged edges from the tart crust while it is still warm.

3 To make the filling, first melt the butter and set aside to cool. Next, finely grind the pistachios in a food processor. Whisk together the eggs, sugar, orange flower water, and honey. Whisk in the cooled, melted butter, then fold in the ground pistachios. Place the tart crust on a baking sheet and carefully pour in the filling. Bake immediately (or it may separate) for 25–30 minutes, until the center has just set but the top is not browning.

4 Set the tart aside to cool for 15 minutes, then dust with confectioners' sugar and serve warm or at room temperature with whipped cream flavored with a little orange flower water. Best eaten on the day it is made.

EQUIPMENT
9in (22cm) tart pan with removable bottom, baking beans

INGREDIENTS

FOR THE DOUGH
(For visual step-by-step instructions, see sweet pie dough p.105)
1 cup all-purpose flour, plus extra for dusting
2 tbsp granulated sugar
7 tbsp unsalted butter, softened
1 large egg yolk, beaten with 2 tbsp cold water

FOR THE FILLING
5 tbsp unsalted butter
7oz (200g) nibbed pistachios (these give the best color, although others can be used)
4 large eggs
½ cup granulated sugar
½ tbsp orange flower water
2 tbsp honey
confectioners' sugar, for dusting

Otherwise known as "Grandmother's Tart," this classic Italian recipe is made using the freshest of ricotta and little else. This tart is fantastic served still warm from the oven and drizzled with honey.

TORTA DELLA NONNA

 SERVES 6   PREP 20 MINS PLUS CHILLING   COOK 1 HR 5 MINS   FREEZE CRUST, UP TO 1 MONTH

EQUIPMENT
8in (20cm) tart pan with removable bottom, baking beans

INGREDIENTS

FOR THE DOUGH
(For visual step-by-step instructions, see sweet pie dough p.105)
1 cup all-purpose flour, plus extra for dusting
7 tbsp unsalted butter, cubed
¼ cup granulated sugar
1 large egg yolk
½ tsp pure vanilla extract

FOR THE FILLING
14oz (400g) ricotta cheese
2 large eggs
zest and juice of 1 lemon
⅔ cup confectioners' sugar, sifted, plus extra for dusting
1 tsp almond extract
1¼oz (70g) roasted pine nuts
1oz (30g) roasted sliced almonds

1 To make the dough, rub the flour and butter together in a bowl with your fingertips until the mixture resembles bread crumbs. Stir in the sugar. Add the egg yolk and vanilla to the flour mixture and bring together to form a smooth dough, adding 1–2 teaspoons cold water if needed. Wrap and chill in the refrigerator for 30 minutes.

2 For the filling, place the ricotta and eggs in a large bowl and whisk until smooth. Stir in the lemon zest and juice, confectioners' sugar, and almond extract. Set aside. Preheat the oven to 350°F (180°C).

3 Roll out the dough on a floured surface to a circle large enough to line the tart pan. Place the dough in the pan, pressing it down firmly into the bottom and around the edges. Trim off any excess dough, prick the bottom with a fork, and line with parchment paper. Place the pan on a baking sheet and fill with baking beans. Bake for 20 minutes. Remove the beans and paper and bake for another 5–10 minutes to crisp.

4 Evenly scatter the pine nuts over the tart crust. Spoon the cheese mixture in, spread it out in an even layer, and sprinkle the almonds over the top. Bake the tart for 30–35 minutes, until the filling is just set. Transfer to a wire rack and set aside to cool for 15 minutes. Serve dusted with confectioners' sugar.